If I
Should Die
Before I Wake

Eileen Munro

MAINSTREAM
PUBLISHING

EDINBURGH AND LONDON

First published in Great Britain in 2011 by
MAINSTREAM PUBLISHING COMPANY
(EDINBURGH) LTD
7 Albany Street
Edinburgh EH1 3UG

ISBN 9781845966164

This book is a work of non-fiction based on the life, experiences and
recollections of the author. In some cases, names of people, places,
dates, sequences or the detail of events have been changed to protect
the privacy of others. The author has stated to the publishers that,
except in such respects, not affecting the substantial accuracy of the
work, the contents of this book are true

A catalogue record for this book is available
from the British Library

Printed in Great Britain by
CPI Cox and Wyman, Reading, Berkshire RG1 8EX

1 3 5 7 9 10 8 6 4 2

For my son, Craig

✳

The moral test of government is how that government treats those who are in the dawn of life, the children; those who are in the twilight of life, the elderly; and those who are in the shadows of life, the sick, the needy and the handicapped.

Hubert Humphrey

Acknowledgements

Once again I would like to thank the incorrigible Paul Lockley, whose humour and continuous encouragement, belief and support sustained me throughout the writing of this second book. I am grateful for the strength of friendship, direction, support and joy brought into my life by Stephen Queen, and for his belief also I could do it. Thanks go to Sandra Brown and Sara Trevelyan for their friendship in the light and dark days, with strength, laughter, tears and love that were just a phone call away. Also to the husband-and-wife team Marcello and Cathy Mega; Adam Ardrey for mutual advice and an ear; Agnes Lambie for keeping 'my house' personally and physically in order with dignity and spiders; Ailsa Bathgate, my long-suffering editor, for her professionalism, kindness and sensitivity; Bill Campbell and the rest of the Mainstream staff; all the staff of the Moira Anderson Foundation; readers of the first book for their support and heartfelt emails; my family past and present.

Contents

Prologue

NOVEMBER 1979

The large utilitarian Lanarkshire building that was Bellshill Maternity, otherwise known as 'the baby factory', was disappearing from view. A 'surprise' bundle slept soundly in my arms in the back seat of a forgotten driver's car. My curly-headed son, now named Craig, was a surprise to everyone but me. I had kept my pregnancy secret for seven and a half months, almost managing to pretend to myself it was not a reality. It had become a way of life, keeping secrets – even from myself.

A white-uniformed nurse had walked both of us to the hospital doors and waved us off – a ritual I had only seen in sentimental black-and-white movies. For that brief moment, although there was no proud father with me, or the baby's grandparents, it felt like the occasion was being acknowledged as special. As we set off for everyday life, had I allowed myself to think about it, I suppose I would have yearned for guidance from a mother – any mother would have done. Yearning would be all I could do. On New Year's Eve in 1974, my adoptive mother had died in front of my eyes from alcoholic asphyxiation while I sat huddled in our coal fire's hearth. I had been 11 years old. Outside my childhood home, the 'bells' had pealed in a New Year and a new hope, while I had shrunk further into my nightdress and the hearth, my eyes fixated on her body as her life and my hope faded. After her death, my little sister Cathleen and I were hastily passed around a succession of different children's homes and relatives, rarely safe and never settled. Now, with my three-day-old baby wrapped in a shawl in my arms, another institutional building disappeared from my sight and a familiar feeling rose in me as I wondered what lay ahead and who I could rely on.

My adoptive father would be drinking in a pub somewhere in the east end of Glasgow, only capable of supporting a bar and dodging a night in the cells for being drunk and disorderly. He had been ashamed of my pregnancy, telling our social worker that I had 'shamed his family'. Craig's father, like me, had been a child in care, but he had left the children's home midway through my pregnancy and headed for London. He had promised to come back for me and the baby once he was settled. With no one else to share my secret, I was left to carry and bear it on my own.

Before my mother's death, my adoptive parents' alcoholism had meant that I was left in charge of the house, and Cathleen and I had been obviously vulnerable. This vulnerability was capitalised on by a man called William Urquhart. He had befriended my father and then my mother by buying them drink. With both parents either sleeping off a stupor or propping up a bar, the path to his target – me – was clear. His name and the shameful acts for which I then had no words were recorded onto a memory tape that haunted my thoughts and played out in my nightmares. I did not know then that I would never forget what he had done to me. I didn't realise that the images would stay imprinted like forensic memories in a colourless cerebral photo album: evidence that would refuse to stay buried. Unlike the cassette recorder that I had hidden under my pillow in order to listen to the radio, my memory had no erase button.

During the years that followed, I experienced further neglect in children's homes, and, worse, I met more Urquharts. Being passed around from pillar to post as well as seeing endless streams of social workers within the childcare system around the west coast of Scotland had left me confused, rootless and further traumatised. I was accused of not trusting my social workers, as I didn't tell them how I felt. They blamed me for not communicating and being evasive. 'She's a thrawn one that one' was a common comment, meaning I was stubborn. Mute with fear when facing a possible confrontation, I found I couldn't summon up a response to these slights. I had a defensive shield of hidden fire smouldering in my belly, but I was seen as 'aloof', or 'a smart arse', as others might say.

For now, a sense of self-preservation had doused the flames to meek embers; I had to remain stoic, keep all my anxiety hidden in case I gave myself away. I thought that I had colluded with Urquhart in committing a crime, and he had threatened to kill me if I told anyone what he had done. My mother had caught him in my bed and called me a whore. I had been seven years old. If they knew about this, 'the authorities' would surely do much worse. They would take my baby away and lock me up. Everything that had ever been said about me would be proven right. I had to keep the crazy cat in the bag, unseen and silent. In my petrified mind, my future and that of my son rested on my enduring silence.

Now, years later, it was approaching the end of 1979 and I was still rootless and unsettled as the car took us towards Hamilton. Our destination was my aunt Helen's house – my dead mother's older sister. She had moved to Hamilton from the east end of Glasgow to create a better life for her family of five. Aunt Helen had come to our rescue several times in the past, her house a safe haven where Cathleen and I could draw breath for short spaces of time between the incidents within the care system. But I had always felt the outsider in this adoptive family of mine, and now I would be a burden again. It did, however, mean I could stay in the same area as Cathleen and would have access to see her as she was still in Fernlea, the children's home I had had to leave when my pregnancy could be kept secret no longer.

The road ahead was as daunting as my experiences in the maternity hospital. Though filled with a new and overwhelming feeling of love and attachment to my baby, fear stitched these new squares of experience to my ever-growing, colourful patchwork quilt of life.

As the car drove onwards, I tried to forget the silent alarm bell that tinkled rather than rang the arrival of a dark cloud. 'What a well-behaved baby you have there; not a peep from him,' another new mother draped in her dressing gown had commented innocently from the door of my hospital room. I should have been pleased. I wasn't. *Tinkle. Tinkle.* My mother's intuition was telling me something was wrong, but with no confidence or confidante I didn't recognise her voice and therefore I didn't know how to act on this suspicion. When I get that feeling now, I *know* something is not as it seems.

1

Crossroads

The isolation of my single room in the maternity ward (I thought I had been put there because I was 16 and unwed, not because I was breastfeeding) could not have been more different from my arrival at my aunt Helen's. With a house full of working people and my cousin Lena still at school, it was mayhem. A welcome mayhem in many ways as it represented ordinary everyday life – a family home in organised chaos like most.

After receiving a lot of attention in the first days, as well as fielding curious questions about Craig and the birth from my astonished cousins – Lena in particular, as she was closest in age to me – I settled into a cautious routine. All the females in the household pulled their weight. My aunt Helen offered practical advice on bathing Craig and sat on her chair by the fire watching me as I did so. All the grandchildren to date had been bathed in a baby bath in front of the gas fire. I have never forgotten the smell of Johnson's baby shampoo and its kind tear-free lather on Craig's wet curls.

My aunt's stews and soups were delicious. Unlike in the homes, I was not forced to eat or punished because I didn't finish what was in front of me. I ate well and without guilt. In the busy household, someone was always either in Hamilton shopping centre picking up food or nipping out to the local store for an essential item like Bisto, ecru-coloured 'bingo' tights or soap powder. My aunt's presence in the household would always be announced by her either opening all the living room windows with the cry of, 'It's like an opium den in here,' cigarette in hand, or closing them, stating, 'It's like fresh air fortnight night in here,' followed by 'Do you think I'm Carnegie, heating the bloody street?' I tried to do my best to pull my weight and earn my keep, but as I was acutely aware of my predicament and very unsure of myself I would wait till everyone was out to do our washing, as well as the dusting and the hoovering.

Aunt Helen's front door was a revolving one, always containing a relative or another visitor. I lost count of the older women who told me, 'Ach, hen, there's worse things than a baby,' with the usual follow-up being, 'You wur'nae fly enough, that's why you got caught.' This felt more like commiseration than comfort, and although I fully understood that it was said out of a certain sense of kindness, kindness was something I couldn't afford. It felt like pity and it hurt. I also found that other curious Scottish phrases were now bestowed on me: '*Ah see you're aw better noo*' and '*You aw by wae?*' meaning I had given birth, not that I had just recovered from an illness.

With the past behind me, I should have finally felt as if I'd escaped from the violence, the children's homes, life-threatening asthma attacks, the social workers and that man who had threatened to kill me – William Urquhart. The future should have held a promise of new beginnings. Although I couldn't understand it, I didn't feel as free and safe as I should have; something somewhere was keeping me prisoner.

Without even being aware of it, I had always felt that way, lacking any sense of security. My life was like a sapling tree with tenacious roots grappling for a piece of ground to grow healthy in its own territory. Ever present, this feeling increased with the recent memories of Craig's arrival, which poignantly occurred on the morning of Remembrance Sunday – at four minutes to eleven on the eleventh of the eleventh.

With the events still fresh in my mind, I had clear visions of being left on my own in a drugged pain, half naked in a cold and sterile room. That feeling – passive, wanting to flee and mute with a fear that was impossible to forget –was added to my pile of life events that persistently but involuntarily paralysed me. The memories induced a racing heartbeat and tightness in my chest.

Eighteen hours my labour lasted; eighteen hours and nobody told me what to expect – as if they could. Yet another sea of women's voices chorused in my ear: '*Ach, it's a pain you'll forget,*' '*it's all worth it in the end, you'll see.*' Of course, this was true. However, although the pain was now forgotten, the fear remained. As I had been only 16, perhaps this had been reinforced by lack of preparation or loving support – birthing partners, videos and antenatal classes were alien to me. I had eventually been rushed to theatre for an emergency caesarean, but it was too late. My baby was in acute foetal distress. The theatre staff had to perform what I now know to be a 'slash and grab' forceps delivery without anaesthetic. I blacked out and came to, only to find I had been literally stitched up. Subsequently, the heat of infected stitches served as a lasting reminder of the experience, and I made a promise to myself that never again would I become that vulnerable.

Though not quite a gymslip mother, I was of the minimal legal age to leave school. All schooling was behind me now, as were my dreams of becoming something respected and worthwhile: somebody, a writer or an artist. As a child who had been in care, expectations were low for me anyway. The army, prison or early motherhood was the expected résumé; I had delivered on the last aspect. While my former classmates were pushing pens, I was pushing a pram. The sadness I felt at losing the chance of a different future through education had to be put to the back of my mind, and I tried hard to accept my new situation.

I rapidly had to become an adult in a scary adult's world. My love at school of modern studies and the escape I found through music continued. My days would typically consist of caring for Craig, watching the news, reading my uncle Charles's newspapers and listening to my aunt's radiogram, humming and singing to myself as I polished the wood. It kept my mind occupied and distracted. I felt I had not completely lost touch with the outside world. My natural curiosity and desire for knowledge was still alive. Margaret Thatcher had come to power, and Pink Floyd was topping the Christmas charts with the ironic 'Another Brick in the Wall', a song about the dangers of education while I was mourning the loss of mine.

While I tried to ignore and hide from the gossiping, one thing was for sure: they were right, those women. There are 'worse things than a baby'. Much worse things!

2

Inheritance

My aunt Helen already had a full house, with my cousin Lena, her older sister Helen, her husband and their new baby boy living there. So, although it was never mentioned, I knew my stay wouldn't last very long.

Uncomfortable at being an imposition and adding to my aunt Helen's burden when she already had her hands full, I worked hard at being practical – cleaning, sweeping, shopping and being forcedly cheery. Although I told myself just to be grateful for the time I would have there, I couldn't stop myself from hoping that if I was good they would let me stay. My dream of being part of a family would always override reality, and I hated myself for it. I suppose it was driven by fear. I knew what was out there and wanted to keep Craig and myself safe. The truth was I was frightened of being frightened.

Practicalities continued as I went about the legal business of registering Craig's birth at Hamilton Registry Office in Almada Street. Here, I discovered that because I was an unwed mother I could not record Craig's father's name on the birth certificate. It was not legal. I was publicly informed of this in the registry office reception in front of other clients who were waiting. I gritted my teeth in the face of this legalised shaming – taking the humiliation on the chin yet again.

The whole process made me wonder about my own birth certificate, which I had never seen. My accessible adoption certificate provided details about both my adoptive parents, but it was devoid of any clue as to who my biological parents were. My maternal grandfather had paid the Salvation Army a nominal fee to secure a child for his daughter. On a good day, I saw it as administration costs. Bought and paid for! That realisation hurt. There was a paper trail of evidence about my existence and life, but this did not tell my full story. It was merely a framework, with no body or heart. I had never considered my adoptive parents as my owners, but, to all intents and purposes, legally they were. In view of the lack of love, this was how it felt. I dealt with this hurt by being pragmatic and made a promise to myself that I would discover who I really was and to whom and where I truly belonged.

A few weeks later, my attention turned from one requirement to another. A date for Craig's check-up appointment arrived in the post, meaning I had to face up to another unknown source of authority.

As far as adapting to being a new mother, all the immediate practicalities were easy to deal with, perhaps because I had cared for my sister and the other young children in the homes. Practicalities were just that – practical; they required no emotion. For the most part, I didn't have time to worry whether I was doing things the right way and, anyway, such insecurities were not part of the working-class ethos with which I had been brought up. They would have been viewed as a weakness, and even as middle-class luxury. '*Too much time on yer hands tae think*' and '*the devil makes work for idle hands*' were two of the mantras that echoed in my mind, and so I got on with it. Having the purpose and routine of bathing, dressing, cooking, washing and feeding was almost a joy. But however confidently I thought I behaved and cared for my baby, my inner turmoil manifested itself when I had to deal with the authorities and the outside world. People could say I was defensive, but in reality I was terrified. I found out the hard way that having a child forces you to integrate and engage with society, and for me it was far from easy. I didn't realise I was frightened that people would get close and find out the truth.

Sometimes, on occasions such as taking Craig to the clinic for tests, I had to give myself a pep talk just to get myself out the door – chin up, shoulders back. Sometimes I had to count numbers and use lamp posts as markers to keep away the urge to run and get me down the street to the end of my journey. But like everyone else, I got through it, and Craig passed the routine baby examinations – clicking hips, measuring of the head and the dreaded heel-prick test. It was explained that the tiny amount of blood taken could identify possible genetic disorders. On hearing this, my mind once again turned to my own birth parents. What if they had any genetic conditions? What if this meant Craig and I were in danger because of my lack of knowledge about my family history? I was a new mother with no mother, and full of fear about the unknown.

Having an uncertain genetic history was just another fear to add to my list. It was fear of a kind I had never experienced before, as the implications now affected more than me. I wasn't just scared for myself; there was so much more to worry about. My isolation, youth and inexperience of good mothering did not equip me for what was natural – a certain amount of worrying was part of being a parent, a prerequisite. However, some people, like me, did have more to worry about. I found that I was trying to uncover details about my beginnings while trying to forget my childhood at the same time. Terrified and ostracised from 'normal' society because of my past, I existed almost totally in the present, and having such an uncertain future made me feel afraid.

Having finished at the clinic, I trundled along to Hamilton Shopping Centre with Craig tucked up in his navy-blue coach-built Silver Cross pram. That pram, which I felt I did not deserve, had caused me embarrassment from a neighbour of my aunt, as I had acquired it with public money from social services. 'Huh, a brand new pram,' she had snorted in disgust.

It was a pram that had never been built for buses or any other form of transport. Only a Sherman tank of a taxi could accommodate such a monster and with a taxi being a financially unaffordable luxury I relied on my own two feet. The large white wheels turned constantly, offering me a lot of time to turn the wheels in my own head. It made me smile to look down at Craig inside this Rolls-Royce of a pram, wrapped in blue, with an elastic string of blue and white plastic toys dangling in front of him. Through the sea of blue fabric it was clear I was advertising the baby was a boy, and not just any boy, he was my boy.

The hype of Christmas and the preparations afforded me some respite from my worries about the future. The hectic shopping centre with all its coloured lights and comforting tunes exuded the ideals of hope, forgiveness and spending. At the Top Cross in Hamilton – across from Pound-Stretcher – an enormous tree twinkled and towered up into an icy sky. Brass bands belted out religious tunes that had the effect of making me feel sad, peaceful and accepting. Multicoloured tinsel scarves decorated every shop door and window.

Making my way down Quarry Street, I stopped at a card shop called Words and Wishes; it was known for having the best cards. Unusual personal verses and designs made them stand out. I consoled myself with the thought that these cards were significant, as they took the place of expensive gifts. I was embarrassed by the fact that I couldn't afford to give to people who would buy gifts for me and Craig. Buying nice cards and making them personal with a sentiment was my way of compensating for my embarrassment and showing appreciation. 'I like a nice card,' I had heard one of my mother's friends once say, and I wholly agreed. Having paid for my agonised-over selection of cards, I stepped back outside the shop and took control of the pram and its sleeping content.

Going shopping was a different experience back then, a time when parents had to leave their prams and babies outside the shop as '*No prams allowed*' signs adorned almost every shop entry. (A pram and baby could also be seen sitting under many house windows, which lay open for the mother to hear if the baby cried.) The result was usually a line of prams at the shop door, with pink or blue discarded bootees lying at the side of the huge wheels – a stray lemon one was an indicator of canny and organised parents. A cry from these ranks would see either a mother rushing from a shop doorway or a passer-by crouching over, shoogling the pram and cooing to soothe the wailing bundle inside. It was in this anonymous atmosphere I would wander and bask, as the sounds, lights and activity elicited intoxicating feelings of goodness. The business of being busy meant that hope, to me, could feel eternal. I did not need to think about the future. The here and now was forever frozen in those filled moments, meaning it would keep and always be present. Or perhaps that *was* hope. The only thing left when all is lost. If I had been given a middle name, perhaps Pandora would have been apt.

I wheeled us both from shop window to shop window, eventually turning predictably into the well-trodden precinct area of Hamilton's Regent Way, passing WHSmith, Marks & Spencer, and Cantor's furniture store to land at the doors of Boots the Chemist. While girls my age crowded the make-up counters, applying samples and laughing about boys, I headed to the baby section. There I collected breast pads for my escaping milk, nappy liners and Napisan to steep Craig's terry towelling nappies before washing them. Breast pads and nappy liners were a luxury; Sudocrem to stop nappy rash a necessity. Prescriptions could also be picked up in Boots, for many mothers like me who were suffering from infernal infected stitches or other common and tolerated birth-related infections. After a few weeks, I also got Craig's milk there. Though it was the beginning of the end of free milk in primary schools, mothers on low incomes received free milk tokens. The Government's rationing had not reached these and I was thankful, as after six weeks of struggling to breastfeed I had reluctantly given up. Cracked nipples, constant pain, infected stitches and having to constantly hide away to feed Craig had seen to that – it was very rare for anyone to breastfeed in public, the '60s and '70s women's rights revolution having either bypassed or been refused entry in working-class Lanarkshire.

For a few weeks after Craig's birth, cushions and bicarbonate-soda-sprinkled baths became a necessity to enable me to sit down. My regular trips to Boots for supplies were part of my new routine, and it was on a return journey from the chemist a few days after Craig's physical check-up that we had to call in at the mother-and-baby clinic at Orchard Street, near the town-centre bus station, for Craig to have some more basic tests. He passed with flying colours.

My memory of this event is short and not so sweet. In an ordinary room, a Mrs Linn had executed the test in no more than 15 minutes.

He was weighed, his head was measured and his joints moved around. While she was conducting these tests, I summoned up enough gumption to stutter my concealed fears about Craig's hearing. 'Neurotic teenage mothers,' was the phrase coined by Mrs Linn when I sheepishly voiced my concern that Craig's responses didn't seem right. With my intuition ignored and my confidence crushed by authority, I left the clinic with a simmering contempt for Mrs Linn. Powerless to do anything with these feelings, I turned them on myself. 'Useless mother,' I whispered. The image of her strutting across the room loudly saying this phrase to an unseen audience kept playing on stop, start, rewind in my head. There was an ornate wooden coat stand behind her in this scene, and I imagined picking her up and hanging her on it.

Arriving home after Craig's test, I retreated to lick my wounds in private, unable to share my gnawing humiliation and fears. After making up a bottle for his feed, I sat in our bedroom, enduring the pain and discomfort of the infected stitches. Humiliation had begun to exude from my stomach outwards and crawl over my skin. Any hopes I had of my worries concerning Craig being taken seriously, discussed and maybe investigated were dashed. I could not properly articulate what I thought the problem was – it was a feeling, and I was perhaps afraid of it becoming a reality.

As I watched Craig sleeping, so beautiful and innocently unaware, there was something indescribable threatening to engulf me. I know now it was rage. I would say it filled me with fear, but surely I was already full. Perhaps it was an overspill that I was frightened of, a loss of control. Craig suckled a plastic teat; I ground my teeth and clicked my jaw. We rocked together, me in a juxtaposition of anger, hurt and subservient gratefulness, with a ribbon of impotence that tied it all together.

3

On the road again

Christmas and New Year 1979 was fast approaching. My world had already been turned upside down after being thrust into motherhood, but more changes were on their way. As I had expected, our time at my aunt Helen's came to an end, though even more quickly than I had anticipated. Five weeks had passed and the bustling household with busy lives made me feel I was in the way. Thankfully, Craig was a wonderfully easy, happy baby, but I was told the pressure of everyone living under the one roof and stepping on top of each other had become too much. My aunt Helen had spoken privately to my social worker Rebecca Mower, although in reality it wasn't much of a secret. I'd become accustomed to being excluded from hush-hush phone calls to and from social services over the years. I would focus on the door of my aunt's living room with its white frame and fern-etched opaque glass, straining to hear, while also dreading what was being said behind it. In this instance, I sat staring into the blue and pink flame of the gas fire, trying to keep alive in me that flame of pretence that all was well. Christmas cards covered the mantelpiece and surrounding walls. When the low-voiced call ended, my aunt came back into the living room. The fact that she wouldn't look at me said more than words. Her avoidance of my gaze told me a move was in the pipeline.

The results of her recent phone call were eventually explained to me a few days later by my social worker in my bedroom. My aunt hadn't been able to look me in the eye, so it was left to Rebecca to tell me what was going on. Now, of course, I realise Aunt Helen felt terribly guilty, but at the time it felt like Craig and I were a burden, causing people pain.

It had been decided that Craig and I should go to live with my cousin Bernadette and her two sons. She had not long separated from her husband and was living in a brewery flat in Hamilton, above Aunt Helen's pub. After being told, I entered the living room and smiled at my aunt, disguising my upset to preserve any future relationship. After all, if I did become upset, what good would it do? Where would I go? I had no choices. Here, my old childhood adage of 'Nothing in, nothing out', when dealing with traumatic or painful events, served me well again. No discussion of the events about to unfold took place between me and my aunt. I felt I had no right to ask about it or mention it. My actions or lack of them meant there was no emotional upset for my aunt. It was just the way things were done: 'Better days are coming' and 'nae point on crying over spilt milk'.

I prepared Craig and packed my belongings for the move, forcing myself not to cry. It would all be for the best. My new residence was a two-bedroom flat in a sandstone tenement building. The main door was hard to open and four flights of stairs would prove difficult, but it was close to the shopping centre. From the living room windows, I could see across Strathclyde Country Park; the view seemed endless. The dome of a mausoleum sat formidably on the winter skyline, breaking up the foreground and background of the landscape. On the opposite side of the street were a church and a nightclub. Behind the club was accommodation for homeless people. I could smell the fresh beer from directly underneath the flat and hear the sounds of bottles chinking, the drone of chattering and the dull thuds of beer barrels being delivered and rolled into the pub. It gave me the feeling of a lively life by proxy. '*A guid joab we don't know whit's roon the corner for us*' served me well and helped me to forge on.

In order to soothe myself, I began exploring my new surroundings. I discovered you could walk onto the roof from the landing of the flat. A place to hang washing out, it became a hiding place for me to escape. It was like a concrete secret garden scented with beer and shared with the birds and the occasional cat. The smells of food wafted up, carried by the cold, icy air. Shoppers and traffic passed continuously, but no one knew I sat above looking down and watching. Although I was hurt by having to leave my aunt Helen's, I was determined by nature and decided I would make the best of it. It was Christmas after all.

However, the move seemed to nudge my anxiety up another notch, and it was here that I can clearly trace that my angst manifested itself again in creating order. At night, in the small galley kitchen before going to sleep, I would make up Craig's bottles: one for the night and another for his early-morning breakfast. Craig's feeding regime played out in my head in order: two bottles, two teats, two caps all placed in the steriliser. (Back then I wasn't aware that I disliked odd numbers.) Six scoops of powdered SMA baby milk, sixty millilitres of boiled water, mixed, and the formula repeated into another bottle that stood on the kitchen bunker. This meant that when Craig woke up for a feed we would not be a bother and end up waking the house. I had also taken to organising Bernadette's multitude of stray earrings, only feeling satisfied when I had successfully matched them all in their pairs. I told myself I was just being practical, but it was really the only way I had to relieve my constant feeling of unease. I had done this as a child at my mother and father's house with my makeshift library, organising and then reorganising my books by name, then title and size.

Holding on to some of my past, Fernlea, the final children's home I had lived in before moving in with my aunt Helen, still figured in my life. For my first visit back there after having Craig, I had made sure Aunt Elspeth, the matron in charge, was on duty. I had been her pet, clever and articulate, but she had used me to further her own agendas. It had been among my tasks to tell tales on other members of staff she had scores to settle with, most of which at the time I was oblivious to, as she was a clever interrogator. On this visit, though I was initially made welcome, it was clear I was in the way and was left sitting on my own with a shawl-wrapped Craig as they ate. Things had moved on and other children had moved into empty rooms. The legal family I had no longer existed: the artificial family concept in children's homes as vulnerable to change as us children. Legally, I did not belong, and they had no legal requirement to make me feel as though I did. I wished my heart was as unsentimental as the law.

The Christmas tree sat in the hallway, between the swing doors, simply and tastefully decorated – to passers-by it was a good image for the home. A few other members of staff seemed pleased to see me, and I felt grateful for that. It meant I didn't have to sever contact completely, which was an unusual situation for me. For years, I had had to move from one home to another, never getting the chance to say goodbye and left wondering what had happened to the other children – instant sisters and brothers who became a fragment of memory just as instantaneously. We were transient children who came and went, and were replaced, sometimes during the night. We could share our history with someone only to find their bed and wardrobe empty when we woke up. So I hung on to this precarious consistency for dear life, even though the events that led up to my leaving Fernlea – my hidden pregnancy being discovered at seven and a half months – left me with feelings of deceitfulness, sadness and, more profoundly, shame.

Passing my old bedroom window, I felt an acute sense of loss. I still cannot imagine what it must be like to leave the security of a loving home while always having the luxury of returning to familiarity when in need of reassurance, to be able to safely have a sulk, an argument and even a hissy fit. Being forcibly passive sure is exhausting.

The relationship between Aunt Elspeth and me had changed. It was now undeniably uncomfortable. I wondered if she felt angry with me for not confiding in her about my pregnancy, as this would no doubt have been professionally embarrassing for her. On another visit, I spotted her car parked outside Fernlea, so I popped in and found her sitting in her office behind her desk, perusing the daily report book. I stood there till she acknowledged me. Following a deliberate pause, she laid the report on the table and looked up at me. Finally, she tackled me, asking me the question, 'Why did you not tell me?' referring to my hidden pregnancy.

'I was afraid that I had let you down,' I replied candidly.

She told me there was to be a shake-up in staff training after

Christmas, and that all the staff were to be sent on courses, and that certain children's homes were being targeted for closures. Taking the news personally, the guilt consumed me. I thought my actions had brought a black mark to Fernlea's public and professional copybook.

In later years, when I got access to my files, I was angry to read that Aunt Elspeth had gone on record at the time stating: 'I knew she was pregnant. I was waiting for her to tell me, but I also wondered if her weight gain was genetic.' She had added: 'As she was adopted, we had no way of knowing.' It was clear that I had dented her professional pride.

Despite this, another reason I hung onto the continuity threads of Fernlea was to keep an eye on my wee sister Cathleen, who remained there. I felt extreme guilt for leaving Cathleen, but being pregnant and past the age of residence meant I had no choice; legally, I had to leave her. I consoled myself with a dream of getting a house and applying for guardianship of her.

It was in Fernlea that my adoptive father first laid eyes on Craig. A pre-festive visit for Cathleen had been arranged, and I had been contacted to be there too, probably to make it easier for the staff to deal with my father if he was drunk, as Cathleen usually disappeared after the pocket money was dished out. On finding out about my pregnancy, my adoptive father had stated in his Donegal brogue to the social worker, 'She has brought shame on my family.' I now find it interesting how he used the word 'my' in the context of family, suggesting he didn't really see me as part of his family. Perhaps on those occasions when he had drunkenly shouted, 'Get those adopted bastards out of here' he had actually been speaking his mind. Perhaps he felt he had been forced to take us in an attempt to justify his marriage and maintain the veneer of a normal family unit. Whatever the case, while he accused me of bringing shame on his family it was I who felt it most sharply. Like the scenario with my aunt Helen, we never spoke about it, though. I have a vague memory of him ignoring Craig, his first grandchild, on this visit. No mention was made by anybody of the shame in his violent and alcoholic behaviour, so I carried the full weight of that corroded can. 'Ach, men are different creatures,' some would say, excusing his behaviour. 'They need a strong woman,' my aunt said. I began to realise how much the odds had been stacked up against my adoptive mother and how she in her weariness, loneliness, disablement and isolation had joined my father in a destructive spiral of despising, depression and drinking. Despite this, I wanted this poor woman to be there for Craig, for me, for her.

It was after I had moved into Bernadette's and had begun to settle into a routine that a visit from Cathleen ended with shocking results. Christmas Day was closing in. The scent of cinnamon and berries from mulled wine wafted through Hamilton. Cathleen and I had been for a brisk walk with Craig in his pram around Strathclyde Country Park.

On our return to the empty flat, cheerful, we both had no idea about what was to unfold. She had been baby talking with Craig, nuzzling into his belly. Watching her with her unruly hair, her trademark blue National Health specs teetering and sitting squint on the end of her nose, I noticed she was very like our adoptive mother, whose National Health glasses had hung lopsided on her face while her unkempt locks dangled loosely like curled ribbons placed on the corner of a gift box. Aunt Helen had brought this likeness to my attention on the odd occasion. Perhaps because of this memory, and enjoying the closeness, I began to make a fuss about her being Craig's aunty. Possibly she felt the same, and she began talking about 'our' mum and dad.

As she talked openly, a lovely, rare ambience of family unity began to surround us, and I decide to use our time alone to gauge how she was in herself. I tentatively enquired how she felt about 'our' dad, starting with him first, as we had never spoken about that night 'our' mother died. Cathleen launched into the story she always did, about 'our' dad being drunk and us running around the house with a pee wee man – the pee wee man being a toy male figure you filled with water and on pulling his trousers down he'd pee a spray of water. Cathleen was not aware of most of the beatings I had received. She only remembered the companionship we had and the manic fun. The pain I felt on hearing Cathleen's fun-filled memories made me angry, but not angry at her. At only ten years old, she deserved to be able to reflect on the happy times she could remember, and I had no intention of trying to fill her head with the miserable moments. No matter how hard it was to sit and listen to her revelling in memories that pained me, I did, and I appreciated the fact that the memories, no matter how distorted, somehow held us together. Thinking I had picked my moment, I gently asked her, 'Do you ever think about our other parents?' hoping to have a craved-for heart-to-heart sister talk.

This was met with a blank look, then silence. Eventually, she said, 'What do you mean?'

Slowly, I said, 'Our real mums and dads.'

'I don't know what you mean,' she replied.

Instantly, the mood changed. The lovely ambience from only seconds ago had vanished. Face to face we stood there staring at each other. With a look of confusion, she withdrew her attention from Craig and turned away. My jaw felt as if it was dropping, but everything just seemed to freeze. My mind was racing until everything halted and the horrible conclusion hit me. Any comfort we had achieved being together that day drained away. I slowly reached over, removed Craig from the couch and put him in his pram in the bedroom. As I did so, the silent voice in my head was shouting, '*Oh no! Oh no! Cathleen doesn't know she's adopted*.' My vision focused on the two large windows behind her, the view over the park never ending. She sat down and then got up again; her stare through her little blue specs bored through me as she waited for an answer. I wanted to throw my arms round her and draw her close, as if this would let us avoid the truth coming out. Part of me wanted to rewind and erase what I had just so stupidly said, but the other part knew I had to tell her the truth. Everyone, including me, had assumed she knew, and now explaining was all I could do. Being her only sister, I had to. After all this time, despite all the schools, social workers, meetings, conferences, children's homes and upheaval to both our lives, no one had ever told her, and now it was down to me. I sat her down and placed myself beside her. I said, 'We were adopted, Cathleen.'

She looked at me and said, 'What does that mean?'

I cautiously told her the rose-tinted story, just as my mother had told it to me: of us being chosen from many children, picked only because we were special, and continued with, 'Our real mothers gave us away to have a better life.'

She just stared at me. My mind's cogs still whirring in a sixth gear, I followed it up quickly with the fact that in the eyes of the law we were sisters and suggested our relationship was perhaps more special because we had been chosen.

Through a fixed gaze, her first question was, 'Does that mean I am not Craig's real aunty?'

'Yes, you are, in the eyes of the law. You are his only aunty,' quickly adding, 'We were brought up together.'

Cathleen got up and went to the toilet, leaving me with my heart thumping, not sure if I had done the right thing, wondering what else I could do to soften the blow. I needed to convince her that I saw her as my sister and for me it really didn't change a thing.

On her return, she had clearly switched off, and she left moments later without even looking at me. I stood in panic mode, unsure what to do. I wanted to cry for her and for me. The door slammed, and I listened to my wee sister's footsteps fading down the stairs. There was no phone in the flat, and I knew I needed to contact my aunt Helen and Fernlea. I rushed into the bedroom to check that Craig was asleep in his pram, then put the snib on the door and ran down the stairs into the street and into my aunt's pub. It was heaving with people eating their pre-Christmas lunches – game pie was on nearly every table and celebratory music blasted from new screens. My aunt, however, was not there, so I pleaded with the barmaid to let me use the phone. With her thumb, she indicated I knew where the office was to make the phone call. Aunt Helen answered and I just blurted out that Cathleen did not know she was adopted. I cannot remember what she said. I then phoned Fernlea and got my aunt Elspeth. I blurted it out to her too. I can't remember what she said either; I only remember my parting sentence, 'Please talk to her, talk to my wee sister.' It never occurred to me then but does now that it would have been better for us if it had been someone else who told her. From that moment, she flatly refused to speak to me about it. We were never the same again. The messenger had been shot at point-blank range.

Gunning for resolve, the next day saw Craig and me marching up to Fernlea to speak to my aunt Elspeth about Cathleen before she went off duty at two o'clock. Also, I had recently received a letter in the post from Alex, Craig's father, to say he was coming up from London to see our son for the first time. I think I needed to talk to someone familiar with all involved.

As I sat babbling the stories about Cathleen and Alex, Aunt Elspeth confessed that Cathleen would not talk to her, then in lower tones she informed me that plans had been discussed at Cathleen's social work review case regarding her being possibly fostered. Another meeting would be put in place after Christmas. This had all been discussed without the presence of me, my aunt Helen or Cathleen.

When our adoptive mother died, Cathleen and I had been placed in care under a Section 15 voluntary care act, granted by our adoptive father, and because of this he still had legal ownership of us, and all the passing aunts and uncles from the children's homes and the social workers had a legal duty of care – so much care on paper, when in reality it was very different. It was deemed that although she had regular contact with my aunt Helen and me, it would be better for Cathleen to be fostered – more legal care – than remain in a children's home.

My aunt Helen had made it clear that she wanted time to think about adopting Cathleen, but despite the fact that she might be willing and able, not to mention the fact that she was the main carer outwith the social work department, bailing them out at every phone call, she was callously told she would have to go through the full assessment procedure before being considered. Aunt Elspeth told me that my aunt Helen's chances of being able to adopt Cathleen were slim. 'Your aunt Helen's is already overcrowded, and her hostility toward the social work department wouldn't help her. I'm sorry, Eileen, but your sister will probably be fostered to someone else.'

When my sister Cathleen and I were younger, my aunt Helen had put us up and tried to keep us at her home, while at the same time her own five children were coming and going with their partners and children. As there wasn't enough room for us all, she had asked for help in finding accommodation for her daughter Bernadette, who had just married and was living at home, and the social work department had accused her of trying to exploit our situation in order to get her daughter a good house in a good area. Aunt Helen had been brought up without the support of a benefit system and had a strong work ethic, so the accusation that she was trying to 'work the system' had stung her pride.

Astonishingly, Aunt Elspeth further told me it was also my father's wish that Cathleen should be fostered. With hindsight, it is clear from the history contained within our social work files that my father was acting out of spite, yet they were at the very least entertaining him. Legally, Cathleen belonged both to the social work department and my father, as it was a voluntary care order. Both had a duty of care towards her. However, it seemed neither party was capable or responsible enough to have her best interests at heart.

I left Fernlea furious and frustrated, pushing Craig at the speed of a petrol lawn mower. There were no more sisterly walks in the park that winter. I headed home to prepare for Alex arriving and Christmas. I knew Aunt Elspeth expected me to pass on the information to my aunt Helen. It was important information, so this I did.

Unsurprisingly my aunt Helen's response was one of anger and resulted in a phone call to the social work department that raged for nearly 30 minutes. I sat petrified but with a shadow of pleasure, not knowing what would happen, and all the while Cathleen was kept in the dark. I wanted to speak to her and let her know, but by delivering the message of her adoption I had hurt her, and she wasn't ready to talk to me, let alone forgive me. Aunt Helen's voice was getting louder by the second: 'When was I going to be consulted? You take the wishes of a drunken violent father over the well-being of a settled child,' she shouted. 'She's nearby us, as is her school. You people think you can do whatever you like, but you can't.' Her parting shot was, 'And a Merry Christmas to you.'

The tension was unbearable as I heard the phone being slammed down, and I sat afraid, feeling I was the cause of the brewing trouble. My aunt stormed past me, slammed the door and went upstairs. Not knowing what to do, I got up and left. A feeling of helplessness and confusion followed me every step of the way home. More decisions were being made that made no sense. The actions of the people involved made me feel like we were labelled products in a system to be shipped and dispatched according to the latest research and theory. On the controlled conveyor belt of hypothesis and conjecture I sat in complete frustration.

4

All out of love

A few days of unrest followed, during which I retreated and stayed out of everyone's way. Then two days before Christmas, the knock on the door came announcing the arrival of Craig's father. Immediately on entering the living room, Alex walked towards Craig's pram. I watched his face; it was beaming. He picked Craig up and instead of feeling happiness at this first father-and-son interaction I felt disappointment. My thoughts and quiet scrutiny were now concentrating on Alex. As I continued to watch and observe him, I felt very confused. This should have been a wonderful moment. But his dark hair and blue eyes that had once been seductive were now just dark hair and blue eyes. In reality, looking back, my fantasy of us being a family had burst. I was experiencing anger mixed with the lack of joy. The confusion was a result of that conflict.

As he held Craig in his arms, looking the image of the proud father, he sat down and asked me, 'Why did you call him Craig?'

'I liked the name. I had three picked,' I replied. 'Anthony or Gregg were the other two,' I added. Suddenly, out of nowhere my teeth were clenching and I began to feel irritation and a rising anger. I tried to ignore these feelings but memories of my aunt visiting me in hospital when it was revealed I was seven and a half months pregnant came to the forefront of my mind. She had whispered to me, 'You don't have to get married.' She had seen it all before and had known the bubble would burst. I now knew what she had been trying to tell me and I knew she was right. '*Dinnae marry for money or convenience – it's a lot mair expensive tae get oot a and ye can get a loan cheaper.*'

I put a brave smile on and scolded myself, '*This was not how it was supposed to be. What is wrong with you, Eileen?*' That persistent and threatening question kept swirling from an omnipotent fog. The romance of it all was dying and in its place was the anger and disappointment emerging as a consequence of being left alone to deal with my hidden pregnancy and Alex's reluctance to tell his mother. He had not appeared at the birth and there had been no card or acknowledgement from him or his family.

It may have been wrong, but I hated the fact that he had left me to carry the baby and agonise for months in secret, yet here he was sitting holding Craig and gaining from the experience without having done any of the hard work. It was maybe just as well he was staying with one of his brothers. It wasn't clear how long he was going to stay in Scotland for or what his plans were. We behaved like a couple and so much was expected, but no discussions had taken place between us. There was a baby, so we floundered around not knowing what else to do. I expected him to tell me his plans, which he never did. Maybe he expected me to tell him what they were to be – what I expected. I never did. My pride would not allow me to be accused of trapping a man, and I was not sure I wanted to. On reflection, I think I wanted him to take a certain amount of control of the situation, to be there because he wanted to be, not because he had to.

Christmas Day came and went in the usual way, only there were an extra three at my aunt and uncle's house for dinner – Craig, Alex and my cousin Helen's baby. My aunt Helen did her shift at the pub and on her return dinner was served. The house was busy and dinner descended into a party with a few extras arriving. The usual insults were traded as jovial banter. The men stood as always with their backs against the wall watching the proceedings. With a few drinks down their necks, they joked in Billy Connolly style with quips like, 'Aye, ye'll no win the pools wi that coupon,' meaning the recipient was ugly and would not win any competitions. Songs were sung, including Glasgow favourites like 'Cod

Liver Oil and the Orange Juice' by Hamish Imlach and 'My Brother Sylveste', where we all joined in the chorus: 'Got an arm like a leg' – at which a wolf whistle would go up, while the line 'lady's leg' would follow, having been eagerly anticipated, and in time be roared out in a bellowed chorus. My cousin Helen's 'Single Girl' by Sandy Posey was scheduled in there somewhere, as was Bernadette's 'Summertime'. My uncle Charles, who was normally quiet, chipped in with the occasional one-liner and his 'moothie' act.

As his harmonica notes sailed into the air like bubbles that burst with melodies, I disappeared into the bedroom that had once been mine to feed Craig. Here, I began to unravel. As I listened to the mingled voices and laughter, my mind led itself down the garden path of hankering. I wanted to be in a home with a mother and father. Not the one I had but the castles-in-the-air home I had dreamt of as a child, and probably still did dream about. As I sat on the bed and held a feeding Craig closer, I felt my heart muscles tighten as he suckled on his bottle. I imagined sitting at my mother's feet, a coal fire in front of me, my mother brushing my hair with colourful ribbons waiting to be braided in. I dreamt I was being told I was special and loved, and imagined a feeling of warm security. Tears were close and about to escape when Alex came looking for me. The door opened, allowing the hilarity and party atmosphere to enter the room and jolt me back to reality. I looked up and smiled, wearing the mask of '*I'm all right*'.

On Boxing Day morning, we began to get organised for an overnight stay with Alex's brother and his family in Larkhall. I packed clean underwear and a toothbrush for myself into Craig's baby bag. I hurriedly made up a bottle and fed him before we left. I had dressed Craig in a lovely blue outfit with a pompom hat my aunt Elspeth had knitted for him and then stuffed him into a lovely Wedgwood-blue-coloured snowsuit that I had proudly bought him for Christmas. Feeling in better spirits, and excited at the prospect of meeting Alex's family, I rallied. Perhaps this was because of hopes of being included instead of bringing shame on a family, as my father had stated.

When we got off the bus, Alex carried Craig's bag and I carried Craig, like a little blue snail with a snowsuit as his shell, from the bus stop to his brother's house. On the way there, we met another of Alex's brothers, who was 'just visiting Larkhall'. He made a few approving sounds about Craig and me, then he was gone. An apparent sadness in this brother is all I really remember, and to this day I don't know why. But it was due to this meeting that I began to feel anxious about the fact that we could not just get up and go home. All the buses had stopped early due to the festive season and there was no other way that we could get back.

Alex and his brother had a drink, and I discovered more cracks in the family. It seemed to be a source of resentment that Alex's mother had gone to London many years ago and had left all the brothers with their dad in Larkhall. Maybe it was all the family history threatening to surface that made me nervous.

As we settled down for the night in makeshift beds, Alex drunk beside me on the floor, we realised that Craig's milk powder had been left at home. We argued in whispers as we tiptoed into the kitchen. His brother had a young child, and we found some Farley's Rusks in a cupboard. I mixed a couple with hot milk and hoped it would suffice till we got home.

I lay awake that night staring at the ceiling, miserable and not wanting to be there. Around four o'clock in the morning, the makeshift bed shook, as did the house. I sat bolt upright, Alex beside me sleeping, Craig between us. I thought a lorry had crashed outside the house, but no one else woke. Later that day, I discovered we had in fact experienced a rare earthquake that had lasted ten seconds and amounted to Mark 2 on the Richter scale. It reflected the volcanic rumblings of fear within me.

Rising early and going home to get Craig's milk, I realised it was over. Any dreams of the three of us becoming a family were gone. In my eyes, I had failed to provide Craig with the loving and caring environment I had longed for him to have. I wanted his life to be better than mine and I had failed. This guilt, coupled with the worry about Alex's homelessness and meeting his friends who were still of a criminal element, made us argue constantly for several weeks. There was nothing too big or small to argue over, so everything was a target, everything, that is, except the truth. The truth being it was over. Nobody wants to take responsibility for ending it. Blame must always be placed elsewhere in a cowardly fashion. 'It's usually long over before the shouting and bawling,' a mature woman told me 30 years later. What real hope did we have with both of us under 20, with very little guidance, thrown together and trying to do the best we could? In my frustration and fear of the inevitable, I wrote Alex a swan song of a sentimental poem from a 16 year old.

The World
I'd lock out the country and town,
Leaving tears behind long ago.
I'd lock out 'them' and never let you down,
I'd be with you no matter how low.

I'd lock out reality,
We would live on dreams.
I'd bring in fantasy,
We have nothing else it seems.

I'd lock out the world except you,
Though sometimes I wish I could do that too.

Inexperienced and anxious, several weeks later I sought guidance. I spoke to my aunt Elspeth on a planned visit to Fernlea and discussed what happened the night we stayed with Alex's family. Years later, I discovered an entry in my social work notes from about this time: 'There is concern over Eileen's ability to look after Craig; she has gone without baby milk for Craig.' There was no mention of where the information came from or my response, and it is betrayals like these that have left me with feelings of powerlessness and mistrust. The anguish is doubled when the source is deemed credible by society – social workers, churchgoing people, charity workers and the like.

I was acutely aware that my status was low – my adoption, my mother's death, my father's behaviour, my own behaviour and now the fact I was an unwed mother all stacked up against me in the reputation stakes. The

All out of love

stakes would take an even bigger beating if I was ever revealed for the person I really was, the person I was made to be by that man, Urquhart. Yes, if my secret crimes were revealed, what would happen to me then? What would be written against my name in the files and folders? My history was still being written by strangers and it was detrimental to my future, as professional strangers read what others had written and formed preconceived opinions about me. Despite every effort I made to blossom and bloom, I was viewed as a weed and a nuisance, social worked and strangled by the system. Also like weeds, my nightmares continued growing in the garbage garden of my sleep.

With or without Alex, I had to get on with my new life as a mother. Leaving the flat to go shopping or out in general meant having to bump Craig's large Silver Cross pram down four flights of stairs, run back up to get him from his cot and get back down the stairs before the pram was nicked. When out strolling with Craig, I would roam around the shopping centre, window shopping and dreaming. Food shopping for essentials was done on a Monday after I had visited the main post office with my benefits book to get my 'supplementary benefit', as it was then called. Which supermarket I went to depended on the weather, how I felt and how much money I had that week. A bright day would see me at the Top Cross shopping at Presto, other times it was Safeway in the precinct.

After that was done, I was then free to dream and window shop in the January sales. After feasting my eyes on the beautifully painted dolls' houses with exquisite accessories in Hobby Horse on Townhead Street, I would move on to Ink Spot in Castle Street. Ink Spot was a shop full of unusual gifts, stocked with row upon row of fabulous paint colours and a whole host of paintbrushes in different sizes. I loved the smell. A terrible urge to open all the oil paint tubes and squeeze colour everywhere like a map of emotional abundance and internal graffiti would see me leaving in a hurry. This was the type of shop I could have run amok in if I'd had any money.

Once a week, I would go into Leisure Land, an amusement arcade that allowed prams and babies. Sitting there amongst the noise, smoke

39

and people, I could give Craig a bottle and have an affordable snack with a cup of tea. Though I never spoke to anyone other than to place my order or to the odd waitress who complimented Craig and his curls, I felt like part of something. When it was time to return to the flat, the Olympic ordeal involving Craig, the pram and the flights of stairs was reversed, only it seemed ten times worse going up than it did down. No wonder I remained so thin!

February passed and as we moved into March I felt my feet had barely touched the ground at Bernadette's when I sensed a change on the way. Eyes began avoiding me while the pretence that all was well carried on. It was noted again in reports by my social worker that she could sense a tension in the household. Both observations proved right. Within weeks, although Alex had found accommodation in a homeless unit sharing with Bernadette's boyfriend, he found the situation too difficult and returned to London. Days later, I found myself packing bags and moving to Hove House, a homeless unit in Blantyre.

Just before we moved, Craig and I attended a required hearing test at the Orchard Street clinic; he passed with flying colours. Mrs Linn was once more the person who conducted the procedure, the same woman who had called me a 'neurotic teenage mother' as I tried to assert myself to suggest during Craig's basic development tests that I had nagging worries over his hearing. I sat silent during the process, muted by her previous public dismissal of my fears. My heart welled with love for Craig as I watched his eyes follow her shadow as she moved about the room, ringing a bell. His bright blue eyes shone sharp and alert as he easily followed her around the room. 'See, he's perfectly fine,' she scolded. Again, I left feeling worthless, ridiculed and angry at myself.

To further my misery, Cathleen was sent to a foster family in the north-east of Glasgow and a new school – the largest secondary school in Scotland at the time. This deeply upset me. How could I keep an eye on her there? Who would take care of her and make sure she was OK? I was frightened for her and frustration led to more self-loathing over my failure to protect her. I briefly discussed Cathleen's situation with my aunt Helen, and we both promised each other we would report back what we found whenever we were allowed to visit. We would collude.

My aunt and I were angry that the social work department would pay these strangers money to look after Cathleen yet had refused and ridiculed my aunt Helen for asking for money for beds and bedding for us. Furthermore, she was never asked to foster Cathleen, the only alternatives offered being to adopt or nothing. My aunt felt this was a slant against her, that people perceived her as seeking to profit financially from the situation.

Money was tight, but I was driven to let Cathleen know that I was still her sister and still around. I phoned Cathleen's foster family and travelled to their home on several buses with Craig, having acquired a second-hand buggy to be more mobile. Arriving freezing cold on my first visit, I seemed to be welcomed by the foster family, who had several other children. In conversations with Rebecca Mower, the foster parents had said that Cathleen was not gelling well with the other kids, 'She is moody,' they added. When Rebecca Mower shared this with me, I wondered if that was just a preconceived perception, as it was possible that someone had written this in her files. Cathleen did not seem displeased to see me but was withdrawn. I told myself it was because I had let her down. We talked off and on for an hour, after which I said goodbye and made the journey back to the homeless unit.

Depression and feelings of uselessness began to overwhelm me. It seemed like my life was a revolving door of despairing upheavals. Yet, paradoxically, it was these same upheavals that rescued me and kept me from being static long enough for the effects of my life's pain to be able to take full control of me and steer me to a place from where there was no return. The chaos kept a tumultuous tide and the inevitable at bay.

5

Back to basics

Raiders of the Lost Ark was the summer of 1980 blockbuster movie. 'Suicide is Painless' the enigmatic hit from the *M*A*S*H* TV series which was hauntingly sung from shop tannoy systems. It would be years before I could go to the movies again or own a video recorder to watch them when they came out on tape. Although I wasn't in a position myself to look for work, as I had to take care of Craig, the headlines about spiralling unemployment and recession were depressing and only added to the gloom I felt. As a teenager, the anger and despair I had felt had found an outlet in the boundless energy of Punk music. Romantic music was a guilty pleasure that I would never have admitted to listening to. However, a cooler kid was now taking Punk's place, and the recession was not felt by all. New Romantics were becoming the 'in' trend and terms such as 'yuppies' were coming into use. I was down but not out, and, although the immediate future seemed to hold no promise, I was still dreaming and determined that change would happen.

Change was always possible, but not always for the good. Hove House was owned and run by the local council. The building was Victorian and reminded me of the children's homes, in particular the Glasgow Church of Scotland hostel Kidron House, where I had almost died of a prolonged asthma attack during which Miss Dunnet, the hostel warden, had whispered in my ear with undisguised satisfaction, 'That's your badness coming out in you.'

Hove House, like Kidron House, was impressive in its architecture yet depressive in its function. It was more of the same and it frightened me without me knowing it. I was in a permanent state of fear, but as this had been the case for most of my life I was almost oblivious to it, and living with my heart sitting high in my chest was normal. Large windows let in light, but the dark-wood furniture stinking of vinegar and the cold, tiled communal toilets with no toiletries or toilet roll shrank its beauty. I later discovered we had to take a toilet roll when we used the toilet and return it to our respective bedrooms.

My large room, which would have been sought after in the west end of Glasgow, smelt of must and mothballs. The large, old double bed, rickety bunk-beds and other mismatched furniture was a permanent reminder I was not a permanent resident here. These were not my belongings. I had once overheard a relative referring to me as a 'cuckoo in the nest,' and I found myself feeling like one again.

On our first day at the unit, I was given a rules and regulations drill by Mrs Woods, the warden. As in previous institutions, I found I was back to making my bed like a nurse – envelope style. I could make a bed tight enough for it to be a struggle to get into it at night. There were grey, itchy, blanket-stitched covers with a bright orange candlewick top cover, like the one Cathleen and I shared as children, when we used ginger bottles as hot-water bottles. Then it went bottom sheet, then top sheet tucked envelope fashion and economically rotated. Only one sheet got washed per week and there was a strict cleaning rota. You either complied with the rules or you were ejected, baby or no baby. The public phone was out of bounds in the evening, and no incoming calls were allowed at any time I was told, with no explanation given as to the reason why. I knew better than to ask.

We were not allowed any visitors without prearrangement and permission, and I had to fill in paperwork to request a visit, giving appropriate notice. But the only person to visit me here was my father, who had rejoined Alcoholics Anonymous. I'm not sure if it was through a sense of remorse or just because he was lonely that he came to visit us, but I was intensely grateful for his sobriety during his visits.

It spared me the heart-crushing humiliation he would have inflicted on us had he arrived in a stupor.

I felt that our lack of visitors was my fault. I had put myself and Craig in this position, and I was shameful. I really did not know how to give myself a break. I had not done enough to prevent the situation, and now Craig was getting the worst possible start in life. The one-line or even one-word answers I gave to those ignorant and less compassionate around me made it look like I was being defensive, or obtuse, ungrateful even. It never occurred to me that people's guilt or my low status within a tenuous family unit helped predetermine how people treated us.

The correct title of our new accommodation was Hove House Rehabilitation Unit for the Homeless; however, it was Dickensian. No single men were allowed; only families and destitute single mothers, as Mrs Woods called us. The seven family rooms were full, one with six people in it: four children and the married couple. Never in my time there did any of the rooms lie empty for more than a few days. Our rehabilitation for the crime of being without a home included being instructed how to iron clothes properly and prepare food, such as pancakes, from scratch. These lessons took the form of a group meeting of all the mothers in the house grudgingly congregating in a freezing old concrete outhouse building. There we were arranged in a semicircle and told by Mrs Woods that we had to learn to be good housekeepers and mothers while the men found work. Our attendance at these meetings was compulsory and was the only break in the strict routine of cleaning, scrubbing and ironing. No one challenged her or responded; they were all emotionally beaten and legally bound by the council rules. Resentments were kept for the communal kitchen later on, when it was felt safe to talk without being overheard and subsequently put on a warning with the fear of being told to leave.

The daily duties consisted of cleaning, scrubbing and ironing. All the brass handles on the doors had to be polished. All floors were hand scrubbed and all windows washed. During the day, little mole mounds of moving women on their knees scrubbed themselves and their cloths across the floors and stairs. As in the Church of Scotland-run Kidron House, work on a Sunday was prohibited. No washing on the line, no smell of cleaning, and dinner had to be prepared the night before. Craig was the youngest child there. The others were at school or nursery. I juggled like any other mother, carrying out tasks and duties while he slept and wheeling him around strapped into his buggy if he was awake.

I'm sure most of the women were more than capable of cooking, cleaning and balancing budgets, but the rules were the rules, and we all had to obediently follow them. The men, however, did no housework, sitting in their rooms while the women cleaned and cooked. Some either secretly drank, though it was no secret, or went out for the day, driven by the search for work or mere escape. We women stayed, only allowed out at certain hours and only after chores were completed. Depression, alcohol and other circumstances had us on our knees, and the cleaning kept us there.

However, I never remained stagnant in my misery; my determination always found that chink in the dark. Sometimes, when the building was staff free, we would find ourselves telling jokes, sliding down banisters and singing. This was our attempt at subordination, a safe protest about our situation. One woman would start us off and the domino-effect choir would be chorusing till we erupted into laughter or a car appeared to shut us up. As well as keeping us busy and distracted from our misfortune, this did serve a common cause, lifting our spirits and relieving tension. Fragile freedom it was: we could secretly sing, though we had no voice. There was a fragile camaraderie of patterned pinnies united by circumstantial cleaning.

This state of affairs, of course, could never be addressed. There was a fearful respect for Mrs Woods. It became clear that she ruled this place with a tight rein, and the harness was called shame. She would regularly slide her fingers across polished wood, revealing a spiteful dust particle, and delight in indicating sloppiness. 'This won't do, no wonder you have found yourself here,' would be her conquering put-down. This was always done in public, and usually when the woman in question was cheerful or distracted by conversation. Lest we forget our station in life!

Curiously, in complete contrast to this tyranny, she would

occasionally invite a select few to the office in the evening. This was deemed a privilege and when it was my turn I would feel guilty about those she didn't invite.

'Come in, ladies, find a seat,' she would say while we were herded inside. Some women were overtly thrilled to receive the invitation, as it offered an escape from the one room in which we lived, breathed, cleaned, ate and slept with husbands and children. This was our big night out. Others accepted only to avoid the hostility that would inevitably have followed rejection. I could only accept if Craig was sleeping.

We were condensed into the small room with a desk, a few comfy chairs and a sofa, and this was the parlour setting where we would play games of bingo – a game I hated. We would all be over exuberant when someone won a line or a full house. 'Wonderful, ladies,' Mrs Woods would say. She reminded me of a distorted Miss Jean Brodie minus the underlying passion and heaving bosom. She took great delight in holding court, and I wondered about her personal life at these times. Resentfully, I wondered how these nights would be retold at her church: did they see her as a saint? Doing society a service? I felt angry with myself for being there.

'Jane, you have won a clothes line,' she would announce, or it could have been a packet of pegs. A well-known brand of cleaning product was usually the prize for a full house. Special prizes appeared occasionally, such as key rings, nail brushes and pumice sets. I admit to beginning to be caught up in the gratefulness of it all. You sure do cut your cloth to suit.

'This is my son, James,' she announced proudly one night. A tall, handsome, fair-haired boy of about 18 entered the room. He joined us without any sign of self-consciousness. As the bingo commenced, it was clear she was the lady of the manor and us her subjects. James flirted and teased us for the duration of the night. I watched older, beaten-down women coming to life, giggling, playing with their hair and covering their faces with their hands. Although he had looks in his favour, in my resentment and shame I thought to myself that in the outside world he would have been known as a mummy's boy.

In the kitchen the next day, the rising resentments would surface.

'See what *that* James said to me, last night,' one woman gushed, blushed and played with her hair. Her glow dimmed as a retort was launched from another cooker stand: 'Ach, you stupid wummin, him upstairs is only playing doonstairs wae the servants.'

On one of these occasions, I returned to my room feeling such anger and hatred at the wretched situation I had found myself in. As I quickly became distanced from the other women, I spent more and more time reading. Books provided the depth and meaning I desperately searched for in life, but as each book concluded I felt a sense of loss until the next cover opened and the cycle started again. It felt like yo-yo dieting: either I was in a feast while reading or a famine when not. A beautiful piece I never forgot and wallowed in for strength was from William Shakespeare's *The Winter's Tale*.

> I am not prone to weeping, as our sex
> Commonly are; the want of which vain dew
> Perchance shall dry your pities: but I have
> That honourable grief lodged here which burns
> Worse than tears drown.

After being ridiculed by staff in Fernlea when I was heard reading aloud in my bedroom, I never did it again even in private. With paper and pen always handy, I would scribble phrases down and keep them, only hearing them in my head. To help feed my reading habit, I located the nearest library and indulged myself in my literary first aid kit – words for wounds. I began to read more war history, and in feminist writings I had found another secret world. Although initially frightened, I quickly became fascinated by the strength of the women whose personalities were bold and strong and who were determined to succeed. Germaine Greer told me from her pages that men hated me; Andrea Dworkin wrote that all sex was rape. It froze my hurting, as she nailed it for me. There it was in black and white, they had given me a hook to hang my hurt hat on. Men hated me and it was my fault for having sex. It strengthened my resolve to never become vulnerable. However, I misinterpreted Dworkin as meaning that my secret history with Urquhart had happened because I had allowed it, and that having sexual feelings was a betrayal of the female strength and a weakness in myself.

Looking back, it was no coincidence that I gravitated towards these readings and feelings. I had the misfortune of having a dark hidden history, and I was reading intellectualised material in isolation. Ineffective, as a member of the underclass, my lowly position among the ranks of the dependent and financially destitute was compounded by my isolation and the fact that I had no peers with whom I could share my thoughts and feelings and put them into context. Like a fish out of water, I floundered.

We women did have one ally in the council camp, a Mrs Mac, or Mac-Mac as she was called by the kids. She was local to the area. Her hair was a soft grey powder-puff, like the ashes left from a wood fire, and she was rotund and motherly. She was Mrs Woods' right-hand woman. She wore a pale-blue checked overall with popper buttons that strained against her large bosom. Mac-Mac worked closely with us in the laundry and instructed us on our cleaning duties. 'Aye, she thinks she is something,' was her opinion of Mrs Woods, and she teased us about fraternising with the big boss on the bingo nights and about the pegs we won. She had no hesitation in sharing her dislike of the woman with us and sometimes gave us advance warning of official visits as a way of undermining her.

'Mr Johnston is coming today,' she would whisper in warning to us as she was excluded from the office. Mr Johnston was the head of the homeless department at the council offices in Hamilton. Having Mrs Mac as an insider, supplying us with information and in-house gossip, gave us underdogs a deluded sense of having the heads up on the council despots.

Usually he would only come on a Monday afternoon, which coincided with most of us getting our benefits. We had to go to the post office early in the day to cash our weekly books then queue up and hand an arranged sum over to Mrs Woods that went into a savings account for when we were re-housed. Or, in other cases, some of it went towards repaying the arrears that had originally led to the payee being evicted from their home. When the money was handed over, a tick would be made next to a list that was made up for us by Mrs Woods. On the list were clotheslines, pegs, buckets, mops and cleaning products: the bare essentials to equip us for good housewifery. On a monthly basis we were given some of our money to buy these essentials from places like What Every Woman Wants.

Throughout my time at Hove House I was still in touch with the social work department as, legally, I was still a child and under their care until I was 18 or my father signed out of the Section 15 voluntary care act. He did none of the caring yet held a certain amount of legal power, part of the trend not to sever contact between children and parents. As a result of this, a woman called Penny Wheeler had come back into my life. I had first encountered her during her visits to Aunt Elspeth at Fernlea. I never knew her job title, just that she worked in the local social work office. On one occasion, she had complimented me to my aunt Elspeth, saying, 'What a wonderful carriage that girl has,' as she watched me walk in from school with that Presbyterian pole of defensiveness strapped to my back. Penny had also given me a very expensive ornate lipstick, highly perfumed. I would swivel it up and down from the bottom of its jewel-encrusted casing. In awe of it, it remained in my bag long after it had run out. It smelt of luxury and cleanliness, and I adored it. (I am compelled to smell things. Even in supermarkets today I can be seen leaving with liquid on my nose if I have squeezed a bottle too hard.) Back then, Aunt Elspeth had been proud of 'her girl'. Now, with no pride in myself, I had to overcome my feelings of shame and speak to Penny myself.

Aunt Elspeth had made me aware that there was an independent living unit being set up for those leaving care, and I was determined to plead my case. The unit was being set up in Lanarkshire but I was still under the voluntary care of Glasgow social work department due to my father's place of residence. This discrepancy, along with the fact that I was an unwed mother, meant that I would probably be excluded. But I was determined to try for a place.

Mac-Mac came to my rescue. She slipped me the number of the

public phone that was situated out on the locked porch. Apparently, the number had been changed months before when a woman had 'discovered' it and been caught using the phone. I could only get to speak to Penny about the project in secret phone calls, so I was dependent on Mac-Mac as my confidante, as well as on my nerve holding out.

We were only allowed to make outgoing calls during the day. No incoming calls were allowed. Any calls outside office hours had to be requested and made in front of Mrs Woods in the office, when she came to do her evening patrol, and only if she deemed them an emergency or if they qualified as important. Although Penny was part of the Hamilton social work department, she refused to go through the official channel of Mrs Woods. I detected she disliked Mrs Woods. 'Eileen, you are a mother, a young woman, I shall deal directly with you, not Mrs Woods,' was one of her first statements in one of our covert calls. She would go to the trouble of phoning me from home after work to ensure our discussions remained private.

Although I was grateful for this advantage, I felt guilty and angry that the other women were excluded from this opportunity. 'Mrs Mac,' I said, as we folded my bed sheets, 'what would happen if one of the children took ill during the night or anything went wrong here?'

In a lowered voice, she sympathised, saying it was barbaric and explaining that on the odd occasion women had had to run the two streets to her house to use her phone when an emergency had occurred.

Mrs Woods usually left at five o'clock, and it was then that room doors would tentatively open and family dinners would begin to be made – the last time of day that we were allowed to use the kitchen. Voices and laughter could be heard as the place came alive with the aroma of hot food. On the occasions she left early, I stood at the tall windows, leaning against the ancient radiators for longer than I had to just to make sure she had actually gone. I stared at the jagged steel fence and gates surrounding us, afraid that she may have forgotten something and return and catch me doing something that broke the bizarre house rules. I couldn't afford for Craig and me to be kicked out, so the extra few minutes taken to stare out the window were well spent.

During my stay at Hove House, I regularly witnessed Mrs Woods' attempts to ring-fence certain women and then elevate them to the rank of favourite. I was stunned by how quickly some of the women would exchange allegiance in the hope of gaining petty privileges, but I was disgusted at how quickly each woman would be discarded to make room for the next selected favourite. They swung from bad mouthing Mrs Woods while in company in the kitchen to running errands for her and snitching on the other residents. They would make tea and bake cakes that they would sit and enjoy with her. Some must have hoped that by being subservient and possibly even through snitching they might get pushed up the housing ladder. No one discussed what they said in the office. Probably due to a sense of humiliation and shame, I did not despise them for this behaviour; I felt angry. It was a classic tactic of 'divide and conquer'.

Having once been in this position with Aunt Elspeth and the staff politics at Fernlea, I knew the signs, so when attempts were made to ring-fence me I was clever enough to move out of the way. Mrs Woods attempted to hold me up as an example in the kitchen. During lunchtime, as we cooked with our backs to her, she circled the kitchen. I was frying an egg on the cooker designated to me when suddenly she took centre stage, saying condescendingly, 'Now, ladies, that is how you fry an egg.' As I turned and looked at her, she nodded 'Tell them how you do it, Eileen.'

Embarrassed and not wanting to be her new favourite, I said, 'Low heat, number 3,' and stared at the egg as it fried. I was not going to separate myself from these women. A sense of loyalty sometimes blind, sometimes principled, was strengthening in me. I refused to toady, thrawn as ever.

After she left that day, I launched myself up the few stairs like a fired cannonball and into the porch, desperate to call Penny. As she understood the situation with the phone and sympathised with me, I knew she would keep the call short. With each call I made, it seemed that getting into the project was more likely. She had told me that having a baby should not count against me, and that day she said, 'It's happening next Monday, only four days to go, Eileen.'

We celebrated quietly over the phone, and I then immediately went into my room and started to declutter. The old record player covered in black tape and found at a nearby dump got binned. Anything else unnecessary got the same treatment. I triumphantly cleaned and cleaned my room with pride as I was leaving.

I was busy doing this over the next few days when Annie, an extremely quiet, thin and dark-haired, sunken-cheeked woman who lived at the top of the house, knocked my door. Her room was right next door to the office. I was surprised, as she was rarely seen.

'Eileen, can I come in?' she whispered.

'Hold on, Annie,' I replied. I ran over to the heavy door and undid the locked snib. Annie stood there looking very frail and anxious. I invited her in. Although I was very curious, this was tempered by anxiety over what had elicited the visit. I thought to myself, 'She never leaves her room.' Her son did all the shopping, leaving the building quietly and returning in the same way. As she walked towards me, I couldn't help but think her body appeared too old for her years. She wore clothes that were worn and looked insipid after years of washing.

'Can I give you these?' she said, holding out a pile of browning A4 paper with writing in blue ink.

'What is it?' I asked.

'Just some writing I have done over the years,' she replied. She held eye contact with me. 'I want you to have them.'

I reached out and took hold of them. I felt somewhat bemused. 'Can I read them?' I asked.

'Yes, please do,' she replied, and then she left. There was no explanation as to why I was given the papers, which left me feeling perplexed by the whole experience. I stood holding the papers for some time, trying to work out what had just gone on, but I could think of nothing that would explain the exchange. Looking down at the pile of papers, I instantly fell in love with the beautiful handwriting that adorned the pages. Anxiety faded and I felt I had been bequeathed something very private and precious. Hiding them under my mattress, I was filled with excitement knowing I would be able to sit down and read them in my bed that night.

After tea and as the hustle and bustle in the kitchen dwindled, one by one the snibs on the room doors could be heard being snubbed shut. Whole families were now preparing to settle down for the evening. Children had been regimentally bathed and the hum of TVs could just be heard. Alone in my room, with Craig fast asleep, I got into my creaking ancient bed and under the institutionally boiled white sheets with the name 'Hove House' clearly written in thick black marker pen. If I took a deep breath, I could almost taste the vinegar and powdered scrub used to clean away the aged smells. But these efforts were in vain, as the smells always returned; like a residue of others' misfortune and sadness they filled the room and offered no comfort.

I reached down and collected the pile of brown papers from the bottom of the bed. Holding them in my hands, I stared at the beautiful handwriting before turning over the first paper and beginning to read. Mesmerised, I read a delightful poem that was a tribute to Al Jolson. Another mourned a dead mother and there was a beautifully affecting poem of a young woman who, after giving birth alone in a cave, left her baby to be found by strangers. One philosophised on the nature of hate.

What is Hate?
What is hate I want to know?
What makes one hate another so?
The answer I do find most clear,
To hate just simply means to fear.

Laying the poems down by my side, I thought about my own writing, which was more abstract so it did not give much away if it was ever discovered by someone else, and I wondered whether these poems were the woman's personal story. I wondered again why she had randomly appointed me as their keeper and why she had given me the originals. This rarely seen or acknowledged woman at the top of the stairs confused me. How would I feel if one day I found myself in her shoes? The pain she must have felt when parting with such personal belongings would have been unbearable to me. I never did get an explanation about why she had given her papers to me. It would not be the last time someone gave me private papers with no explanation. I guess it's possible that she realised more about me at that time than I did.

The situation reminded me of my panic when the Glasgow poet Hamish Whyte, who had taken to writing to me when I was in care, began to point out to me what my poetry was about – that I was trying to deal with the trauma of my past through my writing. Believing he would expose what I had done, I immediately stopped writing to him. He had become a threat; coming too close to uncovering the crimes I felt I had committed, predominantly my crime of 'allowing' Urquhart to have sex with me. Secrets kept at seven were still to be kept at seventeen.

Having read all the pages, I had a desire to go upstairs and tell Annie how wonderful they were. I wanted her to know how much I appreciated the words and stories therein. I wanted to ask her why she had chosen me as their custodian. I played out the imagined conversation I would have liked to have with her in my head time and time again, but my insecurities held me back. Maybe if I had been older and not so scared of people getting too close I would have gone to talk to her. Still just 17, and justifiably untrusting of establishments and terrified that my own secrets would be exposed, my hurt and terror remained bubble wrapped, fragile and as yet never spoken about. I completely believed that if the truth came out about my past I could be locked up in a mental institution and lose Craig. They would never believe a 'homie'.

My mother's horrific and traumatic death that I alone had witnessed had also never been spoken about. Looking back, it occurs to me to wonder whom I would have spoken to about it. Who cared enough to listen, or ask? No one? I could not trust the social workers or any of the random people who came and went in my life. Many decades later, I realised that my silence also protected others from the truth of my life. People could get on with their daily lives with impunity or without having to respond.

The next day was panic stations as I found myself occupied with an appointment with the baby clinic for a hearing test for Craig. Mrs Woods controlled the delivery of the post, just as she controlled everything else at Hove House, and if she was away for the day or off ill we didn't receive our mail till she returned. That morning, Mac-Mac sneaked me a letter that had apparently been sitting up in the office for over a week. It was from another clinic, confirming that the concerns I had been harbouring about Craig were about to be professionally tested. Grateful to her again, I threw my arms around her, thanking her. She thought I was happy and laughed at me, but my impulsive action reflected both relief and fear. I had fought hard to get another hearing test for Craig as, despite feeling humiliated the last time and being so young, I knew something was not as it should be, and if it wasn't for Mac-Mac I would have missed it.

Ironically, it was because I had no respect for the authorities that I had forged on to take action for my son. I had visited my doctor to express my concerns about Craig, but I hadn't told anyone about the visit for fear they would say I was neurotic or paranoid. I was scared of hearing, '*Och you're havering, lass,*' or the more likely, '*What would you know, are you a specialist now?*' My agitated attention swung from packing in preparation for the move and fearing the worst at the clinic. Deep down inside, I knew my fears over Craig were well founded, and I was convinced our visit to the clinic was going to be a momentous event in our lives.

6

Actions speak louder

On the morning of Craig's appointment, though I had swept and hoovered the threadbare rug the day before, I found myself plugging the machine in again, but not for purposes of good housekeeping. Craig lay innocent and unsuspecting in his bed as my foot pressed the metal pedal on the machine. Instantly, the vroom took over the silence. I did not watch the rug to see if the Hoover was picking up any debris; I watched Craig's hands, his body and his eyes. His tiny hands that lay stretched out around his head failed to flinch at the sudden noise, and though I watched his face intently as I banged the Hoover around his bed and directly underneath it, he made no response. Aunt Helen's voice echoed in my mind: 'Tsk, there's nothing wrong with that baby.' Then I could hear Mrs Linn from the antenatal clinic, 'Neurotic teenage mothers.' What if my fears were dismissed by another round of verbal bullets today? Mrs Linn had seemed to take my fears as a personal attack on her authority, and she was determined that I would not undermine her. As my anxiety continued to rise, I remembered another of her verbal bullets that had whizzed by my ear: 'Our tests are very competent and comprehensive.'

After putting away the Hoover, I set about the almost impossible task of trying to get a sleeping child ready to go out without waking him. Craig's limp warm body was stirring by the time the zip was up on his blue all-in-one snowsuit. As we prepared to go out, my bedroom door opened after a brief knock that did not wait to be answered. Before me, towering, stood a doubtfire of a Mrs Woods. She really did remind me of my aunt Elspeth on a bad day. Both staunch and heavily girdled in Marks & Spencer's good churchgoing clothing, the difference between them was that Mrs Woods' aspirations were obvious. 'Hello, Mrs Elizabeth Woods from Bothwell speaking,' she would say when answering the phone.

As the area of Bothwell was an affluent and desirable address to have, she preferred to be known as a resident of that area rather than just the warden in charge of a council homeless unit. A postcode snob! Bothwell was about 15 miles away and in no way related to the homeless unit or surrounding area. In comparison, I thought, at least my aunt Elspeth from Fernlea would answer the phone unpretentiously. 'Elspeth Muir, officer in charge, Fernlea Children's Home,' she would say. However, it was Mrs Woods who now stood, hands on her hips, towerblocking the light from the door in front of me.

'You going out then, Eileen?' she asked rhetorically. Then, without waiting for me to answer her first question, she continued, 'Where are you going to?'

But then she was in charge. I was homeless, under her care. Her actions demonstrated her belief that I and the other residents had no choice but to answer her frequent and intrusive queries. Her brown-patent square-toed and -heeled shoes remained unmoved, demanding my answer. In contrast, I stood in the only pair of shoes I owned, second-hand bright-red brogues, with the scuffs newly coloured in felt-tip pen; my smart beige suede shoes, also second hand, had melted in the oven while I tried to dry them off. Mrs Woods had been on the rampage to find out who had been cooking at night. She never found out. I think she suspected me but not that it was a pair of shoes I had been cooking – sole for supper.

'I have an appointment at the clinic with Craig today,' I replied quickly. I was scared she would ask about the letter that had contained our appointment. I could not reveal my source; I could not grass . . . what would I say? Unable to think of any small talk, I dashed around the room in an overly active manner in the hope that it would distract her. It was futile of course. She snatched Craig up from the buggy that I had been trying to secure him into. 'I will show you there is nothing wrong with this child,' she stated. She had me cornered and knew of the appointment, of course, because the letter had sat on her desk and she had thought it would remain there till she saw fit to give it to me.

To my astonishment, she turned Craig swiftly upside down and swung him from side to side. He looked like a flying squirrel in mid flight and began to cry with fright. 'You see, there's nothing the matter with this child. You are just full of nonsense,' she said.

As I reached out for my son in a contained panic, I thought, is it me that's mad or did I miss something? How did that prove anything? What was I not understanding? My alarm at my son being turned upside down remained unnoticed by her. My subsequent anger remained cold and restrained as I kissed Craig and frantically trussed him as fast as I could into his buggy. My only thoughts were of getting out of this oppressive, miserable place quickly and safely to meet my aunt Helen. She had agreed to come with me to the appointment. She was offering me the moral support I so badly needed, and I took it. It was another success of the surreptitiously obtained phone number that I had been able to call her.

I rushed out of my door, past the barley twisted hefty oak dresser in the hall, hearing Mrs Woods' solid heels on the white-tiled floor behind me. With the tears threatening to escape, I used my self-taught aversion tactics. *One . . . two . . . three . . .* I began counting hard in my head, *four . . . five . . . six . . .* and it did the trick. It wasn't unusual for me to count. Although it would have gone unnoticed by other people, I would count anything and everything if it could help me to detach from a stressful situation – if I could not clean. Street lamps, cars, patterns on wallpaper and tiles were highly countable. This time I was in too much of a rush to find something to fix on, so number counting was my only escape. By the time I reached the bus stop, my eyes were wide and any potential tears had been buried. At least I had avoided the question of the missing letter from her office. In retrospect, she must have known it was Mrs Mac who had given it to me, because if she had suspected that I had gone into her office and taken it I would have been tossed out, no questions asked.

My panic and Craig's fright had settled down by the time we boarded the bus. As I paid my fare, I tried not to stare at the bus driver's hands. Most of his fingers wore an enormous gold ring. I had never seen a grown man wearing so much jewellery or rings that size before. Imprinted in my memory was one that was a lion's head, thickly raised with two glass stones that resembled diamonds as eyes. Even his pinkies had rings!

When I was seated, Craig stood on my knees and, with my arms steadying him, he watched the buildings speeding by through the bus window. Still transfixed by the driver's rings, I kept leaning over slightly and watching his left hand with the lion's head moving up and down the wheel. I still remember this so vividly – like many smells, words and unrelated incidents it transported me elsewhere. I have a faded grey memory in my mind of a tiny photograph of a bus, a driver with rings and Urquhart, but to this day I can't put it in context. I did not know then, but these memories would ebb and flow like the tide, with images bobbing up from the surface like flotsam and jetsam, adrift and disjointed. The older I got, the more I would experience this, particularly under stress.

I was brought back to the present by the bus jarring to a halt as we approached our stop. I tucked Craig under one arm and picked up the folded buggy, swaying precariously till I found a pole to lean on. The doors on the bus flung themselves open, but not before I had another lingering look at those bizarre hands. Then, finding ourselves on steadier ground, I unfolded Craig's buggy with him balanced on my hip and secured him in. We made our way to the clinic.

As we sat in the waiting room after letting the receptionist know I was there, I began to feel anxious. I tried to occupy my mind and amused Craig by playing a tickling game on his hand. Knowing the game well, he started to reveal his near toothless grin. My index finger drew a circle in the palm of his hand, which I held with my other hand.

Round and round the garden
I chased a teddy bear
A one step . . . A two step
And I found it under there.

'Under there' was his armpit, which my fingers reached after they counted and climbed up his arm. He would be open mouthed and giggling in anticipation long before I reached his armpit. Despite attempting to pull his arm away to avoid the tickling, as soon as the game was over he would stick his hand out to repeat the performance.

In between amusing him, I began to study the room. Leather-cushioned and metal-framed square chairs sat empty. As we waited for my aunt Helen to appear, we played alone; no one else came to wait. I scanned posters and brochures, making a mental note that they might come in useful, as I held onto the belief that information was knowledge and that knowledge was power. The quiet in the room seemed to be too loud. Luckily, to break this tension the receptionist was friendly, with no sign of condescension. 'He's a beautiful baby,' she told me. Then a phone rang and she disappeared. I lifted him from the buggy and removed his knitted blue hat that matched his eyes, allowing his blond curls to escape. He'd get the benefit of his warm clothing when we returned to the cold outside. Smiling with a mixture of pride and protectiveness, I ruffled his hair and kissed him again. From his mouth came beautiful noises, gurgles and easy sighs. I whispered to him, 'I love you, my baby boy.'

Just then a heavy glass door opened to my left and I heard Craig's name being called. The slim blonde woman to whom the voice belonged walked towards me, extending her hand. 'Hello, are you Craig's mum? I am Mrs Howard,' she said.

'Yes,' I replied. I shook her hand, something I had not experienced with other professionals, and was led into a room that resembled a DJ's station. It wouldn't have been out of place to have heard the current number one, 'Call Me' by Blondie. There was a large window in front of me that looked through into another room, and in front of the glass stood a machine with dials, knobs, half-moon meters and headphones.

I told her my aunt Helen was supposed to be meeting me here.

'Sarah, the receptionist, will let her know you're both here,' she said.

Smiling, she instructed me to put the headphones on Craig, then she left, closing the door behind her, and appeared in the other room on the other side of the window. She spoke to me through a two-way microphone. Although it was a strange environment, amazingly Craig sat quite contented and didn't attempt to remove the headphones. Everything she instructed me to do was done quietly, with an almost surreally calm air of efficiency. I did all she asked. Looking back, I wonder whether it was the lack of noise in this soundproofed part of the building that made the situation feel dreamlike. Or was it that I never detected any threat from this woman, who actually treated me with some respect as Craig's mother. Perhaps it was the calm before the storm.

Craig smiled wonderfully through the glass window at Mrs Howard, and he beamed at me, accepting the unfamiliar experience without fuss, only trying to reach for dials and knobs. My little son, with his unzipped snowsuit hanging round his waist, looked like a half-peeled banana as he sat with the large black leather headphones covering his perfectly formed ears. He remained unaffected by it all. He was a happy, smiling gurgler. It made me feel like crying.

It felt as though the test was over almost as soon as we began. I was returning to the waiting area when the audiologist spoke to me. 'He really is a beautiful baby, you must be very proud.'

Like any other mother, I believed this to be an absolute truth. His smiles and wide eyes always seemed to elicit that feel-good response from people. However, I sensed something else in her voice . . . that calm before the storm?

I had to wait in the reception area while Mrs Howard evaluated the tests. My aunt Helen was there waiting. She smiled anxiously and gave me her apologies for being late. I was only too glad she had turned up. We talked nervously of nothing that mattered as we waited.

Looking out the main window, I watched as the red single-decker bus with the metal hands on the steering wheel drove noisily past. Black exhaust fumes streamed from the back end, choking the cars behind. The cold air highlighted the pollution from the bus.

Moments later, I was standing outside at the traffic lights on the main street and willing them to change. We had just left the audiology unit, and all I wanted to do was disappear. Aunt Helen stood next to me. I could feel her looking at me, but I couldn't bear to look round.

I knew her eyes had begun to fill with tears. My response was to grip the grey-ridged plastic handles of Craig's buggy with a resolve strong enough to crush them. The lights changed and Aunt Helen walked by my right side as the wheels in my own mind were shifting up a gear and grinding noisily. Her hand reached out and gently squeezed my arm. I froze and tightened my grip on the buggy handles. I was completely unable to respond to her sympathy, as this would mean acknowledging it. 'I am so sorry,' she said.

I looked at her small hand on my arm and over-smiled at her. If I smile, she might not cry, I thought. Perhaps my apparent determination not to weep saddened her even more. Her voice was quiet and had a slight quiver. 'I am so sorry,' she said again.

I knew she was hoping for a normal response from me in the face of the news we had just received. Purposefully, I watched the red bus disappear into the distance. Its departure left the showy purple-and-yellow signs of the shop What Every Woman Wants in my view. Aunt Helen was still speaking, but the words didn't register until she made me stop and hear them again. 'What are you going to do?'

There was little I could say, little I wanted to say. All I could do was keep moving. She appeared anxious, possibly at my fixed smile and my long silence, but she could not hear my heart. I focused on the wheels of Craig's buggy as they trundled along, the noise gathering momentum over the paving stones. I concentrated on the noise, which sounded like the rhythmic running of a train on a long journey. I did this in order to avoid answering her question or maybe to buy me time in which to give a considered answer.

I had been right! The memories in my head replayed in a seamless stream, and certain phrases repeated themselves like a stuck record: '*Neurotic teenage mothers*', '*Our tests are very competent and comprehensive*', '*Nothing wrong with that baby*', '*See, he can hear*', '*Neurotic teenage mothers.*'

I had no time for the flavour of that bitter pill that I was swallowing, more afraid perhaps that its unpalatable taste might consume me. The leaflets I had been scanning at the audiology unit flashed through my head. I looked my aunt square in the eyes, with a no-point-crying-over-spilt-milk smile, and said, 'Well, I will just need to learn sign language.' This was followed with a whispered determination: 'I won't let Craig down.' My naive pragmatism coated that pill and stopped our tears.

On reaching Hamilton's shopping precinct, we headed for my aunt Helen's favourite cafe and meeting haunt, a little Italian-owned place called The Capocci Man. Over fish and chips, I began to fill the silence that threatened to overwhelm us with frantic prattling chat. The hot vinegar fumes from the food rose and stung my nostrils, and I was eating too fast. Craig ate the fish I had cut up for him and put on a separate plate. We both laughed as this perfect little boy tried to scoop up renegade peas with his hands. I excused my watery eyes with the smell of the vinegar. I don't think she believed me. I feared her tears would only add water to my own banks that were promising to burst.

As we finished our meal and left a table covered in mushy chips and stray peas, Aunt Helen left me to go to her work. She insisted on paying for the food, and I tried to erase the image of the sadness in her eyes by striding away – as if by moving more quickly I would sever myself from the inevitable and the less chance her sadness would have of attaching itself to my consciousness. Also, the less chance she would have to witness mine.

I decided not to get the bus home but to keep striding. The thought of the bus just seemed too claustrophobic. The thought of people speaking to me or of being in close proximity even with strangers was something I wanted to avoid. I had to get something out of my system, so I kept on walking.

We journeyed on in silence along Hamilton Road and onto the Old Glasgow Road that runs from Burnbank in Hamilton to Blantyre. Passing the Corns DIY shop, I remembered the owners had a connection with one of the children's homes I had been in. These memories were relatively new in comparison with my Glasgow ones. I hankered to revisit other scenes from my past. It was a way of reminding myself I had existed.

On I pressed, pushing Craig in his buggy, my heart continually falling as we frequently looked at each other. Forging on past Springwells, where the Robertson's 'ginger' factory was located, I thought of my own past. It was their bright-green limeade and bottles of pineapple juice that stuck out in my memory owing to their exotic colour. Irn Bru was too popular to be exotic!

I hankered for a time past that was not a grim memory but a consistent, continuous feeling with no drama. That would always be wishful thinking – I had not yet understood I could never forget or go back. Going back would certainly not solve anything, but I just did not want to be where I was – I craved good memories. Maybe I was even harbouring a fantasy that by rewinding I could somehow change the past. It's surely not true that you don't miss what you never had. I often wonder what it would be like to leave a home setting and be able to return at any time for comfort and parental love, to have a permanent family and bedroom. The children's homes, the social workers, the friends, the schools – once the connections to these places and people were severed, those doors were closed to me. Moving on and starting from scratch was what I did. How I envied the fact that some children grew up but still had a bedroom full of cuddly toys awaiting them. I thought of those fairy-tale books where children were rescued and taken in to a good home with a loving mother and father – that would never happen to me now. I could only regret Craig would have no grandparents, genetic or otherwise. Alex had disappeared from our lives completely and I had no knowledge of his past.

As I strode further along Blantyre's Glasgow Road and past the Memorial Park, the long walk allowed me to think freely and randomly. I thought of the young boy I had pulled out of the pond there earlier in the summer. I had been frozen after that, too. Dripping wet, I walked home with Craig and the boy with his mother, not wanting to speak of it, embarrassed by the show of gratefulness I received. Thinking of them and other unrelated thoughts distracted and cushioned me from my current situation.

Almost 20 minutes away from the homeless unit, I was running out of striding steam as the rain began. As it was not torrential but drizzling and cool it was welcomed. Cold and fresh on my face, it took me out of myself. I put my face up to catch it. Past the pubs and churches I continued. With his transparent buggy cover protecting him from the weather, an oblivious Craig had now fallen asleep, his wee hatted head keeled to one side.

I knew Mrs Woods would now have probably finished her shift and gone home. That was a relief to me and had I suspected that she was still there I would have kept walking till it was safe to go back to my room without her standing there waiting to press me for information. Turning a corner, the street and house were in sight, but not before I saw the single-decker red bus pass me by. This time I could see the rings of his right hand on the steering wheel. The feat of beating the bus back would normally have been a source of great satisfaction, but not today.

Craig had slept for the last ten minutes of our marathon trundle, no doubt content with a wee belly full of fish and chips and free from any knowledge of what today's events had revealed. As we arrived through the doors and passed the oak dresser on our way to my room, I could hear the other homeless families in their rooms. It was teatime, and the smell of cooking seeped into the hall. I removed my key from the old heavy door, and it closed behind me. I would be on my own till the next day.

Only in the early hours of the morning, as Craig lay once again safe in his cot and I in my bed, did the exhaustion weaken me to allow a taste of that pill. Denial gave way to self-pity as I lay in the solitude of darkness watching a silhouetted Craig sleeping. My love for him filled me with a physical ache and new fears. I cried silent, heavy tears that were few but agonising.

Only then could I relent and recall the moment Mrs Howard reappeared with Craig's hearing test results. Smiling, she had taken both my aunt and me into a side room. Facing me directly, and clearly feeling full of compassion, she was straight to the point, saying, 'I'm sorry, Eileen, but Craig is profoundly deaf.'

Her voice began to fade, with phrases like 'appointment for hearing-aid moulds' only just registering. I had only wanted to snuggle my son close to me. I wanted privacy to apologise to my baby. A snapshot of the rash I had during my secret pregnancy came and went quickly – it flickered in and out of my consciousness several times. A darker memory also threatened to engulf me, but I managed to close down and force it back into my subconscious.

All along I was right when I so wanted to be wrong. I could see in my mind the faces of all the people who had either ridiculed or doubted me. As my bitter tears fell, I played out scenarios in which I angrily told them the results of the tests. It was my impotent way of seeking vengeance for my son and me. My anger raged as I thought of all the appointments I had attended with Craig after which I had to push him home dejected. He was completely dependent on me to fight his corner, and while I had done my best, enduring the fear and ridicule, I felt I had failed in my attempts to be taken seriously and that this had affected my son. I had let him down. He had been denied the proper medical intervention that might have made a difference. No one had heard or listened to me. Their own fear or ignorance had made them deaf, and as a result my son was the one being ultimately punished. A defenceless child left damaged by the ignorance of others and at the centre was me. When it came down to it, I was the one to blame, and I'd never forgive myself for succumbing so easily, when all along I knew.

There was no point in ranting and raving; crying would just create embarrassment for me and others witnessing the scene. I had to be practical, and sign language seemed to be the logical solution. I was 17 and terrified but desperately trying to behave like I thought I should. I was always afraid to break down in case there would be no return from that place, no comforting witness, and no safety. Presbyterian pole up the back and chin out. Words like succour, sympathy and sanctuary were alien and were to be avoided like the plague.

As I lay there in the dark, my responsibilities seemed immense. I wanted to scoop my son up and return him to the cotton-wool womb. Instead, I began to sing.

> Hush little baby, don't say a word,
> Mama's gonna buy you a mocking bird.

Realisations were sinking in. Would Craig never hear me telling him I loved him? Would my son never utter the words 'I love you'? How could I tell him about the dangers of the world? How could I teach him self-protection from the bad people that I knew existed?

> If that mocking bird don't sing
> Mama's gonna buy you a diamond ring.

I was singing myself to sleep in an attempt to comfort myself. It never occurred to me that it was the system that had failed and that Craig would now be labelled as one who had fallen through the net. As far as I was concerned, it was me as his mother who had failed. I had simply not been able to get them to listen. It was my duty to my son, not theirs to their profession. Useless and hating myself, I carved myself up with my own knife of self-loathing.

Morning finally came. Rising, I knew I had to pull myself together for my son's sake. Self-pity had dissipated into my pillow. Questions would be asked; I would have to seek out solutions. I could not afford to feel like the useless mother I had in the dark hours of the night. If my son could not hear me telling him I love him, I would find a way to make him feel it. Shoulders back, chin out. A brilliantly comforting cliché sprang to mind: actions speak louder than words.

7

On the road yet again

The summer of 1980 was fading into autumn and finally the day of our move to pastures new had arrived. Hope rose on the horizon in the shape of this new house, which seemed to offer progression in the way of freedom and a place in the community of Hamilton. Penny had told me that I would be sharing the house with two other girls and that Craig would be the only child. Job advertisements had also been placed to find two volunteers to live in with us. Hoping for friends of a similar age and from a similar background, I was keen to meet them.

We travelled there in a taxi arranged by the social work department, and along with Craig's baby stuff I carted cleaning materials and a clothesline I had won at the prize bingo in Hove House. The only personal possessions I had managed to keep to remind me of a family life I once had were a mink brooch of my mother's and a small unframed watercolour painting that she had acquired from somewhere. Now added to my treasures were the poems from Annie, the nearly-there woman. Her precious history!

I never looked back at Hove House for fear that Mrs Woods would come running out and put a stop to the proceedings. The last thing I did before leaving was to pass on to my cleaning companions the acquired phone number in the hope that someone else might benefit from it. Throughout the summer, I'd had to listen to the other residents' building resentments and anger, and I was relieved to be leaving all that behind along with the constant feeling of humiliation that we'd had to endure. Now my shoulders relaxed and sank into the leaving taxi. I did feel a small triumph for me and for them as I envisaged the phone in the porch ringing off the hook, and it made me smile inside.

Arriving at the new house, we were met, as arranged, by a heavy blonde woman cloaked in a multicoloured cardigan with matching beads round her neck. 'Hello, Eileen and Craig,' she said, helping me get my belongings from the taxi. 'I am Emma Lyons,' she added, and extended her hand for me to shake. Penny had told me that Emma was to play the role of homemaker for us girls, and with her briefcase adding to her attire she looked the part.

The taxi drew away, and with Craig secured in his buggy we both chatted away as we lifted my bags into our new home. Our new address was Bark Avenue, Hamilton, and the large white house that she led me to was positioned in the right-hand corner of a cul-de-sac. This new housing scheme, I learned, had been recently built for the Glasgow overspill. The social work department had secured a house from the Scottish Special Housing Association. It secretly pleased me that all the residents would be from my home town; perhaps I thought I might find a connection to my past.

Looking around me, I could see a whole scheme that was spanking new; the houses were very modern. Nobody had lived in 'ours' before; it felt positive and exciting to me. Trees were planted everywhere, breaking up the concrete maze of streets. It was like a Lego labyrinth. There was no front garden but rectangles of bushes and plants outside almost every front door. The front door was separated from the quiet pavement by a doorstep. The street lamps I noticed were very stylised too: straight from the set of *War of the Worlds*, they looked futuristic. I felt full of hope for the future and relief to have escaped the draconian Hove House.

As I was first there, I was lucky enough to be able to get first pick of the bedrooms. The largest room was reserved for the volunteers, whose job it would be to offer guidance and support, so I chose the second-largest room. It made sense to Emma and me, as there had to be room for Craig's large cot.

As I ran up and down the stairs with my plastic bags of belongings,

Emma boiled a pot of water, as there was no kettle yet, while telling me the house was not actually ready for us to move into as all the furnishings had not arrived. I noticed a box of basics such as teabags, coffee, milk and bread on the bunker in the kitchen. 'We wanted to get you out of Hove House as soon as possible,' she said. Then added, 'Penny was so upset for you stuck in there; it's notorious.' I stopped just long enough to tell her I hated it. I also felt fleetingly guilty that my despair had possibly pressurised Penny, as I liked her and was ashamed of my desperation.

The bedroom furniture for all the rooms had arrived and was in place, but there was no furniture in the living room. In the dining room, though, there sat a large teak dining table and chairs. Wow – we had a proper dining room, with a hatch from the kitchen!

Emma and I sat having a cup of tea in the dining room on chairs still encased in plastic, and she explained her role to me. She brought papers and folders out of her briefcase. I noticed the rings on her hands were as colourful as her beads. She began, 'My role is to help you girls budget your money, learn about economic cooking and manage bills.' I listened, tapping my feet, but I really just wanted to open the new quilt cover and duvet lying upstairs and make my bed.

It seemed that Penny had got the keys just that day, and the other girls as well as the volunteer were not ready to move in. 'Will you be OK on your own for a few days?' she enquired.

'Yes, I'll be fine,' I replied, momentarily disappointed but not enough to quell my excitement about escaping Hove House. I shrugged it off. We had a general chat, with Emma questioning me about my background, details of which, as usual, I kept to a minimum, before I asked about hers. Emma then gave me her office phone number and told me to call if I needed anything. As the phone was not connected yet, she told me where I would find the nearest phone box and handed me my set of two house keys. All I could think about was that I had house keys and was to have a house phone! I was buzzing and adding rapidly to the list in my head – new quilt, new bed, new pillows, curtains. Everything was new, clean and untainted.

As Emma left, I watched her walk to her car. The big, multicoloured, briefcase-carrying cardigan squeezed herself into a tiny black car and waved before pulling out of the cul-de-sac. I stood at the front door, waiting a while before I shut it. I gazed over the surrounding houses. They all looked lovely. Everything looked faultless. On display were elaborate curtains, flowers, ornaments and new blinds that decorated the window frames. I breathed in the fresh start and shut my door.

Rushing round the house like a precocious child in a pre-Christmas present hunt, I went from room to room opening doors and windows. Craig sat strapped into his buggy, watching the amazement on my face as the windows opened and spun right round on themselves, which made for easier and safer cleaning I later found out. We also had our own back garden, fenced off, and a gate. In the garden, I noticed there was not a clothesline on the lawn but a whirly gig. So much for my prize clothesline from Hove House! I can't remember, but I like to think that made me smile. Sarcastically, I thought, 'Well, at least the pegs will be useful!'

I enthusiastically opened every cupboard door in the kitchen. Top doors, bottom doors, big doors and small doors! Then long drawers, short drawers and deep drawers that I opened and shut several times, revealing nothing in them but newness. I used my latest keys in the back door; it was glass, without the usual council wire mesh threaded through it. What I thought was a cupboard in the downstairs hall turned out to be a toilet. Two toilets in the one house! This thrilled me. What a start for Craig this would be.

In each room and in both up- and downstairs hallways were small metal grilles. These were part of the underfloor heating system that was the signature of SSHA housing. The house smelt of nothing but newness and was hollow sounding owing to the industrial carpets and lack of furnishing, personal or functional. To me, the whole house and area was unblemished, full of potential and promise. It represented a new blank canvas just waiting to be coloured in and lived in. Nothing bad could happen to me here, and no one would guess how bad I had been. That night I ran a bath, swanked about the empty house and believed I had escaped. I had a home. The cuckoo had finally landed. She who had dared, had won.

8

Settlement

Two days later, with Craig's cot and my bed made up, and some shopping done, I awaited the arrival of the other two girls. Linda was the first to appear. She was a plump, long frizzy-haired blonde girl in colour-coordinated clothes. With her was a slim woman dressed like a catalogue model for Scottish knitwear. I assumed she was Linda's social worker. Matching blue luggage lay at Linda's feet; I was now glad I had got my plastic bags emptied before she arrived.

Initially, she had beamed a smile at me. As the usual 'hiyas' were exchanged, I explained the bedroom situation and also that I had already been here for two days. She looked me up and down and then with a sideways glance seemed to withdraw. 'This is Meg,' she said of her companion, then, lifting her luggage, she disappeared upstairs.

'Want a cup of tea or coffee?' I asked Meg.

'No, thanks, Eileen,' she replied. 'How's your aunt Elspeth?' she asked.

Trying to hide my shock at this stranger obviously knowing who I was and that I had lived in Fernlea Children's Home, I chatted away. Meg did not stay long; in fact, she seemed in a hurry to leave. I overheard Linda asking her if she needed to go so soon.

Later on, as I helped Linda make up her bed, we exchanged information. I found out that Meg was the matron of the children's home Linda had been in. I had heard my aunt Elspeth talk of that children's home many times, always in a derogatory manner, implying there was a high criminal element. Reflecting back, I suppose there must have been professional competition between the matrons or officers-in-charge as to whose home was better run.

Linda had taken the room next to the bathroom. 'Suits me this one,' she had said, for reasons I would discover later. As we chatted, she unzipped her luggage. The brown and twill case seemed to double up as a Tardis – from it, apart from clothes, she produced ornaments, perfumes, lotions and framed photos. She placed and then replaced them carefully around her room. In comparison to me, she had many 'nice things', but we obviously shared a compulsion to arrange and for things to be orderly.

She spoke vaguely about her background, shying from giving anything away. Her parents were still alive, but she did not have any contact with them. She had a younger sister who still lived with them. I didn't ask why, as she skipped over this subject quickly, signalling to me not to ask. I responded in kind, saying my mother had died but giving no factual details. Meg was the main topic of conversation, and Linda seemed very attached to her. I envied their relationship but felt a fellow 'homie' deserved that.

Then we moved on to the next subject, which was Wendy, our new housemate to be. Linda was a wealth of knowledge and eager to share it. 'Do you know her?' she asked me. When it was established I had no previous knowledge of Wendy, the gossip began. As Linda sat cross-legged on the bed, the tale unfolded.

'Wendy's a bit of a nutcase, and so is her fiancé. He's a wrestler,' she said.

Stunned but intrigued at both revelations – I had never pictured a nutcase or a wrestler fiancé in my paradise – I listened to the monologue that unravelled from her. Apparently, Wendy had been on drugs and had jumped in front of car, smashing through the windscreen. 'Shards of glass were embedded in her head, injuring her so badly that she now has a stutter.' She further told me that after leaving hospital, Wendy had left the children's home and was now living in the hostel that was attached to the children's unit where Linda had been a resident. 'She has tons of family everywhere, they're dodgy and always coming out the woodwork.' It was food for thought as I made tea for Craig and me.

Linda stayed in her room arranging and rearranging for the rest of the night. I never went near; I didn't know what to make of the information. I fed my hungry son and rearranged our room – it must have been contagious. Craig took it all in his stride, never seeming to be unsettled for now by moves or new people. I wondered about the other girls' past. Where did they originate from? And what had happened to bring them to this point in their lives? Craig was not even a year old, and in that short time his father had come and gone and we had three addresses under our belts. Twice I had been labelled neurotic for thinking my child had hearing difficulties but he had been diagnosed as profoundly deaf. I was sure Wendy and Linda also had difficult stories to tell and hide.

For the first two honeymoon weeks, it was just Linda, Craig and me. As we began to settle in, Linda appeared to be really taken by Craig, allowing him to crawl about her newly made bed. The peace was shattered by Wendy's arrival, which saw the front door burst open. I heard a few 'F-f-f-fuck sakes' and 'S-s-shits' being blurted out. What I saw in front of me was an almost pretty, slim but busty dark-haired girl. On her left arm were a few plastic bags bursting with possessions that were swinging erratically in jolting movements. She launched into a rant about the 'f-f-fucking price of the taxi'; all the while the plastic bags were being swung about, hitting the glass front door and surrounding walls. It was almost comical, but I dared not laugh.

More and more stuffed plastic bags were whirlwinded and trailed in the door, and eventually an old battered case appeared courtesy of a thick-set young man with a fighter's nose that was 'her Jamie'. An extra large amount of Tupperware dishes was dumped at the bottom of the stairs, and the plastic bags kept coming. Wendy had no choice of room, and Jamie carted the entire luggage pile to the smallest room in the house. A trail of escaped possessions littered the stairs like gingerbread crumbs and led to her room. Wendy picked them up, swearing on each stair and at each recovered item.

In the hurricane that was Wendy, and the ensuing hustle and bustle, I helped with the last of her belongings as Linda put the kettle on. Questions flew back and forth and quickly became quite personal as we attempted to bond and find out about one another. Linda's questions focused intently on information Wendy might have about Meg. 'Did you see Meg before you left?' she asked.

'Aye, she came to see me and says she will see me later,' Wendy answered, following up with, 'How?' obviously irritated. It's a curious Scottish language trait that we say how when we mean why.

'When, when did you see her? When is she coming to see you?'

Had I had more understanding of jealousy and its possible dangers, these questions would have put me on guard. As it was, I just assumed our shared history and current situation meant us outsiders would automatically gel. In my mind, we had a common ground that should have united us, and I thought naively that it would. It was partly the result of reading history and politics and believing in Idealism. Underneath it all I was using this fantasy of a perfect home situation to try to relieve my anxiety. I longed for peace, safety and security. Having never lived in a 'normal' home, I did not know what was and was not possible.

After tea was drunk, an announcement made by Wendy really pissed Linda off. 'Right,' Wendy said, 'Ah'm off.'

Linda looked aghast. 'Where to?' she asked.

'Staying at Jamie's,' Wendy stated. That was Wendy, abrupt and straight to the point. She offered no explanation. On reflection, though, perhaps her brash 'not answerable to anyone attitude' was due to her stutter as much as it was to her personality, as this led her to speak in short, sharp and simple sentences.

Linda clattered around in the kitchen, her dissatisfaction evident to me that night. 'See what I mean?' she said with regard to her previous description of Wendy. That retort concluded the meeting of us 'homies'. We all had a past, were settling into the present and looking for a future.

The next gossip on the agenda was anticipation and speculation as we waited for the volunteers. When Hannah arrived, Linda looked her slim figure up and down then seemed to dismiss her. As far as I was concerned, Hannah was probably the epitome of the 'jolly hockey sticks girl'. She was sporty, an active outdoor person, and I was curious about her. I wanted to know all about this person; to me it was a new experience, a way to find out about other ways in life. It was also a reaction to feeling constantly judged myself. Linda, however, instantly hated her, and I did not fully understand why. Was it because Hannah came across as a confident, positive person? Or was it because she was English and slim – or was it all of the above? I did eventually agree with Linda's theory that Hannah was a spy in the camp – our conclusion resulting from her continual use of the phone and habit of locking herself away. Hannah perhaps felt she had bitten off more than she could chew, and Linda's frostiness unsettled her. Whatever the case, she did not last long. Within weeks, she had left. 'Skinny bitch' and 'good riddance to bad rubbish' was Linda's triumphant response.

At this point, I bumped into a guy called Joe, whom I had met while living in Fernlea. He lived two streets away. To my mind he held both a threat, being male, and an allure. Into music, he wore eyeliner and trilby hats, and he was in a band. Gary Numan and David Bowie were among his idols, and he told me he played the synthesiser. Eager and enthusiastic in his storytelling, his eyes widened excitedly when talking about his music. He had recently lost his job but was going to make it in the music industry. He chuckled and was attentive with Craig, adding for good measure that I was looking good. This fervour and flattery suited my current desire for a new beginning. However, I was anxiously waiting for an appointment to take Craig to Yorkhill Hospital and only half-heartedly accepted Joe's invitation to come over and listen to music sometime. Reality had bitten. I had responsibilities, and I lost my eye contact with him. With a resigned wave goodbye, I headed home.

Craig and I had got into a routine of me awaking to him gnawing on the bars of his cot, a clear sign he was teething. With only two bottom teeth in, he had already bitten through the blue plastic teething ring I kept in the fridge for him. Like a little caged hamster gnawing away on a feeding sticking, he greeted me with a smile every morning as I stirred in my bed and lifted my head off the pillow. Our routine was a morning bath for him, a feed and then he was placed back in his cot till I got ready. Though his deafness was now diagnosed as profound, I still spoke and sang to him as I organised myself. I did not know what else to do. Silence would mean ignoring him. My singing and chatting antics were always animated, and he would laugh. It was the only way I could feel emotionally connected with him, to stop that horrible feeling of not having a mother-and-son bond. He would sometimes ape my antics and dance along with me; it was bittersweet, both joyful and sad.

I was left in limbo as what to do or where to go. I had been informed that I would receive a letter about an appointment, but for now it was antics and love that sustained us. Practicalities too. A bucket of soiled nappies was first on the agenda, then household chores. Walks to the shop for bread and milk passed our day, as did arranging who would be in for the arrival of furniture. I was nearly always in, not being footloose and fancy-free.

Wendy was easy come, easy go. She was always at her old haunts and Jamie's parents' place. She did not need this unit like Linda and I did, as she had strong outside connections. Wendy barely acknowledged Craig, mostly because she was not there and certainly was not giving lip service to the coo-cooing brigade. Linda did seem to enjoy him, though, when he was smiling, and she spent time amusing him. 'I'd love to be a mother,' she said on more than one occasion. I got the feeling she wanted that elusive home setting that many of us from children's homes dream about. She wanted to be happily married and have children, and for it to be a better home than the one she had come from, of course.

Linda was attending the doctor regularly. She would not say what for, though I did sometimes hear her throwing up in the bathroom. It was becoming apparent why she had wanted the room next to the toilet.

I felt fortunate to have Barbara, the residential social worker from Fernlea, whom I felt had been a good friend. She had kept in touch and had begun visiting me here. Also, my cousin Bernadette had begun to ask me to babysit for her. She had started college, hoping to go to university, and lived only 15 minutes' walk from me through a park that separated the two schemes. She had got the marital home back after her divorce and had moved from the pub flat we had previously shared. In between the humour, the nappy pins and gurgling, I had hopes of 'getting a life'.

In Bark Avenue, the house began to smell lived in. The hollow newness and pristine paintwork gave way to scuffs, shampoo and bleach. We muddled along while waiting for the arrival of new volunteers – more strangers to have input and walk in and out of our lives. Craig and I revelled in our new-found freedom from signing in and out or having to ask permission to leave, and we walked everywhere. We could go for miles with him gurgling and pointing at anything that moved. I never knew then that exercise was purported to be good for depression or stress. I do know I walked my socks off. If Craig's buggy had required the same checks as a car, the mileage would have been high and the wheels would have had no tread left. I had turned the seat in Craig's buggy round so that he could face me as I pushed him. I was aware I needed to make facial contact with him and also wanted to see his own facial expressions; it was one of the few practical things I could think of to do. At least while we walked the communication in our eyes and smiles kept us connected. The word handicapped I could not envisage as applying to my boy as he sat looking every bit the perfect child. I had no idea what I was to do other than wait for a hospital appointment.

One particular day's walk had a purpose. I had a doctor's appointment. Still full of allergies, I snorted and sneezed my way down the main street like a retired set of bagpipes, then carried on down past the Philips Lighting factory and the large cemetery, heading for my doctor's surgery next to Viking Sports at Peacock Cross. My appointment was to discuss the letter I had received from the audiology unit confirming Craig's profound deafness, and I also wanted to enquire why I suddenly had developed this wheezing and itching reaction that my inhalers did not help.

The appointment lasted minutes. I was informed I had hayfever, a prescription was written, and it was confirmed that I would be receiving an appointment for Yorkhill Children's Hospital for genetic counselling. I had no idea what the implications of this would be for us, or indeed the reason for it. But I knew I had to go. I had nothing else to work towards but this appointment; all I had was hope. Hope for what, I did not know.

Crossing the road in front of the doctor's surgery, I made a beeline to the chemist. On getting my prescription, I opened the packet of pills outside and took the one pill as instructed. After I swallowed the pill quickly without water, Craig and I began the long walk home. My puffed red eyes itched and my nose was so bunged up I had not a hope of breathing through it. Up until then, I would have prescribed myself pan scourers to get some respite from the itch in the roof of my mouth and throat; however, by the time I had got back to the Philips Lighting factory, exhaustion was overcoming me. The traffic was whizzing by me on the road, and the noise of the vehicles coming and going was making me feel faint and dizzy. By this stage, I was finding it difficult to walk, never mind push Craig. Aware I still had a long way to go uphill, I talked to myself and began counting to focus my mind on getting home. When I eventually reached Bark Avenue, I stumbled in the door, ignoring Linda in the kitchen, unstrapped a thankfully contented Craig from his buggy and staggered up the stairs to my bedroom. After dumping Craig in his cot, I fell fully clothed onto my bed and did not wake up for hours. I couldn't remember the last leg of my journey home, just the concentration it took to stay upright and get my feet to move.

Through the bars of his cot, I saw Craig watching me, and, guilt racked and fearful of what we had just experienced, I scooped him up and fussed over him. We were safe. In the kitchen, I fed him a well overdue meal. After that, I went about consuming large amounts of tea and toast. In my bedroom later on, I read the instructions on the pill packet. It read: 'Can cause drowsiness. Do not operate machinery.' There was nothing about driving or being in charge of babies in buggies!

9

Papering, plastering, placating

After Hannah's sudden though not surprising resignation, we soon found out that two new volunteers were arriving. All we knew was that one was from Perth and the other from down south. We began to talk and wonder what they would be like. 'Hope we don't have another Hannah,' Linda said. 'Don't f-fucking care,' was Wendy's response. I, on the other hand, was looking forward to them arriving. I was keen to break the intensity of the house by having more people around.

I wish I had been more territorial and protective of my space, but I was frightened I would upset the apple cart and lose my hard-fought-for place, as I had got into the house by default. A pyramid of facts was turning into wild fantasy of me being thrown out. Part of the regime and one of the rules of the unit was that we had to have regular house meetings to ensure all was well with us girls and that we were coping with our finances and being out on our own. Emma was to see to issues that would crop up on a daily or weekly basis, and we would have a monthly house meeting to raise any issues we felt pressing. At the first one, the agenda included checking to see if all the furniture had arrived, whether we wanted to do any decorating to make the place our own and other generalities. However, on a few occasions during the conversation, Linda mentioned that I had not been around very much. She had said, 'Oh, Eileen was not here, she was staying at her cousin's.' I didn't know why at the time, but this rankled me. On another occasion, as I was preparing to visit Bernadette, Linda had asked me if I really had to go. Although I found this request strange, my immediate response was sympathetic. I knew what loneliness was and I stayed in with her. In this way, I unwittingly made a rod for my own back.

On one of my rambling walks with Craig in his buggy, I bumped into Harry, a guy that I had dated briefly when I was at Fernlea whom my aunt Elspeth thought was a 'hoot'. We dated only briefly because after I met his sister she had spied me in my school uniform from the bus she was on going to work one morning. She suitably embarrassed him about dating a 'schoolie', and I never saw him again after that. Now, we chatted quite easily with any queries as to the whys and what fors of his disappearance left unsaid. He spoke about his nightshift job packing shelves in Tesco. 'I just can't sleep at night, so my body clock is suited to this work,' he said. The conversation moved on to family – his and mine. He had gone to school with my older cousin Helen and knew my family. As we parted, he asked if he could pop in and see me. I took this to be a friendship gesture and nodded.

Three days later, Harry appeared at my door. Anxious about what Linda would say, as she had been hinting she was afraid of men, I took him into the dining room, where we sat round the dining table several chairs apart. Tea and biscuits helped to distract me from the tension I had begun to sense. I was keen to know what was happening in his life and hear news of anybody we knew. It became clear he was looking for more than friendship when he stated, 'You are looking good, Eileen, and Craig is lovely.'

Not really knowing how to, or if I wanted to, respond, perhaps afraid where it might go, I avoided replying. I craved friendship and probably male attention, though I found it hard to admit this to myself. I had a distorted perception that it was wrong to seek male attention of any kind – a view that seemed to be supported by the feminist books I was reading at that time. What happened next did nothing to dispel this idea.

Linda's room door opened and I heard her come down the stair. My nerves started to flare. When she entered the dining room, I was overly cheerful and pleasant. I was unsure how she would react. Would she see Harry as an intruder?

'Hiya, Linda. This is Harry, an old friend of mine,' I said.

She stood there in her symmetrical blue and burgundy top with matching burgundy trousers. (I had now discovered she was getting all her 'nice' things from catalogues: the sad-faced clown of Pierrot that perched on her pillows and quilt cover now also hung from the curtains; the pink and black design also covered her walls; ornaments, lamps and a mask appeared. A picture frame had been the latest in many parcels that had arrived. Pierrot and Sara Moon pictures became the '80s answer to the Crying Boy and Spanish Lady pictures of my childhood – they were everywhere.)

A strange smirk spread across her face, which I mistook for nerves. 'Want a cup of tea, Linda?' I asked.

'Yes,' she replied.

I left her and Harry chatting and hurriedly made her tea. I was feeling uneasy and sensitive about some of the things she had brought up at the house meeting. I remembered her words. 'Eileen stays at her cousin's, and I am left here myself,' she had said. It unsettled me, and I was afraid, somehow, she was going to get me into trouble. As I had been sympathetic to her fears of being in the house alone due to my own fears of 'something bad happening', I had somehow got caught in a web of pandering and tiptoeing around her insecurities. If I could somehow do the right thing, people would not die, like my mother; bad men like Urquhart would not exist and all would be well. I just had to be good.

Harry left shortly after we finished the next cup and said he'd like to come back. 'See you soon,' he shouted. His black post-Punk hair and short stocky body disappeared round the corner. After I closed the door, I collected the empty cups and plates, passing them through our posh hatch to the kitchen, and tried to avoid Linda's gaze. Something was unsettling me about the whole interaction and about Linda herself.

In the next few days, my dad was due for a visit. He had visited on a few occasions, and it was much the same as when he saw me in the children's homes. We would sit together for a few hours, with him always stinking of drink and neither of us having much to say. It seemed like we had had the same conversation for years. On the occasions he disappeared to the toilet we had downstairs, I knew he was having a fly drink from a cheap half bottle of El Dorado that fitted almost perfectly inside the poaching pocket of his gabardine coat. I could smell the drink lingering in the toilet, just as it had at home when I was a child.

He nearly always arrived at the same time, but on this occasion I was not quick enough to get back from the shops with a cake for him and he had arrived without me being there. On my return, the front door was locked and I had no key, as Linda had been in and said she was not going out. I knocked and eventually hammered to get in. When Linda finally opened the door, I heard cars arriving. I turned and saw that a social worker and the homemaker Emma were getting out of their cars. It was obvious that something very serious had happened. Linda dashed up the stair, screaming, 'No, no, go away.' In total bewilderment, I stood in the hallway and looked to the authorities to explain.

'Eileen, your dad turned up drunk and Linda phoned us. She was terrified.'

This had all taken place within 20 minutes. I was horrified and full of shame. We sat at the dining table and discussed what had happened; Linda refused to come out of her room. As we were talking, the door opened and Meg, Linda's matron from her old children's home, entered. Linda had phoned her too. My mortification and guilt were complete. I felt like the perpetrator of a crime. Within the hour, all the authority figures had left. Meg had visited Linda in her room for about 15 minutes and exited abruptly. I took it to be because she was angry with me. My dad had just disappeared. The conclusion was that he was not to visit again till we had a full house meeting.

Two days later, Harry visited in the early evening, bringing green-foil-covered Viscount biscuits. I was in my bedroom painting designs on the wallpaper round my bed. I listened as Linda answered the door and froze as I heard Harry's voice. '*Oh God,*' I thought, '*I'm going to be in deep shit now.*' I had apologised to Linda, but she had given very little response back. That strange little smile appeared again on the corner

83

of her mouth as she said, 'Maybe we could go out for walks together, Eileen, you, me and Craig?' Eagerly I said yes, glad I had been forgiven for my crime and all would be well. Now, I did not think so.

I rushed down the stairs with the intention of getting rid of Harry. I found Linda in the kitchen, opening the biscuits he had brought and beaming away, kettle on and chat flowing. Now I was the one who felt awkward.

Harry asked to use the toilet. 'Use the one upstairs, I have not cleaned the downstairs one yet,' Linda said.

I began to open a biscuit when Linda said, 'You want to make the tea, Eileen?'

Incredibly, in my naivety I felt relief and cheerily agreed. Linda disappeared. I finished making and pouring the tea. When I opened the hatch to the dining room, there was no one there. That unsettled feeling returned. I slowly and quietly began to climb the stairs. Halfway up, I stopped. Linda's bedroom door was shut, and I could hear her giggling and Harry talking. Stunned, I returned to the dining room. 'What the fuck?' I repeated to myself over and over. Linda's smile, I now knew, was a smirk.

Wendy returned and as usual burst through the door after seeing off a taxi. She asked, 'Where's Linda?'

I looked her square in the eye and said, 'In her bedroom with Harry.'

Wendy was momentarily silent. Then she replied with her expected panache, 'Huh, fuck's sake, and I'm no f-f-fucking allowed Jamie in m-m-ma bedroom.' Two days later, Wendy put a lock on her bedroom door.

Linda beamed at me all next morning. As I felt I had no right to anything or anybody, I said nothing. She made a fuss of Craig and offered me tea several times. My anxiety levels were rising, and anything strong or highly scented began to make me vomit.

Barbara phoned me and must have sensed my despondency as she came to visit the next day after finishing her overnight shift at Fernlea at two o'clock. I don't remember telling her about the incident with my father. Rightly or wrongly, I believed that somehow I had been responsible for more trouble. It's easy to reflect now and see that my father was the one who was wrong, but at the time I felt as though it was me who was at fault. As Linda had pre-warned me about Wendy's dodgy family, I burned with shame over my father's actions – and of course blamed myself. I also didn't mention the incident with Harry. What people get away with when you keep your mouth shut.

Linda and I had picked up some cheap rolls of wallpaper from the Asda in Blantyre. We hadn't even considered asking for anyone's consent before decorating, we just hoped it would be fine. Barbara wasn't too happy that we were hanging it without permission, but she pushed her common sense to one side and offered a helping hand. In no time, we were slapping paste on paper and working our way along the upstairs landing while chatting away about what was happening in the outside world and sipping glasses of wine from a bottle that Barbara had brought with her. The chat centred on where Barbara had gone last weekend and who she had seen, who she fancied and no longer did. She had no hang-ups, it seemed, and appeared so amazingly normal.

As she chatted about herself openly and freely, Linda began to pull faces to me behind Barbara's back. But I enjoyed Barbara's chat and in retrospect it took me out of myself and lifted away the depression, although only for a short time. We were very different in our origins. Barbara came from a comfortable middle-class background but had a great ability to make me feel completely at ease with her. On the occasions we would go out together, when it was my cousin Bernadette's turn to babysit, more often than not she paid all the taxi fares and any extras other than a few drinks, pooh-poohing any refusals by me. Getting drunk with Barbara was always fun, it was natural, with no signs of judgement on her part. Always laughing and without an agenda, that's how Barbara seemed. She never made me feel obliged or in any way a lesser person. Barbara was as skinny as I was, and she would casually leave clothes in my room for me that I might like, but I never felt beholden to her, just very appreciative. I really related to that and loved her for it. That was Barbara in my eyes; she was not as self-conscious as me, she just danced and shone.

Though she was the drunkest, ironically it was Barbara that noticed the wallpaper. She had drunk more than a few glasses of wine from the bottle that she had brought when she let out a shriek: 'It's all upside down.' After standing back to look, we then collapsed onto the landing floor and laughed and laughed. The paper *was* upside down. I can't remember if we ripped it off or continued. But I do remember that Linda didn't find it the least bit funny and eventually went to bed. Barbara's visits were invaluable to me; however, they too were soon to come to an end.

10

Patterns by design

The volunteers had now arrived. Angela came from Perth and Jackie from somewhere down south. Jackie came first, then a week later Angela arrived. Jackie was petite, slim with short blonde hair, boyish in physique; apart from my friend Barbara I had never seen someone with 'fried eggs' for breasts before. Babs joked in her self-deprecating way that hers were medium range and Jackie's small. Jackie, unlike Babs, had very little humour but, like Hannah, was English and appeared very confident. Linda unsurprisingly took an instant dislike to her. Angela was rotund and attractive in a Vivienne Westwood way. She had been an accountant, and now said she 'wanted to do something meaningful with her life', adding 'and get out of the rat race'. She had cropped her long hair and packed one bag. It never occurred to me then but does now that maybe these people were running away from something. They too were looking for a new start.

There was tension in the house, and I felt constantly anxious. I felt I had to smooth over the dissatisfaction, though this caused me a lot of personal stress. I could not exhibit the same strength of character and opinionated backbone as before; I had to be careful, as I had a child to consider. But of course my idealistic attempts at peacekeeping never worked for long. My resilient humour and forced patience only deflected the inevitable for a short while.

Some kind of pattern was emerging with Linda – I could not explain it, only feel it. Most of the issues that arose seemed to centre on her – my drunken dad, Hannah, and now Jackie. I was also aware that Harry had only returned to see her once after a promise to go to the pictures had somehow fallen through. I was waiting for some kind of eruptive climax to her mounting resentment. Astoundingly, I never felt any satisfaction about the situation with Harry, just angst and responsibility.

On reflection, there was not a great deal of unity in the house. We did not gather, do girly gossip or watch TV together. The ironically named living room remained largely unlived in, no pyjamas-and-slipper movies planned or enjoyed. Cuppas in the dining room and squeezing past each other in the small kitchen at the rare shared mealtimes had become the routine for us girls. With Wendy never part of the household and the volunteers bustling to and fro to offices and settling in, the only real together times were sneaky secret bitching sessions in our bedrooms. That's where Linda retreated and where I spent my nights in listening to the radio, reading or scribbling poetry as Craig slept.

One night, Linda appeared in my doorway and whispered for me to come into her room. In order to avoid waking Craig, I complied. Craig had become sensitive to movement and had also taken to launching himself out of his cot, landing with a thud that could be heard downstairs and running across the floor to my bed. He was both wiry and fast. Closing my door, I walked to her bedroom. Hushing me into her room, as I sat on her bed she shut her door, signifying it was going to be a bitching session.

Whispering, I asked Linda, 'What are you thinking?'

Instantly she replied, 'I don't like them.'

I knew that this meant there would be trouble ahead. I knew she was talking about Angela and Jackie, and I also knew she was looking for me to agree with her. I never took what she said at face value, as by now I had learned that nothing she said was straightforward, so I kept my comments neutral. 'Don't know yet, hard to say this early,' was my guarded reply. I don't remember most of what we talked about, but Linda's comments about Jackie were along the lines of 'too snobby, too bossy', and of Angela, 'a bit mad and mental, no right in the head'.

I could agree that Angela was a bit zany. She wore second-hand clothes, and her hairstyle made her look impish. She would snip off random pieces of her fringe, and she often wrestled with a mirror whilst trying to cut the back of her hair. For all she was slightly bizarre, I was intrigued by her and liked her, but I decided against revealing this to Linda.

As the conversation about Jackie and Angela faded, I was about to go and make some tea when out of the blue Linda suggested we break into Wendy's room, saying, 'I'm convinced Jamie is staying overnight and they're using drugs. I'll bet there's tins of gas in there and all sorts.'

When I didn't instantly reply, she furthered her case by stating, 'I mean, Eileen, we might be in danger, you, me and Craig.'

I can't remember what I said, but I know I was feeling incredibly anxious and mistrustful of all sides. I stood and looked at the large framed painting of the Pierrot clown that hung on her wall and sympathised with the tears that rolled down its cheek. Like the clown, I felt contained within a frame, the only difference being my tears were not for public show.

After I somehow managed to deflect the suggestion of breaking into Wendy's room, Linda continued to chat and confessed that she had got into debt with her catalogues and had asked for Emma's help. She was appealing for sympathy and clearing the way for what was on the agenda to be revealed the next day at the arranged house meeting.

Returning to my bed, I lay awake, wishing I could stay there, cosseted by the duvet, protected and drama free. I wanted to live in a happy bubble with Craig. There was just too much for me to face up to. Catalogue debts, bloody catalogue debts – was that all she had to worry about? I just wanted doctors to look at Craig and say they had made a mistake or tell me what to do.

The next day, shortly after lunchtime, everyone either arrived or was already present as the meeting began. When the issue of her catalogue debt was raised, Linda immediately welled up and Emma leaned over the table and touched her hand. She stroked it in a soothing way and said, 'We will sort it out.' Linda went on to state that all she was eating was packet soup. There was no mention of her vomiting or dieting. She mumbled and sniffed on about missing Meg, saying, 'She has hardly been in touch.'

I sat silent, wondering how this was all going to be resolved. Then Emma turned to me. Out of the blue, she said, 'Eileen, there is concern that you are not participating in the household as much as you could.'

I was totally shocked by this and sat bewildered. I was verbally slapped speechless. '*The house is spotless,*' was all I could think in my head, but I found it almost impossible to summon a response.

'You stay at your cousin's some weekends,' she continued, only she wasn't asking me, she was merely trying to clarify what she had been told.

Linda couldn't look at me. The penny dropped. She had been making covert calls, pleading how miserable this all was and how the house wasn't the place she thought it would be. I looked at Emma and wanted to wrestle everything out in the open, but I couldn't. In fact, I said next to nothing, only, 'No one told me it was a problem to visit my cousin, but if it is, tell me.'

'It's not creating a homely atmosphere,' Emma replied.

I couldn't believe how selfish Linda had been, could not believe how I had been stitched up. Her lack of friends and her ability to make people dislike her meant that I was the only person in her life. But it seemed that living in the same house and spending most of the day together were not enough. Although on occasion she said she had applied for work in local stores, for the most part Linda played at keeping house; her room was her palace, her kingdom. I think I knew she was afraid of socialising. But I had never heard of social phobias or, indeed, anxiety. 'Highly strung' or 'over-sensitive' were the common phrases I was aware of, which had been included in descriptions of myself. Knowing fine well that she would never have been able to pull this stunt with Wendy for fear of a broken nose or burst eardrum, Linda had tried it with me.

Interestingly on reflection, not one person in authority or indeed Linda really questioned Wendy's coming and goings. Wendy, it seemed, was entitled to build a life of her own. Linda, it appeared, would use whatever and whoever around her to get what she wanted. Whatever had happened in her past, something drove her to crave this attention. My feelings didn't appear to have been taken into consideration. I didn't shout loud enough.

Each one of us in the house had similarities between our life stories. Naively, I thought that counted for something. However, my romantic view of the situation was just that, romantic. We owed each other nothing. Never did Craig's diagnosis or my feelings feature on any of the agendas of the house meetings. Now the insensitivity to a new mother and child facing such a mountain astonishes me.

Silent I sat, but a cold rage smouldered. Strangely, though, it was not directed at Linda but at the social workers round the table. Perhaps it was because of their stupidity. When I should have been singing like a canary, I was keeping shtum about Jamie's secret overnight stays in Wendy's room and Linda's bedroom rendezvous with Harry. I kept silent regarding Linda's dislike of Hannah, the volunteer who eventually left, and her accusations about Wendy's activities and that master plan to break into her bedroom. All of these things frantically buzzed about inside my head and I could have and should have said something, but I didn't because I was silenced by the word 'grass'. I was content to do my own thing and leave everyone else to get on, but Linda was making things difficult. Her mounting dislike of the new volunteers was unbelievable, and so was her dislike of the very people round the table who were supporting her wholly in her wonderful play of misery. Shouting the loudest and whimpering sure had everyone eating out of her hand.

It was a jaw-dropping performance to watch. Inside, I was distraught. My dad could now only meet me in town, having been banned from coming near the house. His drunken behaviour had warranted this, but I sensed that Linda's fear was also mixed with a perverse pleasure that I could not understand. No longer could I go and stay with my cousin on the occasional weekend, yet Wendy was to carry on doing what she pleased. I felt frightened that I was living in an independent living unit with no independence and with deceptive and allegedly drug-dependent inmates. Overwhelmed by Linda's manipulation, as she sat there smiling at me through her tears, I was speechless. In my head, the mantra was playing, '*You don't grass.*' My nothing-in, nothing-out behaviour took hold.

I sat there looking at the authoritative faces around the table. At the time, I probably thought I was being mature, keeping control. Of course, the opposite was true. I was controlled and silenced, but not by choice. In my life, I had been threatened with violence, I had been conditioned, social worked, textbooked, recorded, filed and labelled. A house in chaos and turmoil had me running for shutdown mode. Terrified of violence and homelessness, the only response I had left was the depression that resulted from not having the ability to stand up for myself. From fear – with the natural gauntlet of emotions in between quickly skimmed over – to depression. Consequently, self-hatred quickly followed, but I was a good girl, a good 'homie'.

I have no idea to this day how it would have gone had I spoken up. I stayed silent, afraid I would be attacked or worse. Desperation also played a part in me trying to keep my head. I could keep the delusion of a family environment going if I did not break the silence. Life had taught me that when you are in a position of dependency, so many variables can control the outcome. It was soon to teach me that again.

Later, I mustered up all the self-control I could gather and called my cousin Bernadette. When she answered her phone, I cracked and blurted everything out about Linda, and eventually I simpered, 'I'm not allowed to come and stay any more at the weekends, Bernadette.'

'OK,' she calmly accepted.

I couldn't be sure that I wasn't being listened to, so I cut the call short and told her I'd explain everything when I saw her next. I put the olive-coloured phone down on the teak and glass cabinet, leaned against the door and, without fully understanding why, my throat ached and lips quivered. No tears appeared.

11

Hoodwinked

In the following days, I did two things. I visited Fernlea, probably craving some familiarity, and I put my name down on the council housing list. As I was now 17, I could legally apply. At Fernlea, I knew John was on duty as I had seen his car. John had been the residential social worker closest to my age, and I thought I could rely on him. Hamish, my social worker during my time at Fernlea, had noted in my casework file: 'John can hardly stand on his own two feet never mind look after children.' Despite this, as always, I forgave John for being less than he should have been as a social worker, and remained close to him, blaming myself, not him, for events in the past. We chatted for a short time, but of nothing relevant. When I mentioned the two new volunteers we had at the house, he could tell I felt some kind of discomfort and was itching to talk. He questioned me about them. I recognised the same glint in his eye as I had seen when I was in Fernlea and he had a fancy for one of my schoolmates. I told him briefly of what had happened round the dining table. I tried not to appear upset, but I was desperately seeking his support. 'Phone your social worker,' he replied. With this advice and a renewed resolve, this is what I decided to do. As I was leaving, he called out, 'I will pop up and see you.'

Feeling supported, I notched Craig's pram up a gear and headed home with a real sense of strength. We passed the park where I had been given a beating when I lived in Fernlea, then travelled down Mill Road to Laighstonehall and took a shortcut bypassing the long swooping street through the park to the back end of our scheme. On the last leg of the journey, I met Joe again, and a fleeting memory of him 'winching' Alison, my friend from school when I lived in Fernlea, flashed in my head.

'How ya doing, Eileen?' he shouted as he jogged over. As I knew he lived only two streets away, I had been sure we would bump into each other again. He asked if I had heard from Alison.

'No, I didn't even know she had gone to London till you said,' I replied. I asked how the band was going.

'We are going into a studio to do recordings,' he told me. Naively, I was impressed.

We walked together. On the sly, I looked at his dark pinstripe suit, black shirt and black tie. I noticed remnants of eyeliner under his eyelashes. It was our respective families, Craig and music that were the topics till I reached my front door. As I said goodbye, he shouted, 'I am having a party Saturday night, want to come?'

'Yeah, I might,' I replied.

I set to work as soon as I got in the door. I made what felt like a clandestine call to my now rarely seen or heard-from social worker. Fortunately, she was in her office and answered my call. I was thankful for this, as it meant no one else in the house would receive her return call. I leant against the door and knelt down as though to contain my whispering from travelling. My nail-bitten fingers fiddled with the grille of the underfloor heating and the coiled cord of the phone. Try as I might, I could not stop my voice quivering at certain points as I tried to rationally explain what had happened at the house meeting. This phone call undoubtedly broke my code of not grassing, and it left a silence on the other end of the phone.

Finally Rebecca spoke: 'Leave this with me, Eileen. It's not on.' There was no real emotion in her voice, but a sharp enough conviction in her statement convinced me she would look into it. I felt a sudden relief, but it was overshadowed by the thought of what might happen as a result. Before going on the phone, I had half expected to hear, 'What do you want me to do about it?' or 'That's Hamilton's jurisdiction, I can't interfere,' but I didn't and that was a good sign.

Although it was now nearing the end of autumn, I found a new spring in my step. I had received the appointment for Craig to go to Yorkhill Children's Hospital, although I had no idea what it would involve. Apart from the words 'genetic counselling department' printed in bold text there was nothing else within the letter that offered any clue as to what the appointment would entail. Craig, oblivious to all difficulties around him, gurgled, smiled, laughed and crawled curiously into any space he could find. He was at the stage of 'being into everything', opening low cupboards, pouring shampoo down toilets and talc into the bath. I became obsessed with taking photos of him at this point. I had searched in vain for photographic evidence of my own childhood, even ransacking my aunt's collection in an old battered case to no avail. There were many photos of babies in prams but none of them was me. I didn't want Craig to wonder what he had looked like as a child, so I got a cheap camera and began recording his development. I reflect now on the wonderful photos I have of him at this time.

John from Fernlea appeared the next week. I was delighted that he had kept his word and also that I had a visitor. As I made us tea in the kitchen, I shared quietly with him that I had phoned Rebecca my social worker and related her response. Linda had disappeared to her room. She was still ordering stuff from the catalogues and didn't seem one bit concerned. The bathroom upstairs was filled with fancy toiletries, and I knew she had plenty more in her bedroom. My luxury toiletries were Boots' own brand, and Craig's baby lotions doubled up for both of us.

John, still as long and thin as he had always been, gangled his way into the dining room, which had become the hub of the house, his elbows stabbing the table. I confided in him about the Harry incident, partly because we were close in age and he already knew about him. Aunt Elspeth had continued to relate with great hilarity the tales about his visits to Fernlea, especially when he had flattered her as a good laugh and told embroidered and elaborate tales of work and the goings on, such as falling asleep on the shelves where he was supposed to be stacking cornflakes.

Looking back, I see that she loved to hold court and be entertained.

As John and I chatted, Jackie returned home from a training course. The volunteers always seemed to be called to the office for some course or meeting. As she entered the room, John's eyes lit up. She joined us, and it became obvious they were flirting with each other. A few nights before, she had, among other things, confided in me that she had begun dating a head social worker, so I presumed she was flirting more for fun than anything serious.

I left them to it and busied myself doing everyday things. I was feeling quite good, but the forthcoming hospital visit nagged away at me. In my heart, I knew there was no cure for Craig's deafness, no pill, no operation or change of behaviour that would mend things. So what was there? My fear was that the answer was nothing, the paradox being I would sooner want to know than continue to hang in limbo, waiting to be told what I already knew. But I would have to go through the motions and wait for the professionals' response.

Medical answers were one thing that would be eventually available, but emotional support and understanding would not be. That rash I had during the months of my secret pregnancy haunted me and flashbacks to it were triggered when there was a query about the origins of Craig's deafness. However, with no one to talk to, it remained unspoken about.

With his usual jiggling, John then left with a promise to return soon. Thereafter, Jackie began to question me about him. I was answering all her questions without a thought when from upstairs we heard shouting. We both ran up. Linda was standing at the bottom of her bed in her colour-coordinated pyjamas and slippers, her hair still wet from her bath. She was ranting about a prescription she had got that morning from the chemist. 'I don't know what these are. These are not my usual pills, and this is not even my name on them,' she shouted. In tears, she offered them over to us.

I took them from her and read the packet. It was not her name or address; they were prescribed to a Mrs something or other and were tablets for heart problems.

'What were you supposed to have?' I asked.

'I get Ativan, and they're blue,' she cried.

'*Ativan, Ativan,*' I repeated in my head, and then I remembered what they were. I had come across the name when a year previously I had visited the library and looked up drugs after my doctor had prescribed me with Valium. I had binned the prescription but read up on the drug. It was my way of informing myself of the dangers and convincing myself my fear of them was justified.

'Shit, that means that possibly an old person has got your prescription.'

Everyone stopped for a second and considered what I'd just said. 'And if that's the case, it could bloody kill them if they take it.' I lifted the packet and ran down the stairs. 'We better phone the chemist, we better phone the chemist,' I repeated.

Frantically dialling the number of the chemist, I hoped that some poor old woman with a heart condition hadn't been given Linda's pills and was now lying half dead in her house. Ring after ring passed before eventually a male voice answered. In my panic, I must have sounded as though I had run round the block. Ranting and anxious, I wasted no time in explaining they had mixed up a prescription, telling them the names of the drugs and the names of the people affected. Profuse apologies were offered. Mrs something or other would be contacted right away, and Linda was asked to go and get her correct prescription.

By late afternoon, Linda had calmed down and was putting the kettle on. Jackie went into the dining room and closed the door, indicating she was making a private call. As the kettle boiled, Linda leaned towards the hatch and tried to listen. Her right elbow leaned on the bunker and with her fingers on her lips she grinned and mouthed to me, 'I think it's a guy.'

I could not help but grin back, amazed at her recovery and gall, then her elbow slipped and she rattled her chin off the bunker. Through her pain, we both tried to contain our laughter by doubling up and making frantic 'shut up' faces at each other when Angela breenged through the door. Her battered second-hand school satchel was dumped on the kitchen floor and she was bombarded by the drug tale simultaneously from myself and Linda. We would have to wait to find out what Jackie was up to.

12

Loose screws

John returned on the Thursday afternoon and chatted with Linda, Jackie, Angela and myself. Wendy was where Wendy always was – nobody really knew. Meg had called Linda and they had arranged to have lunch together. A delighted Linda had been up and ready for hours before leaving to meet her. I spoke to the others about Craig's hospital appointment and the party I had been invited to. Angela said she would babysit Craig, as she was not going out. Jumping around like a cat on a hot tin roof as was John's way, he said, 'I am going away camping for the weekend.' It was a sure bet he would be meeting up with some of his birdwatching mates and would probably sit for hours peeking through a camouflaged hideout in hopes of spotting some feathered rarity. Jackie stated she had to visit relatives down south but never said much more about why. While we drank tea and chatted, I set about removing the collar from a grey silk shirt I had bought at a second-hand shop, to make it more modern. I always loved the mandarin-collar style.

Thursday night saw Linda distraught in her bedroom. It turned out the purpose of the lunch meeting with Meg had been to tell Linda she was leaving her job and returning to the islands. She had originated in the Hebrides and was returning to help her sick mother. As Craig and I sat in Linda's bedroom, she talked and wept, and I genuinely felt for her. I knew that feeling well. It is devastating when people you have become attached to leave. I was about to ask her if she wanted to come to the party on Saturday when she announced that she was going to break into Wendy's room tonight, stating, 'This is not on.'

I kept my mouth shut. She went on a rant about Craig's safety, our home here and how unfair it all was. Picking up a nappyless Craig, she said to him, 'Is that no right, wee man?' She buried her face into his giggling belly and blew raspberries. Linda's mood swings amazed me, and maybe I even admired them because I was so blank and stoic. However, the fact she was seeking retribution for the loss of Meg by attacking Wendy scared me too. I did not understand Linda's reaction to loss of control; she avenged by any means, while my response to difficult situations was to retreat, use humour or just tough it out, keeping my fears private and eventually slipping into depression. I did not know I was behaving in such a pattern; I did not know that I was depressed. I simply did not know who or what I was.

Stretched out on top of my bed with Craig asleep in his cot nearby, I was reading when the ominous though expected knock came on my bedroom door. A few minutes later, Linda and I stood at the top of the upstairs landing at Wendy's padlocked bedroom door. We were alone in the house, and Linda had made sure that both outside doors were locked in case anyone returned soon. In pyjamas and dressing gowns, we stood huddled over the padlock like children breaking into the locked cupboard in the kitchen where the chocolate was kept. Although alone, we spoke in whispers. Producing from her dressing-gown pocket a few yellow-handled screwdrivers, she said, 'One of these should fit,' adding, 'If not I have more in my room.' No doubt a matching set from some catalogue.

One of the two screws that held the padlock onto the frame of the door was coming loose when she turned to me and said, 'I can't concentrate, I think it's my medication, you have a go.' Caught up in the moment, I did so and managed to release too easily the first screw. As I handed her the loosened screw to hold, I saw in her eyes a real excitement; while I was petrified, she was rejoicing. Her voice whispered in my ear, 'Watch the paintwork and don't scratch it.'

I stopped in my tracks and a long-awaited penny dropped. I handed her back the screwdriver, using the excuse that my hand was sore. My thoughts filled with the next house meeting we were having on Monday. I had visions of me having to reveal what I had found when I had unscrewed the lock and broken into Wendy's room. I went to the toilet, sat there and whispered to myself, 'You bloody idiot.' As I left the toilet, Linda was entering Wendy's room. From the doorway, I could see there were piles of boxes lying around. With a thirst for finding something illegal, Linda searched through all the drawers, under the bed and inside the wardrobe. On the bedside cabinet sat a can of lighter fuel. 'See, I told you,' she said when her eyes finally rested on it. She seemed overly pleased to have found her evidence.

'One can of lighter fuel, Linda,' I said, and then added, 'Wendy and Jamie both smoke.' I pictured the heavy square Zippo lighter Jamie used and knew the fuel had an innocent use.

Going back to Wendy's wardrobe, Linda pulled out several boxes with the Avon cosmetics name on them. 'Bet this is knock-off stuff!' she said.

I shrugged my shoulders. At this point I was past caring. With the air of craziness in the bedroom deflated, and Linda obviously sated, she placed the boxes back in the wardrobe, still scanning as we walked out of the room. I took charge of the screwdriver and was extremely careful not to scratch the paintwork. Swearing a few times, as Linda had disappeared downstairs and I was left to complete the dirty work, I tightened the hinge to the frame of the door in the exact position it had been before. After going back to my room, I sat on my bed staring at the wall. If I could have articulated complicity and being set up as a stool pigeon I would have, at least if only to myself.

13

It's not my party

The weekend came, as did my party. My silk shirt was ready, and I poured myself into a pair of Barbara's jeans, which were probably a size six; I was an eight. Having done my roots the night before, I was now a true bottled blonde from a Born Blonde box bought from Boots, and I was excited.

Joe came to the door for me and we walked together the few short streets to his house. Once inside, he introduced me to his sister, Louise. She was a beautician and naturally commented on my make-up and hair. 'It's a great colour,' she said. I met neighbours from a few doors away. Kerry was a tall girl just younger than me and she was a trainee hairdresser. I enjoyed mixing with people, chatting energetically and laughing. Joe spent a lot of time by my side. He showed me his collection of records, rattling off artists like David Bowie, Mick Ronson, some Punk, New Romantic, rock and, of course, Gary Numan. He spoke so energetically that my replies in comparison were microscopic. 'I like them, and him . . . Oh, she's great,' I cooed.

Joe disappeared to get some drinks, and I got the chance to chat some more with Kerry. She invited me to her house, giving me her number, and after several glasses of lager it was almost midnight. Though I didn't want to go, I knew I had to. Joe left the lively party that had erupted in the kitchen and reluctantly walked me home after realising that pleading with me to stay on was fruitless. Although reluctant to leave myself, I responded with a continuous, 'No, no, I can't. I have to get back.'

Passing under the street lamps, Joe asked, 'Craig's father, who was he? Where is he?'

I gave simple, factual replies. My heart was thumping and by the time we got to the front door I could feel myself getting lightheaded. I wondered and worried if he would try to kiss me. He did. On opening my front door and saying good night, I stared at the ground, too scared and shy to look him directly in the eyes. He stood up on the front door step and kissed me again. I can't say it was awful; I can't say it was like the heavenly kiss I had received from a boy called Sean one night while on holiday in Switzerland with the school. It was prolonged and felt good. Hearing footsteps from inside the house, I pulled away. 'Want to go for a walk tomorrow?' he asked, with a sense of urgency.

'Yes,' I instantly replied, wanting to get inside the house and close the door before whoever's footsteps found us. As I was closing the door, I promised that I would phone him.

'Who was that?' Linda asked as I turned from the now closed door. The question was immediate and direct.

'Just a guy I knew before,' I said. There were no questions about the party or whether I had enjoyed myself. I wondered if she thought it had been Harry at the door.

I glided up the stairs, passed my bedroom and saw Craig lying sleeping soundly. Creeping a few steps along the hallway, I knocked lightly on Angela's door. Her head peeked round and she invited me in. As Jackie had said she needed to visit relatives, she had the bedroom to herself. 'How was Craig?' I asked.

Climbing back into bed, Angela answered, 'He hasn't woken up once. How did it go?'

The smile on my face at being asked this question was answer enough, but Angela wanted to hear the details. 'It was fantastic. I met some really nice people, and he kissed me.'

'Whoopdee-doo!' she half screamed, half whispered.

Encouraged by this and her throwing her quilt in the air, I carried on, 'He has asked to see me again tomorrow.'

'Whoopdee fucking doo,' she replied, teasing me affectionately.

I laughed with embarrassment and glee, then pinned the quilt down on top on her in a joking attempt to shut her up, as I knew Linda would be straining next door to hear us.

My news over, Angela began to confide in me about a guy she had met in one of the social work offices, whom she really quite liked. While she rattled animatedly on, I noticed a pair of green nylon tights stuck to her wall. I stopped her mid sentence and, gawking at the tights hanging from the wall like nylon ivy, I said, 'What's all that about?'

She grinned. 'I took them off and that's where they landed. I quite like it. Do you like it?'

'Yeah,' I said.

Angela's hand and arm movements became more animated and affected, and her lips pursed in slight mockery. To me, it seemed like she was describing an accidental abstract piece of art. She probably was doing that while also taking the piss. That's why I liked her. As I sneaked off to bed, she lowered her voice and looked glum, 'Remember, there is another house meeting on Monday.'

Sighing, I replied, 'Yeah, I know.'

With that acknowledged, we both smiled at each other and said goodnight. Screwing my face up as if it would help me click her door shut more quietly, I turned and saw Linda just a few feet away in her room door. 'Want a cuppa, Eileen?' she asked.

'No thanks, Linda,' I replied as pleasantly as I could. 'I'm tired. See you in the morning.'

The house meeting played on my mind. As I lay awake, I could think of nothing that would be more negative than usual. I knew Linda was planning on bringing up the possibility of all of us pitching in for the basics, such as sugar and tea bags. Wendy was never here and would stand against that plan, so I couldn't see it going far. I wondered if Linda would dare reveal what she had seen in Wendy's room, but how could she without getting herself into trouble?

On Monday, our house meeting started in the afternoon. Emma was there, as were the two volunteers, Jackie and Angela. An independent social worker, Jan, was also in attendance to oversee things. She headed up the project but we had never met her before. Even Wendy was there.

Cars had arrived, doors opened and shut, the kettle boiled, and we started gathering in the dining room.

Jan stated that we were all doing well and the project seemed to be a success. 'The next-door neighbours have no complaints and seem supportive of the house,' she said. This was true. A relatively young couple lived next door and had often said if we needed anything just to ask. We had chatted in the street and out in the garden, but other than that there was no real interaction with the neighbours.

Emma sat with paperwork in front of her and brought up the issue of us having a kitty for the basics in the house, such as tea, coffee and toilet rolls. 'N-no way,' was Wendy's predictable reply.

Emma tried to reason that it was a good idea for the community of the house.

'I think that's a good idea,' said Jackie.

'Well, you f-f-f-fucking wid,' Wendy replied. The ash from her cigarette fell onto the table. She had a habit of missing ashtrays, and the everlasting picture in my mind of her is of someone never out of trainers, always hauling up her jeans and spreading fag ash everywhere. Annoyed, she swept the ash away with the sleeve of her jumper and knocked the glass ashtray onto the floor. 'Ah'm gonna f-f-f-fucking move out and live with Jamie if that's the case.' Wendy was incensed. She got up, leaving the ashtray on the floor, and had a fight with the door on the way out of the dining room. Smashing the door against the wall, she thumped her way up the stairs, cursing and swearing all the way. 'F-f-fucking bastards, think you kin t-t-t-tell me wit tae dae.'

Linda got up, stared at everyone and said while she shut the door, 'That's what we have to put up with.' Her 'butter-wouldn't-melt' face appeared as she looked at everyone, shaking her head.

The atmosphere was already awkward, then we heard Wendy flouncing down the stairs still muttering swear words. The front door then opened and was battered shut. The house shook. So did Linda's head in mock righteous disgust.

The meeting ended without much more happening other than the social workers making phone calls and cups getting cleared away. Later on, in the early evening, Barbara came visiting, smiling as she came through the door with a bottle of wine poking out of her bag. She took my mind off the day's events and produced a fabulous jumpsuit of hers that I had previously admired and had borrowed in the past. Made of a black shiny material, lined, with zips across the breasts and at the sides of the arms and legs, it looked like something Diana Rigg, the original Lara Croft, would have worn in *The Avengers*. 'Keep it,' she said. 'It looks way better on you.'

As always, she cheered me up, I whispered the details of the meeting to her and finished just as Angela arrived declaring, 'Oh goody, wine.' But as the bottle was almost empty, it was decided we should go out and get another. The three of us along with Craig in his buggy trundled to the nearest shop. Both Angela and Barbara took turns at pushing Craig. Several bottles of wine were purchased along with sweets, snacks and the cheapest chocolate Angela could find. She had a thing about cheap chocolate – she adored it. We munched our way back to the house, and, after the day's events and the worry of what was to come, it felt good to be in relaxed company.

Barbara and Angela opened the wine as I got Craig ready for bed. Linda had shut herself away in her room, refusing a glass of wine. With Craig tucked up and sleeping, I joined the other two, who had already finished a full bottle. Linda eventually joined us in the living room, but not for long. Angela's laugh got louder and louder, Barbara's tales got funnier, and Linda left the room with a quick sneer. I knew she was thinking that they were 'mental' or 'crazy', and in particular Angela. It bothered neither of them what she clearly thought. Her bedroom door slammed in indignation and protest.

Jackie returned home and popped her head in. She quickly retreated, saying she was away for a bath. She had gone out after the meeting, nobody knew where. That was the freedom she and others had to do as they pleased. I was glad Angela had joined us as it meant it would not just be me that was answerable for having a night in. Amongst the hilarity of the evening, I could feel the ominous tension building in the house.

I had had several glasses of wine by the time we decided to call it a night. After clearing up, Angela was using the downstairs toilet, singing her head off, while Barbara had bolted upstairs and barged into the main bathroom, where Jackie was relaxing in the bath, and started to vomit. The sound of raised voices made Angela stop singing, and seconds later it was all over when Jackie walked semi-naked and wet into her room and slammed the door. The whole situation must have been music to Linda's ears. She appeared at her door and offered the widest grin she could muster before slowly edging the door closed. Now, I thought, I am really for it!

I lay awake biting my nails till they bled, then had to get up and run them under the cold tap to stop the bleeding and take the pain away. I watched as red-stained watery streams kept appearing from my nails when I removed them from the running water.

Morning came and Barbara apologised to Jackie. The apology was sniffed at. Angela turned her mouth down as if to say, 'What's the problem?' Linda gave us all the silent treatment but did so with a smile. Barbara left for work, and I got on with my day.

Craig was coming up to his first birthday. Poppy sales and rattling collecting tins always evoke memories of his birthday. He was red cheeked with teething as well as staggering around on wobbly wee legs, using the furniture like crutches for balancing and guidance. The wood on his cot was gnawed like the wood around a mouse hole. He curiously never cried when teething, just woke me up with a gnawing noise and a beaming smile as I lifted my head and turned towards him in his cot in the morning. His curls were getting longer and remained blond. The expression in his bright and brilliant blue eyes was always alert, and they had not changed from the cornflower blue at his birth. He was in his walkie pen, which allowed him to stand up and whizz about the place. It was steel, with wheels, coloured beads on the tubes and a tartan seat.

While preparing his lunch in the kitchen, I heard Linda shout from the living room, 'Eileen, Eileen!'

Dropping what I was doing, I rushed into the room. Linda was kneeling beside Craig and the walkie pen. 'He stopped breathing, he is going blue, he stopped breathing. I just pulled him away from the TV,' she rambled.

Craig sat motionless in the pen, pale and staring at me. Frightened, I picked him up. 'Why?' I gasped to Linda,. 'What was he doing?'

'He kept turning the TV off when I turned it back on and was laughing, so I grabbed the pen and pulled him away,' she replied.

I went to the kitchen clutching Craig, instinctively murmuring in his ear while trying to stem my tears. I sat him in his highchair and frantically rubbed his hands and feet. Moments later, he was laughing and eating his lunch. It took a lot longer for me to recover.

After lunch, I walked to my aunt Helen's to escape. When I got there, I was confronted with a very upset Aunt Helen. She told me she had been to see Cathleen several days before at her foster home, and the foster parents had kept her at the door. She and my uncle waited in the car as Cathleen had got ready, and then they took her out for the day. Dropping her off, again Aunt Helen was kept at the door. The next day, she had received an abrupt phone call from the social work department. She was told in no uncertain terms by Rebecca Mower that she was not to appear there again with a drink in her! She was inconsolable with rage.

Stunned, I forgot about my own misery and got angry myself. I found it so easy to be furious on behalf of someone else, especially when you know what has happened to them has been vindictive. I had never seen my aunt with a drink in her; even at New Year I had only ever witnessed her having one drink at the stroke of midnight.

'Can I phone her right now?' I said, referring to Rebecca Mower, my social worker. I was incensed. I was terrified that my aunt would feel she could not take any more of the personal politics she had become involved in, which had nothing to do with child welfare and what was best practice. I had to make this right; I had an almost insane fear of losing my aunt. This attack on her was personal and had come from Cathleen's foster parents and was backed up by my alcoholic father's previous malicious accusations. My aunt's character had been assassinated by a vendetta and personal agendas, and the authorities were accepting it.

When my mother died, my aunt had insisted the money collected at her funeral should go to buying us children necessities such as vests and pants. She had further antagonised the social worker at the time by asking for help in the way of bedding for us two girls. The issue was not about us children or good social work practice; it was a personal war about who had control. Furthermore, she had told them exactly what she thought of them for returning us to our violent drunken father, stating correctly that he was not a capable man. Not only had the social worker at the time recorded that my aunt was hostile and aggressive, he had also reportedly gone out drinking with my father. Moreover, his records only gave a one-sided opinion of my aunt's behaviour. To me and to all others who knew my aunt, it was not a one-sided opinion, it was an outright lie and personal attack.

I phoned Rebecca Mower and left a message asking her to phone me at my aunt's. It took her an hour or so to return my call, during which time I listened to my aunt expending her anger as she got ready to go work. I remember the tongs, the hairbrush and hairspray all getting banged on the kitchen bunker in time to her retelling of the tale.

When the phone rang, my aunt and I looked at each other, then, taking the initiative, I ran to the phone and Rebecca Mower was on the other end of the line. I sat there in the hall on the seated part of the wooden telephone table and garbled about how I had never seen my aunt Helen drunk in my entire lifetime and how wrong this all was.

'We have to take all reports seriously, Eileen,' she said, adding that she was glad she caught me as she had been planning to phone me at home today anyway. I twiddled with the phone cord and shuffled on the seat. Staring out of the hall window, my heart began sinking as I heard her say, 'It's been decided that Barbara can't come and stay overnight at Bark Avenue any more.' Before I could reply, not that I could, as I was without a voice, she went on, 'As John and Jackie are a couple, it is not in John or Jackie's professional interest to have a colleague of John's visiting.'

Reeling from this, I finished the phone call subdued. After asking my aunt Helen to please visit Cathleen again and bring her out to see me, I left meekly. I didn't have the strength to tell her what was happening with me having to cut ties with Bernadette and the house politics, as I felt she was still too angry to hear me. I did not want to add my nonsense to her fire.

I walked home slowly and with a heavy heart. As I walked through the door, the phone was ringing. Linda answered it. 'It's Jan for you, Eileen,' she said.

Taking the phone from her and pulling Craig into the dining room in his buggy, I closed the door and listened to the same story over again. The twinkle in John's eyes, his visits, Jackie's weekend away at her 'family' – it all now made sense. Feeling used, the isolation and betrayal I felt burned deep. I was going to lose Barbara as a friend too. My friends, my home and my feelings were all subject to far too many variables.

I stayed in my room after teatime, listening to music from my clock radio and wondering how I could tell Barbara. As I settled Craig down for the evening, I was changing his nappy when my stomach wrenched at the smell. I ran to the toilet and holding Craig on my right thigh I vomited. Over the next year, this was to become a developing hidden habit.

Back in my room, I opened a letter that had arrived for me. It was from the then Department of Health and Security, otherwise known as 'the broo' or 'the dole'. I was to be interviewed in a week's time to assess my claim for supplementary benefit. Linda popped her head into my room. I could hardly look at her, but I did tell her the news about Barbara, as I suspected she already knew. Her mock astonishment told me she did. You just know sometimes when someone is being disingenuous. I said nothing of my suspicions. What good would it do? What could I do? I was a 'nobody' in my eyes, and it seemed I was to others as well.

The next day saw John bustling in the door and Jackie rushing to meet him. They were excited and bursting to be seen as a couple. Jangling about, all arms and legs in his usual manner, he darted into the kitchen and whispered to me, 'We were away camping.' I was apparently to be excited and pleased for them too, and I did pretend to be, afraid to appear to be anything else. I would have been genuinely pleased if it had not cost me a good friend and been executed in a less underhand manner. I can't remember how I put it to Barbara or how she felt. I wonder now how our friendship impacted on her at work – was she taken less seriously or gossiped about behind her back?

Over the course of the next few days, I wandered down to Fernlea, hoping to see my aunt Elspeth, perhaps driven by a need to tell someone

I hoped would listen to my hurt. I still never really had a sense of why I went to places or to particular people. My physical and emotional foundations were weak, and, as recent events had reinforced, I had no real stake or claim anywhere. I sat wistfully in the office, thinking again that as new kids had arrived in Fernlea and my bed had been taken, the truth was that the staff were no longer legally obliged to care for me. I had once been answerable to them for all my actions, and we had had late-night conversations about my feelings and about their lives. We had shared laughs, and tears too, but that was all gone. That feeling of being feral stabbed at me. I was at the mercy of the whims of the changing social work seasons, like dry leaves that fall from trees only to be replaced next time round with fresh new ones, and I had no roots to hang on to.

As I sat in my usual place in the office, bum on radiator, my aunt Elspeth glanced over the daily report book, reading the written accounts of what had happened the day before. I had read it before, sneaking off to look when the staff were not there. It mainly contained negative judgements and jargon. 'Peter was moody today'; 'Peter would not cooperate'; 'Laura was acting out and spiteful.' I had never read anything kind or considered.

Feeling self-pitying, I recounted my tales of woe. First, about my aunt being accused of being a drunk, about which Elspeth was horrified. She had known my aunt Helen and had been witness to some of the difficulties arising from the past. When I told her about John and Jackie, her jaw just about hit the report book. You know, too, when someone is totally in the dark! She had spent several years supporting John through his personal difficulties. 'Got him in a tent for a weekend and caught him,' she fumed.

Eventually, I left and walked home, realising that while there may have been a lot of covert calls in recent weeks, they had not come from Fernlea. Feeling slightly better than dreadful, I walked home the long way, down past the Bent Cemetery, past the Cosy Corner pub, stopping there for juice for both Craig and me, then continuing up through long streets and avenues, eventually reaching our scheme. John rarely came to visit me again; it felt like my purpose had been served.

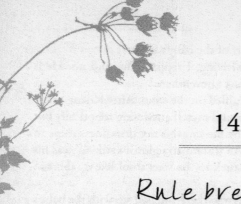

14

Rule breaking

Leaves were falling from trees and wild walks into the off-the-beaten-track countryside had become almost impossible for me and Craig. It was time to hibernate in libraries. Summer had gone, leaving me only with memories of picnics of sandwiches made with a funny-faced cold meat called 'Billy', that we shared with curious strolling horses during intimate days where we lay on an old sheet gazing through grass and wildflowers, blowing the dandelion clocks that floated back to the earth like daytime stars. Snow had shown itself with its first flutter, the clocks were ticking down to winter, and it was around this time that my interview took place with the representative from the DHSS.

The male interviewer arrived, black briefcase in hand. I was alone in the house and Craig was down for his afternoon nap. Everything was in hand, and I felt confident. I showed him into the kitchen, as I was preparing dinner, and offered him a stool. He opened his briefcase and brought out a notebook and pen. I was not prepared for what came next. It was supposed to be a straightforward interview about my circumstances in order that the DHSS could determine what financial assistance I was entitled to.

We sat face to face on stools like opposing Wally dugs. 'Right, Miss Cooke,' he began, 'can you tell me who the baby's father is?'

Feeling a bit uneasy, but knowing I had to answer the questions of this source of authority, I complied.

'Do you know the whereabouts of the baby's father?'

Terrified I could be accused of lying, I replied, 'Yes and no. He is down south somewhere, but I don't know where.'

His pen scribbled away as I shuffled on the stool. After having many random questions fired at me, I found myself answering robotically but with a rising panic. An attempt by me to avert my uneasiness came in the offer to him of a cup of tea. An instant straightforward 'no' was his answer. His abruptness saw me stuck to the steel stool like a rabbit in the headlights.

'Now, Miss Cooke, can you tell me where you had sex with the baby's father?'

Mortified, with shame beginning to wash over me, I again complied while inwardly crumpling.

He and his pen scribbled away. 'How many times did you have sex there?'

Frightened not to give an answer, I made a number up.

'Was there anyone else involved?' he asked.

I knew what he meant. Meekly, I replied no. Why did I not say, 'How dare you?' or ask for him to come back when I had a witness?

'This is state money, other people's, you know.' The implication was clear: be grateful. No replies, no money! 'Where else did you have sex?' he continued, as I burned with shame. 'How many times did you have sex there?'

The rabbit in the headlights that I was had been run over. Like a captured and wounded animal, I complied with steely replies in the pathetic hope I would get the financial assistance needed for myself and my son to survive. My face remained composed and my replies were merely automated responses to this man. As his questions became more intense and probing, I remember getting off the stool to turn off the boiling potatoes, willing him to finish his emotional cull. His eyes were as steely as the stool as they bored into my back, and I began to feel very frightened. I never got back on that stool.

'What type of sex did you have?' he asked.

I did not reply. I just stared at him with a look that said, 'I don't know what you are talking about.'

He refused to let go of his roadkill and rearranged his question. 'Did you have oral sex?' was the last question I remember him asking.

The shame burnt deep. I remember that and the fear in me stacking up, but with my humiliation almost complete I can't remember how I replied.

Putting his 'notes' in his briefcase, he looked amicably at me and said, 'We will be in touch.'

Alone in the kitchen, my humiliation screamed loud; it was deafening. Not able to think or know what to feel, and not knowing why my jaw and body was in the grip of so much tension, I was sick in the posh downstairs toilet. Not yet 18, and with no witnesses, I knew only how it felt but had no words to nail it. My aloneness was crushing, as dreaded memories swamped the emptiness, and I was glad when Linda came home. I could not tell anyone – what would I tell them? My feelings frozen and disposed of down the toilet, I was empty apart from disgust and self-loathing. How could I share that? I felt as violated by him as I did by others from my childhood.

I had just finished feeding Craig in his highchair when Linda lifted him out and dropped him on the floor. He was crying hard, and I picked him up from the floor and ran up the stairs to comfort him in my arms. Rocking on my bed, I was comforting myself too. I vowed I would have to get away from here. I did not know that wherever I went I would be taking myself and my feelings with me. My list, with its heading 'Nothing in – Nothing out' read in my head as:

Say nothing.
This will pass.
It will go away.
Get out.
It's over.

That night, with my duvet wrapped round me, I gnawed intently until I ripped off my toenails with my teeth and they throbbed and bled. It diverted thoughts of the DHSS man and images of him reading his notes.

15

Protective custody

Straight after the humiliating incident with the DHSS man, I became Joe's girlfriend. I had obviously sought comfort somewhere and someone to supply more Elastoplasts on the concealed sores of self-loathing and disgust. I wanted to be normal. Twice a week I would go to his house, and the rest of the time I remained at Bark Avenue. After the experiences with Harry and my dad, I would not invite him there, and I also had the duty of being company for Linda imposed on me.

My friendship with Barbara had dwindled, and I saw her only on the odd occasion now. I missed her. Adding to the madness and bias, John and Jackie sometimes stayed together in the house. Astonishingly, Linda thought it was terrible that I had lost a friend due to their relationship, or so she told me. Her part in me not being able to stay at my cousin's on the weekend remained undiscussed.

In this limbo time, some good times and milestones were shared. For example, Craig was walking unaided, and his front teeth were coming through in parallel with his laughter. He laughed with his belly. As with a lot of children, it was infectious. His whole body would shake, and the purity of a belly laugh would reach his eyes. This in turn would reach my heart or anyone else's who was witnessing it. Listening to my deaf child giggle unreservedly while I played peek-a-boo behind my hands was an innocent delight – and heartbreaking. I was so unsure of our future and afraid of everything. Weeks and months passed for me in yet another bubble – another movie with another director sitting in the passenger seat of my life. I got on with it.

One night on a trip to the local chip shop with Linda, we met Jack and Charlene. Charlene was Harry's sister. Nothing was mentioned of his visit or absence from Bark Avenue. We joked and laughed, with Jack playing the fool to us girls. They walked us back some of the way. Wrapped up against the cold, we chatted away unsuspectingly in the moonlight. Jack and Charlene left us at the split between the park and lane that separated the schemes.

Minutes after separating from our company and nearing home with the warm chips held close to us in newspaper wrapping, Linda let out a shriek. We had both heard a cough. Turning round, she had seen a man standing in the near distance. He was standing in the freezing cold . . . naked! As I turned to look at her in astonishment, she ran screaming in the direction of the nearest houses. I turned again and stared at the naked man. He stood near bushes and under a lamp for maximum viewing. We locked eyes. In my head, I could hear Linda screaming and the sound of a door getting battered by her fists. Events happened in slow motion and without feeling for me. I felt no fear, and I felt disconnected to everything around me. It was a surreal scene. I should have taken flight or responded in some way.

I turned to see where Linda had run and turned back again to stare at the guy. Linda's chip bag lay with its contents scattered on the ground and the street lamp stood alone; he was gone. It was as if he had never been there. By the time I had got to the house where Linda had run to – I knew which one it was by the screaming – the police had been called by the householders. Linda was hysterical; I was, on reflection, unsettlingly calm. As Linda talked incoherently in the living room of the people's house we had invaded, the police arrived. Linda became even more disjointed and confused, and sympathy tea was administered as we were interviewed over the incident. After questioning both of us and taking notes, the police had to take us home, as Linda was refusing to go out the door. The police drove us the short distance in their car. As we arrived, Jack and Charlene were anxiously waiting for us. They had heard the screams and rushed to our house. Jack felt guilty for leaving us to go the short distance alone.

A few days later, we received a phone call to go to Hamilton police station to attend an identity parade. On the day we attended, I could not get a babysitter for Craig, so we had to take him with us. As we entered the room set aside for victims, I was gobsmacked. The smoke-filled room contained about 20 women, all there to identify the same man! I had Craig in my arms and paced the room, shooshing him up and down. When my name was called, I was led out of the room by a policeman. He said, 'Just this way, girl,' as I followed, entering a lift and still wondering what I was going to do with Craig. 'Just go into the room and take your time. Point him out and say his number. I'll take the baby for you. What's his name?'

Almost without warning, I found myself in a room with five or six men in a line and two policemen. Shocked, I faltered slightly as I had thought I would be able to identify the offender through the two-way mirrors I had seen on the TV. Trying not to look at the line of prospective flashers, I noticed the room was cold, or perhaps it was me. It was a large white and grey room with no mirrors and only one door. However, I remained calm as I walked towards one of the policemen. He spoke in a low voice and instructed me to take my time. He said, 'Walk up and down the line. If you see the man you saw on the night, stop and say his number.'

I walked up and down the line-up. I could see a man with bare feet in his brown sandals. Then I came face to face with him. My eyes flitted over him. '*That's him, that's him,*' my voice was whispering to me. Afraid to blurt it out, I walked up and down the line again while trying to plan how to deal with this. I could not run or walk away. There were two policemen, six potential flashers and only one door; I was stuck until I made a decision. Aware that the police were also watching me, I eventually came to a stop near them, perhaps as security.

'Can you identify a suspect?' one policeman asked.

'Yes,' I whispered.

'Walk down the line, stop and shout out his number clearly,' he said.

Though I was terrified, I robotically did as I was told. Inwardly, I felt as though my world was going to spin into an angry chaos and it would be me in trouble when I said his number. Stepping deliberately and surefooted as if to steady myself against the consequences, my heart pounded as I passed each man in the line-up. They all looked straight ahead, avoiding my gaze. I stopped and said, 'Number three.'

To be sure, the policeman asked again, 'What number?'

'Number three,' I repeated. Our eyes did not lock this time but flitted over each other as I stood in front of him; just a few feet separated us. I imagined all the others exhaling in relief that they had not been chosen. Leaving the room, I was met by the first policeman who was carrying Craig. Craig threw his arms towards me, and I grabbed him gratefully. As we re-entered the stainless-steel lift, the policeman asked me, 'What number did you pick, hen?'

'Number three,' I said, pulling Craig close to me.

'Good girl,' he said. 'That's our man.'

I felt a strange sense of relief. I had not incriminated the wrong man, and the unforeseen ordeal without the two-way mirrors was over. As the lift rattled, shuddered and came to a stop, I was ushered down to reception in order not to meet any of the other witnesses so I could not contaminate evidence. The policeman offered me some unorthodox advice: 'If that ever happens to you again, hen, just look him straight in the eye and say, "I see you have a straw. Want a can of Coke to go with it?"' He laughed and I joined in nervously. It was no joke, though; I was now shaking with delayed fear and grateful for any diversion such as humour. I wondered then if he would have thought I was a good girl, a nice person, if he had known about me and my crime. It's that peculiar feeling that surfaces when you see a policeman or police car: you immediately feel guilty. Perhaps it's the adult version of the childhood chastisement that 'God is watching you and he sees if you are being bad.'

I waited for Linda at the station reception, bouncing Craig on my knees. I still felt astonished by all those women I had seen down in the witness room and wondered how many had not come forward. I also wondered how this would all go in court. The last time I had been in court I was 14 and was giving evidence against my father, who had been charged with the physical abuse and neglect of me and my sister. At least this time I wouldn't be in a situation where it was just my word against this man. I also reflected on the fact that the last time I was in Hamilton police station I had got a beating from two of the policemen when I had run away from the children's home. Here I was now, helping them. It could have been one of the policemen I was beside in the identity parade who had assaulted me. It highlighted to me how people in general had many facets to their behaviour.

Soon Linda appeared; she appeared quite ashen. When I asked her what number she had picked, she said, 'Number four.' I asked her why she had thought that it was number four, and she replied, 'Because he had no socks on.'

I was speechless. What could I say to that? What I did realise then and there was that if Linda had known what number he really was she still would not have said. She was too scared to confront him, and I was too scared not to.

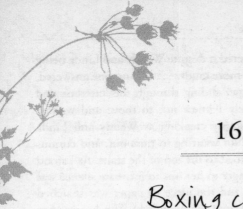

16

Boxing clever

As well as the continuous stream of catalogue parcels that still arrived for Linda, it seemed Wendy was now in competition with her. Smaller parcels would arrive for her too. Wendy had given Linda the key to the lock on her bedroom door. There was no more mention of breaking into Wendy's room and no more bitter accusations came from Linda. The boxes were, however, mounting up in her unused bedroom. It all came to a head when Wendy came home and stayed for a night.

The noise of laughter and Wendy's usual swearing could be heard from her bedroom as she and Linda chatted. There was also the noise of boxes being opened and packaging rustling. Later, when I met Linda in the kitchen, she shook her head at me and rolled her eyes. She was indicating that what Wendy was up to was wrong. I smiled but thought of Linda's ability to play all sides. Even though I had probably heard of the words 'collusive' and 'manipulative', I could not tie them to actions. I could barely understand how I felt, never mind give the emotions a name. We girls were probably all the same on that score. It was always a feeling in my gut, a flinch or a tension anywhere if not everywhere in my body that flagged up a feeling of being uncomfortable. How could I figure out this emotionally indeterminate state if I did not know what it was . . . how could it be figured out?

One day shortly after this, the front-door letterbox was rattled. I could hear it from my bedroom as Craig and I played on the floor with his building bricks. No one answered it despite Wendy and Linda being downstairs. The letterbox rattled more loudly . . . still no one answered. Next there was the sound of paper sliding through the letterbox and landing on the floor. Instinctively I knew not to move and waited. Eventually I heard a door cautiously creaking as Wendy and Linda sneaked toward the front door. Not wanting to miss out, and curious about what was happening, I tiptoed to the top of the stairs. As I stood there, Wendy raised a shaking finger to her lips to intimate silence was required. A few minutes passed and the piece of paper was snatched from the floor. It had been a visit from the Avon lady. Wendy owed her a lot of money for the spectacular pile of orders she had been getting and not paying for. Most of us in the house had ordered Avon goods from Wendy. My favourite of the perfume samples that Wendy had was Sweet Honesty, and I had a bottle one week and then the matching talc the following fortnight. Wendy seemed unperturbed by this near miss and warned us never to let the woman in. We all began chorusing, 'Ding dong, Avon calling,' taken from Avon's TV advert.

Other even less wanted visitors and news came to our door. A letter had been left to say that the police had visited us. They had been bringing news of our court date, which unbelievably was to be in several days' time. Both Linda and I were astounded and anxious that it was to happen so quickly and with little warning. All those women as witnesses and incredibly he did not plead guilty. I am sure the court date was a Monday morning, and all weekend Linda displayed distress. She phoned people constantly for reassurance, and we discussed it at length. 'I don't know why I have to go; I didn't identify him,' she said. I knew then what I had suspected at the police station: she had probably misidentified him on purpose.

At the eleventh hour, the police phoned us and we were informed he had just pleaded guilty to all charges. 'He has taken his power trip over his victims right to the wire,' the policeman said on the phone. Linda's head tilted to the side, her mouth pursed and dropped on one side as was her way when she got what she wanted. While we had a general protest about the flasher being able to play the system like that, we were both relieved.

There is an old superstitious saying: 'Things comes in threes,' and indeed they did. A third letter appeared. However, this time it was wanted and personal. It was Craig's appointment for Yorkhill Children's Hospital to attend for tests and genetic counselling.

My aunt Helen had recently been in touch with me and I had visited her. I told her about the appointment. She apologised that she would not be able to come with me. I shrugged. 'It's OK,' I replied. I had got used to not having the support that most of my peers had – the unconditional support that was expected of family members. I'd make do with what I could get and not complain. I felt I had no right to complain or anyone really to complain to anyway. Keeping 'shtum' meant I did not rock the boat of relationships. It also meant I could keep my fears to myself. Any sign of weakness might signal I was not coping. I also harboured tenuous thoughts that perhaps more in-depth tests would reveal Craig's deafness could be explained and corrected. I left my aunt's after informing her I was going to visit Cathleen soon and would let her know how I got on at the hospital. The next day she called me, saying her next-door neighbour Mrs Shaw would come to the hospital appointment with me.

As we sat in the waiting room of the hospital, full of quiet desperate hope, a young girl not much older than me appeared. She swivelled round the buggy she was pushing and we saw a mass of pink and white frilly lace sitting motionless. My heart sank, as the baby girl's head was at first glance hugely swollen, then I realised it was not swollen but deformed. A little lace bow sat on her head. Nobody spoke, and I felt empathy, perhaps because of our similar age, then frightened for my son. I began to think: what if whatever caused his deafness cannot be corrected and will cause future complications? No time for tears. No time for fears. No weaknesses, just a tension setting in my jaw. It clicked away as it usually did. The pain was a good distraction.

Craig's name was shouted, and I responded. Soon we were in a room with two nurses. Craig was stripped, and naked he was placed on the floor. He had his curly head measured as well as his height, and his blood was taken. He remained, as always, happy, unaffected and grinning beautifully with his few teeth. In the middle of the room, he went from tottering about on his feet to crawling towards random toys. Mrs Shaw and I chatted to each other about him. One of the nurses clapped her hands and began saying his name. The senior nurse present turned to her and said tactlessly, 'There's no point in speaking to that child; he is deaf.' Feeling as though she had just grabbed me by my windpipe and slapped my heart, my body tensed up and I froze. Nobody said a word. I had nowhere to hide and cry.

After I had got Craig dressed, all the while afraid to look at Mrs Shaw in case I broke down, we were ushered into a room to see a consultant. In contrast to the nurse, his manner was genial and his questioning courteous. He tested Craig's eyes and heart, then asked me about my medical history. 'I am adopted,' I said, and that investigation reached its dead end immediately. Further discussions about genetics touched briefly on Craig's father, but again it went nowhere as there was very little I knew.

The consultant read letters in front of him that I now realise contained information about my pregnancy and birth experience. Thoughtfully, he took my hand and said he did not think Craig's deafness was genetic, but he would like to see me again when the results came through. He finished by telling me there was nothing they could do about his deafness.

On the mostly silent journey home, Mrs Shaw mentioned the senior nurse, 'Appalling,' she said. I no longer cared. The damage had been done; she had hurt me, and I had furthered it by saying nothing. I still wanted to say nothing. The only expression I had was that I vomited when I returned home.

Later in my room, with Craig sleeping soundly in bed, people's words flew around my head, voices saying, '*Helen Keller was deaf, she was taught to speak, there are things you can do, and they discover new things every day.*' What these 'things' were and who Helen Keller was I did not know. What I had to do next was to find out what I could about my adoption and my birth parents, and get relevant books about deafness from the library.

17

Collateral damage

The house dynamics were blindly and manically roller-coasting along on a one-way track. The demented and sardonic words of the Siouxsie and the Banshees song 'The Happy House' remind me of our artificial family environment at that time. It was a simmering madness. While on the fragile surface of our household the project was supposedly based on democratic living, the opposite was true. There was no unity. Project social workers made most decisions. Wendy did what she liked, opting out of house rules, while Linda controlled what she could. I did not get to place a vote. In my distress, I said nothing. In hindsight, no one knew what they were doing in this experimental new project, which would have given Channel 4's *Big Brother* a run for its money. The house meetings that were supposed to give us all a voice took place erratically, and the untrained support workers living with us to 'assist' us didn't seem to know what they were supposed to be doing either. On paper it looked good, but in practice it was falling apart. I was crying out for familial bonds with memories like an umbilical cord attached to an anchor – a mother.

Our 'family' consisted of a Tourette's-suffering gas sniffer, a bulimic prescription drug addict and me, a terrified, disassociated single mother. And those were just the inmates; the volunteers had their own issues. I did not know then that certain jobs attract certain people for different reasons. It was indeed a happy house, where we were all in a melting pot, quite manically happy and quite sane. These words described our house and the delicate foundation of madness that held us all together like a stack of shaky stickle bricks.

Social workers did not talk to you, they talked about you, and they wrote about you, all with textbook precision, buzzwords and jargon. They appeared career driven on the surface, but some, as I was to find out much later in life, were crippled – like us girls – by their own agendas and their past. It's no wonder we were all cracking up.

It was in this environment that Linda continued to spiral in and out of debt and vomit to keep her weight down. I continued to remain fearful, muted and in continual confusion, while vomiting when the adrenalin forced the food from my body. Nightmares played on '*repeat*' in my sleep. Old ingrained messages continued to play like stuck records from my own top-ten hits in my head:

> *Bad girl.*
> *Ask for forgiveness.*
> *Pull your socks up.*
> *Get on with it.*
> *No point crying over spilt milk.*
> *You've made your bed so you will lie in it.*
> *Damaged goods.*
> *Nobody's child.*
> *You have brought it on yourself.*

And perhaps at number one, the most-played demonic ditty would be: You asked for it!

I had a very disjointed and fragmented perception of the world. It was overwhelmed and sculpted by past events. I identified easily with international conflicts and horrors in the past, specifically the First and Second World Wars, the Holocaust, Hiroshima and Vietnam, for reasons I could not understand. My empathy for war poetry had remained with me. The terrors that I had suffered would not be recognised as a hidden epidemic till decades later, but I found comfort and connections in the written word. Counselling, if it had been in existence then, would have been seen as a weakness by others and by me, as well as a threat to my sanity. It might reveal my secrets. In my isolation, I had only snippets of stoicism to support me. And these were reinforced by the black-and-white images I had seen of walking skeletons in the concentration camps and the nauseating sight of naked children running in Vietnam with skin peeling off their bodies. These left me pulling my proverbial socks up; no one else could. I was left thinking, 'Well, I am alive, and better off than them – what the hell do I have to complain about?' My troubles, I thought, amounted to being sometimes unable to wear shoes and walk properly owing to the fact I had stripped my toenails with my teeth to the point they bled and throbbed, sometimes becoming infected – all bloody self-inflicted. It was the same situation with my teeth. I'd never smile in photographs due to the damage that neglect had caused. No responsibility had been taken for my dental care. The legacy made me feel ugly; every tooth in my mouth now ached, partly because of the way I clenched my jaw. Again, I blamed myself and punished myself by not getting the attention that I needed. These people and children were innocent; I was not, and I wanted to keep my crimes private. My nightmares remained torturous and random, and I could make no sense of why other than thinking it must be because I had a guilty conscience. My war was with myself, and I battled it privately and almost daily. I just did not know it, and I was not going to find out any time soon.

18

It's a giving time

As we would not be spending Christmas together, we girls gave our presents to each other early. The parcels were ripped open and the paper, bows and boxes piled up and placed neatly at our bins, as we were all going our separate ways for the holiday. Linda was spending it with Meg at her old children's home, Wendy at her fiancé's, John and Jackie had announced their engagement, Angela went home to Perth, and I was free to go to my aunt and uncle's for dinner. I ended up staying overnight on Christmas Eve. Perhaps in the hope she would ask me, I had given enough away to let my aunt know I would be on my own in the house.

My gifts that year were predominantly, if not completely, courtesy of Wendy from the Avon catalogue. Wendy was selling her acquired stock at knockdown prices, and Linda and I and the neighbours all snapped some up. It felt good to be able to give some decent gifts. The cliché 'it's better to give than to receive' sure rang true to me, though I would have been horrified if my aunt and cousins had learned the provenance of their presents. I remember perfumes called Timeless, Moonwind and, my favourite, Sweet Honesty. I had a bottle in the shape of an owl. There was a honeysuckle scent that I had committed to memory from one childhood Christmas. Rose and lilac scents came in special novelty shapes for the festive season – green stocking-shaped bottles with red stoppers, a glass Christmas tree with a gold star for a stopper, and there was also the phenomenon of Soap-on-a-Rope.

On Christmas morning at my aunt's, I felt a part of something – as though I was holding my own by giving decent gifts. My son unwrapped books, crayons, cars and floating bath toys, and every time he opened a new present his face lit up and his mouth became as round and wide as his eyes. It was truly a joy.

Then, as now, my joys, though short lived, always seared the heart. I had found from a very early age that when I experienced a complete joy, tears always threatened to steal the shine. I could hardly wait to see Craig rip open his presents whilst eating chocolate money that I, as Santa, had wrapped with excitement on Christmas Eve. It gave me such pleasure to create a wonderful sight and experience for him to wake up to in the morning, but the experience was tainted due to stress about money, my own memories of that time and panic about it all coming right on the day, and left me with the sense of trying to catch an elusive moment amongst stressful mayhem. This anti-climatic feeling confused me and I was never able to fully experience the moment for what it was.

For me, joy seemed like a double-edged sword. I had learned far too young, and without any redress to cushion me, that there was always a price to pay – guilt and sadness. Sometimes this was due to the interference of others, as it seemed that people could extract perverse pleasure from ridiculing you in your moment of happiness. I never realised then that they too could be experiencing misery and therefore want to rain on your parade. *'Whit are you so happy about?'*, *'There's a want about you'* – I remember many voices saying this kind of thing to me, suggesting I had no right to be happy and that if I was there must be something wrong in the head with me.

Maturity has brought the knowledge that sheer joy is such a pleasure that it does evoke tears. However, getting so many negative responses when I let my guard down when I was younger taught me that you could never trust in anything or anyone fully. Never get too attached. Never be too happy. Never state your fears. But most of all: show no weakness. It will all either be used against you or be taken away from you.

Humour was and still is for me and others an inherent anaesthetic to take the edge off the truth and pain. Like many from my area and background, self-expression came by way of humour, and my Glasgow wit and quirky turn of phrase enabled me to keep my social head just above water. Quick to see the funny side of things to turn a situation around, I could have had a black belt in conflict resolution.

I always chose what would seem the obvious solution such as keeping my mouth shut and skimming over problems, but like a plasterer I was only skimming the cracks. This was obvious at occasions like New Year, which we passed at my aunt's. It was another momentary dulling experience of bringing in the bells at Hogmanay with a skimmed cheer. No mention was ever made of the visions that would seep through the cracks . . . of a dead mother in a living room chair.

Craig and I bunked down in a single bed under a mound of coats while the party continued. In a few hours I was up, feeding Craig his breakfast and heading home. The festivities were all over and now my aloneness hit me like a ton of bricks, weighing me down for days.

With Craig to look after, however, pragmatic concern soon had me back on track, determined to deal with the diagnosis of profound deafness, and I set out on the search to find out where to learn sign language. My sense of purpose waxed and waned at each door I knocked. Approaches to doctors, social workers and my ever-steady source of information the library drummed up nothing. There simply were no classes for parents, no parents' groups, no pre-school groups, no clubs. Nothing! I was, however, informed by a health visitor attached to the audiology unit that at three years of age he would start school and begin his education. Until then we were left with homemade signs such as rubbing tummies for food, and other obvious signs for drink, sleep, toilet and love.

With a feeling that our life was in limbo, and with no professional or parental information as guidance, we lived in an animated wilderness, waiting. Through exaggerated actions such as finger pointing, dramatic facial expressions and body movements, Craig and I communicated: that was our language and emotional development. We both had no place to belong other than ourselves.

I had no real idea what had caused Craig's deafness. I believed the genetic counselling had been brief because of the fact that I had been adopted and the absence of information about Craig's father. Left hanging and very much alone, a terrible thought that I had been keeping at bay was getting stronger. I secretly held the belief that I had caused his deafness by taking an overdose in the last stages of my hidden pregnancy. The image of the rash I had had also stood out in my mind and I worried about both of these as potential causes.

It was to be decades later, after much pain and heartbreak, that I was to find out the truth. For now, I was told by the medical profession that they could not be sure what had caused his deafness but I was assured it would not happen again. The consultant at the hospital had casually told me that any future child I might have should not be affected. This offered no comfort at all.

In recent years, I gained access to my medical records and in them I discovered a letter written by the genetic consultant which read: 'This is, indeed, a tragedy for this mother and baby. It should not be allowed to happen again.' He was referring to the fact that I had not been immunised against German measles while in care, and in fact it was the unidentified rash I had had during my pregnancy that had very likely caused Craig's deafness.

As nobody told me this at the time, I tortured myself for 30 years that I had been responsible and done this terrible thing to my son. I would probably still be despising and punishing myself if I had not accessed my records.

Time in Bark Avenue was passing and my 18th birthday came and went. Wendy was rarely seen at the house and Barbara was still banished. Aunt Elspeth perhaps had said something to John, as he rarely appeared now.

Spring was turning into summer 1981 when my sister Cathleen, whom I had trekked with Craig on and off buses for hours to gladly visit, was allowed at last to visit me. I think it was around March, as Cathleen, Joe and I, with Craig in his buggy, walked for miles in streaming sunshine to Strathclyde Park. Trundling along, the chat evolved as easily as Craig's buggy wheels turned. Cathleen skipped around Joe and occasionally pushed Craig.

The swans swamped us at the waterside in the hope of food. Craig's lack of fear became apparent as he lunged into what must have seemed to him a fascinating swarm of animals. As I raced to rescue him, the white elegant necks stretched to pinch his ice-cream cone and their beaks pecked him, nudging him onto his back. I picked him up, with solid yellow beaks sniping at my legs as if to chastise me, and plonked him safely into his buggy. Craig was belly laughing, stretching his arms out to reach them and offering them his cone.

We laughed and moved on to the playpark area, where Craig and Cathleen raced around and up the steps of chutes to hurl themselves down the sheet metal and whizz off the edge, either to be caught by myself or land on their bums. A few hours had passed, and passing the swans we brought an end to the day as we embarked on the journey home. Cathleen walked close by Joe's side on the way back. Having never been a wee sister or heard of sibling rivalry, the normal behaviour of 'walking in my big sister's shoes' was unknown to me. It had just been a great day – it felt like we had been the family unit that I craved but always found elusive.

Pleased at giving myself and Cathleen a real family day out, we arrived home happy. Joe and I parted company as we reached my front door. A kiss, promises of a phone call and he was gone. Exhausted, Cathleen, Craig and I went up to my room and changed Craig. Cathleen stared out the window and went quiet. Downstairs, we quickly made and ate our food. Cathleen helping to feed Craig made me feel I had my wee sister back. I dared not ask her how she felt about her foster family, perhaps because I was afraid to know the truth or break the spell of contentment I thought we had. Her wee glasses slipping down her nose and her lazy turned eye elicited my restrained feelings for my sister. I had missed her and guilt still swirled around because I was not there for her in my role as protector.

'Can I put Craig in his cot?' she asked.

'Yes,' I replied, eager to keep the momentum of the day going. I turned to the sink, filling it with our dishes as she sat him on her hip and began to walk upstairs. As the basin filled up with water, I turned the tap off and slowly followed them. Standing at the bottom of the stairs,

I looked up. Cathleen stood there with Craig in her arms. Towering above me, she stared down at me and shouted, 'I hate him. I am not his real aunty.'

Seconds later, Craig was in my arms. She had thrown him down at me and luckily I had managed to catch him. Clutching Craig in shock, I have very little memory of what happened next. A vague vision of the front door being slammed and a call to my aunt stays with me. My aunt was applying to adopt Cathleen, perhaps finally galvanised by the accusations against her and scores to settle, and also I reported to her after my visits.

My aunt Helen did eventually adopt Cathleen, and I saw less rather than more of her. Never again did she acknowledge who I was to anyone. It was an indication of how she perceived me – a dirty reminder from the past – but, confused again, I could not work it out. I was not equipped with the maturity to understand it. Applying an ostrich-in-the-sand style of conflict resolution, I convinced myself it was not happening and pacified myself by ignoring it.

My relationship with Joe intensified, and the sexual pressure was building. I made an appointment with the family planning clinic to speak about birth control, forever trying to find the mature and adult solution. I listened to the nurse at the clinic run through my options as pragmatically as I thought I was being, and soon I had the coil fitted. The pill had many health scares, she had informed me, then we spoke of the lack of information about my medical history due to my adoption. As a result, it was decided to fit a coil. I did not know clinics got paid for every coil they fitted. I left feeling like an adult, in control and informed. Pragmatic I may have been, informed I was not, nor was I prepared for the emotions of a sexual relationship.

An unwed mother, my baby born out of wedlock, I'm sure some viewed me as a pariah, others pitied me and others despised me. I was only just aware of the sexual subtext to my world by instinct and not by name. I had no idea of the role hormones played in evolution, and the inherent power of their drive. I had no idea I was surrounded by them. Like the child that never wants to think of its parents having sex, bizarrely I never thought of anyone having sex. That ignorance and denial, born of shame and being shamed, left me pretty much skill-less as well as vulnerable to every waking, walking hormone that surrounded me, including my own.

As quickly as the intensity grew, so did a dark side to my relationship. First, it was a hand round my throat against the fence of my house, then a slap. The rage of this man, who seemed so alive with creative ideas and plans, was not so attractive.

I never told anyone in the beginning, and I tried to end the relationship several times. When a split occurred, the phone calls would start, initially pleading with me to take him back: 'I am sorry. I love you.' The threat of suicide was raised in one phone call, so I took him back, frightened and believing it might happen, and failing to see the now obvious pattern that was emerging.

During this time, I was offered a flat by Hamilton District Council. Joe was delighted, and so was I. However, it turned out to be a bottom flat in a 'hard to let area', which meant poor housing conditions and many social problems.

Craig and I trundled off to the grey council offices with the delusion in my mind I was going to discuss my offer. After sitting huddled with others in an extremely small reception area, my name was called from behind a sliding hatch door.

'Hello,' I said, always wanting to be taken seriously, yet smiling so as not to get people's backs up.

'How can I help you?' a blonde woman replied.

I began to enquire about the flat I had been offered: if there was work that needed to be done internally, when would the workmen be finished? What else would be available to me in the future? 'If I refuse this offer,' I asked, 'what will happen?' The discussion took all of 15 minutes with no privacy and no offer to view the flat, and I learned that if I refused it I would go right to the back of the housing queue.

'Families are desperate for houses,' she said. Her tone told me that by families she was referring to anything other than an unwed mother.

I left, walking with my shoulders back and eyes fixed ahead. She may have made me feel like something you wiped off a shoe, but I was not going to let her see it. Acknowledgement of humiliation was in itself a humiliation. I was always making mental mantra notes to myself, and I have no doubt that on that day it would have been along the lines of '*Crumpling only happens in private if it has to happen at all*'.

I felt under a great deal of pressure to make a decision and my thoughts drifted to our house move after my mother's death in 1974. A family in an even rougher area had capitalised on my father's grief and offered him a swap. He took it, and it had only added to our problems. I worried that I was getting myself into a similar situation but I also felt that it was my only choice.

My aunt Helen had frequently told me that my father was a weak man and he would have done better with a strong woman. It never occurred to me that these were her slanted thoughts and not necessarily the facts. I accepted them, and the Presbyterian public pole on which I unknowingly but frequently martyred myself remained erect. So I got it into my head it was not my father's behaviour I had to avoid but my mother's. I had to be strong. It was almost like she was lacking in some way and even responsible for his behaviour because she had been weak and therefore it was acceptable for him as a man to be so.

I had not yet read Glaswegian R.D. Laing's book *The Divided Self*, about past experiences and current behaviour, but I had read Robert Louis Stevenson's *The Strange Case of Dr Jekyll and Mr Hyde*. I understood the concept of duality: in Glasgow terminology, 'street angel–house devil'. I understood the parameters of hypocrisy and cowardice that this duality operated within. In private, without witnesses, much devastation was caused and suffered in silence. Women, it seemed, had to be the moral gatekeepers of our society, and I had failed miserably, between, among other situations, Urquhart, getting pregnant and shaming my father's name. So I had to be a stronger woman and make the decisions without complaint. However, my emotional and intellectual conflict battled daily with this. Why should I suppress my needs and feelings because I was born a female? The truth was I didn't really need to do that, it had already been done for me.

19

Another home

Within three weeks, I had signed the missives to the tenancy of the flat, had the keys pocketed and, armed with bleach, began a scrubbing assault. Our new home consisted of two bedrooms, a hallway, bathroom, living room and a burnt-out kitchen. The back garden was small, with a communal close, washing area and bins.

Joe's mum visited within days, with the offer of help. She was probably curious to see the flat her son would be spending time in, as Joe had just asked to marry me. The question had been popped on a walk home from cleaning the flat one night, and as naively as he asked, I accepted. We parted company as he headed for home to tell his parents, while I toddled a few streets feeling wanted but uneasy. The pull of being wanted and belonging was stronger, as Joe called the house almost as soon as I stepped through the door. 'I have told them,' he said. Sensing perhaps my hesitation, he added, 'They are cool with it.'

I was to visit the next night, which I did. As I suspected, it was not as 'cool' as he had made out. It was clear that his mum was less than happy. I can understand that now. At the time, I was convinced it was because of my background and the shame attached to being an unwed mother; I was not good enough stock. As we stood in the living room of the family home, a drink was poured and toasted to us, with the dry and unenthusiastic comment from his mother, 'Well, you're the one he has chosen.' Despite this obviously unhappy reaction, she readily got down on her hands and knees in my new flat and set to work, lifting filthy stapled-down linoleum from the bathroom floor to reveal a chequered layer of black-and-white tiles. She set about the task with vigour, scrubbing them clean till they looked and smelt presentable. The burnt-out kitchen was another matter. It took several days to clean the smoke damage from the walls, and exhaustive sleep would follow. I could not get the ceiling clean to my satisfaction. I gave up after several days standing on a wobbly, second-hand Formica table, similar to the one I remembered in my childhood home. All my furniture was second hand, and I added knick-knacks I bought from charity shops. The antique wardrobe, dressing table, couch and chairs came from a second-hand shop that the social work used because it accepted benefit cheques. I roller painted over the wood chip and damp areas growing up the walls several times after washing with vinegar.

There were parallels to the move my father made after my mother's death – there were certainly clear reasons why it was a hard-to-let area. There was no garden, and the rubbish from other households piled up. Old chairs and bikes lay discarded in the shared washing green. A murder had recently taken place a few streets away. I accepted this, as my status kept me low on the housing list back then, but I was determined to make the flat itself hospitable and homely. Craig settled in to his new bedroom well, the first time he had a bedroom of his own. His toys could be left out and the room personalised for a wee boy.

Cleaning and painting, plus fitting a carpet myself, filled in the weeks and kept us busy, and me from thinking too deeply. Far from enjoying a happy engagement, Joe's violent behaviour continued and he began to threaten suicide any time I attempted to break free and find some sanity. However, this was easier said than done, as I was alone in a dismal flat with no means to contact the outside world, living a silent existence with Craig.

One sunny day found us both out. I had pushed him for miles, Craig chomping on a banana, when we found ourselves in fields far behind an area called Little Earnock. Forging on, looking for countryside adventure rather than being stuck alone in the flat, we climbed fences, with me lifting his buggy over, then leaning in a balancing act and placing him in it, before I then climbed over. We wandered as I had done as a child. Dodging the country pancakes the cows and bulls had deposited behind them, we eventually rested in an idyllic field. Lush in its greenness, it was surrounded by lots of different types of trees, and there were many different delicate wildflowers for which I had no name but appreciated their exquisite beauty. Here, like in the homemade dens and back-door bedsheet tents of my childhood, I could escape ugliness.

We picked flowers for each other and did the buttercup test, although I could not explain the theory of how it worked. You liked butter if yellow reflected when its small flower was held underneath your chin. Craig just copied me and stuck several under my chin. We could have been residents of a country estate or a smallholding, but we were not. I picked scissor-sharp blades of grass and whistled through them, as my father had taught me in our garden, which had led to many a bloody split lip. Together, Craig and I were escapees for the day.

I remember that day so clearly. Craig had tiny trainers on with brightly coloured laces, and the sun shone through the spaces in his curls. After a while, I noticed some cows appearing over the hill and moving quickly down towards us. I became uneasy, as usually they never bothered us or came close. I picked Craig up and placed him on my hip. Then I grabbed one of the curved handles of his buggy and moved with pace, trailing it behind me. I could hear and feel a thunderous stampede behind me as I literally chucked Craig's buggy over the wire fence; Craig went the same way and I followed. My T-shirt, which had a black and white zigzag pattern, got snagged, and my black cloth paddy sandals squelched after I stepped in one of those country pancakes. Leaning over the wire fence was a raging bull with a distinct smell emanating from it, snorting foam and steam from its nostrils like a boiling kettle. My heart was thumping with fear; I could hear it in my head. Craig was none the wiser, and with a hand full of dying flowers and his head lapsing to one side in his buggy in near sleep, we began the trek home.

The thunder I had heard in the stampede dissipated but another significant symbol of stormy weather appeared on my horizon. As we walked home, Joe appeared from now where. He had been out looking for, as I heard it, 'silly sibins'.

The Latin, I was later to find out, was *Psilocybin*; the domestic name was magic mushrooms. Dreams of love and the happy ever after with a talented creative mind had been slipping away, but giving up on the hope takes longer when dreams are all you have. I listened to him describing the best type, the best time and the best trips. Like an anorak trainspotter raving about the latest model, the latest colour or time of arrival, his obsession was no different. I was now aware that his volatile behaviour was down to drugs. It was not an epiphany plucked out of the soil of reality like his mushrooms but a growing realisation that brought with it fear for Craig's and my own safety. Joe had tried to reassure me that cannabis was the drug of creative people, citing David Bowie as his main defence. I remained unconvinced.

'I'll walk you home,' he said now, tickling Craig and talking incessantly. Partly out of fear of saying no, and partly still clinging to a wisp of a dream, I agreed. As we passed a red phone box on the way home, he said, 'I'll just jump in here and phone Jim. All's cool.' Jim was one of his friends I liked. After the call, Joe said, 'Meeting Jim at the train station. He's coming through from Glasgow. See you at yours.' I walked the short distance home myself. Sadly, I was looking forward to the company after weeks on my own. How I would regret that decision.

20

Unhinged

My shaky front door was knocked and I let them in. It was shaky because the frame that held the door in place had no strength. On reflection, it probably meant it had been kicked in many times before. Pleased to see me, Jim hugged and pecked me on the cheek. This was the wrong thing to do in Joe's presence.

I had recently papered the hall and living room, having acquired some cheap wallpaper from Asda in Blantyre. This was the same place that Linda and I had bought paper for Bark Avenue, which, with the help of Barbara, we had pasted on upside down. I had also painted murals of sunshine, clouds and trees on Craig's blue walls. Outside his window was a small patch of grass, bins and concrete. Tonight, he was fast asleep.

Jim asked the usual questions about how Craig I and were. I spoke honestly about my hopes for the future and how we were waiting for him to get a place at school, explaining that deaf children started school earlier than other kids. After making a toast and omelette supper, I noticed Joe and Jim behaving strangely. Jim, skinny and wearing more eyeliner than Joe, curled up on the floor in front of the electric wall fire. Soon they admitted they had taken 'silly sibins'. The words 'cool', and 'amazing' did not settle my sense of unease. I had watched Joe sit on the same couch with my father and sneak a drink with him as I made tea. My father's obvious disregard for his shameful daughter and resulting grandson gave Joe the green light to treat me in the same way as my father did.

Tension began mounting as I watched Jim laugh nervously and Joe's expressions darken. Making tea in the kitchen to escape and maintain normality had the opposite effect. After Joe had spat on Jim and made him lie on the floor, I knew he would head for the kitchen. As I attempted to put the kettle on the electric ring of the cooker, I was pinned up against the kitchen wall, and I could see Jim curling up on the floor after being humiliated by Joe.

The image of Jim cowering on the floor was the last thing I remember before being dragged along the hall by my hair into the bedroom. I heard a tearing noise and felt a hot sensation on my head. As I sat up from the floor, I touched my head and felt the pain. In front of me, sitting at the bottom of my bed, was Joe, holding a large clump of my hair. The pain on my head was coming from a large bald patch.

'You know what I will do with this?' he said, holding up my stolen hair.

I stared, giving no reply. Then I watched as he plaited it and attached it to a brooch from his lapel. Re-pinning the brooch to his jacket, he stood up and from my place of silence he pulled me onto the bed. Though I was mute, something snapped in me, and I attempted to fight him off. I was hoping against all odds that Jim would come from the living room and stop the assault. That never happened. As I slid from the bed onto the floor, my hand hit all the ornaments on my dresser; I could hear them smashing. I found myself jammed between the side of the bed and the wall. As I was there, with Joe on top of me, his hands round my throat, I can remember screaming only once. Jim later told me it was several times. Eventually, with no strength left to fight, I lay on the floor, his hands still round my throat, and my arms flopped as the fight left them and I began to faint.

As I was passing out, I heard a shout. My body felt relieved as Joe's weight was removed from me. A policeman, not much older than myself, stood above me and was reaching his hands out to me. I could hear other male voices and the distinct drone of intermittent radios. As Joe was dragged away, shouting, 'I did nothing, man. What have I done ma-a-a-n?' the young policeman was aside me on the bed. 'You don't deserve this, you can do better,' he said to me in several different ways. 'He's nothing but rubbish' and 'You're smart but vulnerable.'

Wincing at the word vulnerable, at my predicament and feeling ashamed, I looked around for clothing to cover myself, as I realised I was sitting half naked. Unable to look him in the eyes and feebly trying to hold my top around me, I scanned the floor for something to cover me. It was then I noticed my skirt. I had been wearing it! The feeling of humiliation hit me like another punch, only this time I could barely contain my tears. The policeman touched my shoulder as he left, and that hurt too. A small kindness, a slither of compassion, doesn't seem to go down well with a particular Scottish psyche. Pity, an emotion that was the second cousin to despise, was not welcome. The self-hatred burned in me and at me.

Jim and I had the mess and evidence cleared up within an hour, the broken ornaments swept up, clothes gathered and binned. We arranged the furniture back the way it had been, had tea and talked, realising it must have been the neighbours who had phoned the police. I was lucky they had, and I fully appreciated why they had. I understood that it was me who had put them in that position. My only sense of relief in this situation was that Craig had not heard or witnessed the violence. Looking at him sleeping under his blue quilt cover, I promised this would never happen again.

Later, in the small hours of the morning, Jim and I sat while he cried with his own shame. I comforted him with weak words of 'It's all right' and 'It's over.' I knew I had allowed myself to become a victim of domestic violence; it was nobody's fault but my own. I had not been strong enough for him. I was the weak one, and in an attempt to gain some strength back, there I was bruised, bleeding, partially bald and comforting Jim.

Around five o'clock and with Jim on the couch, I crawled into my bed. My mind was still turning on the rollercoaster of the events, and thoughts of worthlessness and feelings of shame began to roll in, as did my aches and pains. I just did not know how I was going to be able to step out of my front door and face people. Nursing myself and my self-hatred under my own quilt, I heard footsteps in the communal close. Joe had returned.

I had never heard of the words sexual discrimination or domestic violence while growing up. In my adoptive mother's era, not too far into the past, I am led to believe that a woman could not have her name on the rent book of her council home. This was only allowed to happen if there was no male of the household. The mindset then, and which still exists to some extent today, was that 'You canny get in between a man and his wife.' Men did not hit women – it was a rule, so when it did happen, the counter defence was 'She was asking for it', 'She pushed him to it', 'Why did she not leave him then?', 'She would try the patience of a saint.' I grew up thinking my mother was either weak for staying or that the weakness inherent in her could not prevent my father's violence. After all, even my mother had blamed me for what William Urquhart had done, though I was only seven at the time. 'Whore,' she had called me. It seemed that, being female, I was at fault by default.

As Joe stood outside my door, shouting through the letterbox, fear paralysed me as I lay in my bed. Anticipating violence, I did nothing for what seemed like an eternity. Jim came into my room, his face clearly full of fear. 'Get out of here, get out,' I whispered. I was afraid it would fuel Joe's rage if he found Jim in my bedroom.

Jim rushed away from my terror just as Joe burst the shaky door in. I had been waiting for months for the door to be repaired by the council, and it gave way with ease, like a paper door in a comedy sketch. No laughter was to be heard, though, only the opening of my living room window. I knew it was Jim making his escape. Knowing I was now on my own with no witnesses and with Craig still sleeping, I lunged from my bed, still fully clothed, and met Joe in the hallway.

'Where is he? Where is he?' Joe rasped repeatedly.

'Who?' I replied, knowing full well he meant Jim but intent on buying time, as I did not know what else to do.

Into the bedroom he stormed, then into the living room. Jim's presence was evident by the crumpled blankets on the couch. As I stood with him in the room, I saw that he was still wearing the hair he had ripped from my head plaited and attached to a badge on his jacket. His clear lack of remorse and the displaying of a trophy made my already high levels of anxiety rise. True to form, though, I remained outwardly calm.

Joe asked me for a cup of tea. I complied. As the kettle was boiling, I stayed in the kitchen, and the tension simmered away. I cannot remember the rest of the conversation we had. As I set the requested cup of tea down on a small side table and went to walk away, I felt a horribly painful blow to my back. Lying on the floor in agony, with Joe standing above me, he stated matter of factly, 'Kidney punch.' Next came a punch to my eye. I was panting, as I found it difficult to breathe, and the effect was a strange combination of dull yet excruciating pain. No survival skills were coming to my rescue; I simply could not get up. As I lay flat out on the floor, he stooped towards me and said, 'Ah'm off to get Jim, and here is what I wanted to give you last night.' He held a cassette tape in his hovering hand till I managed to reach up and take it. Leaving, he kissed me and said, 'I love you.'

I cleared up the splinters and folded the blankets away, then carried on as if all was normal. I told no one. It wasn't until days later that I listened to the tape Joe had given me. *'A dark and dangerous dimness . . . a mind frozen, hard like ice . . . a woman tough and spectacular . . . the bullets ready in their device.'* Had I been older, more aware, these words, with his voice overlapping a synthesizer, would have elicited a different reaction in me other than to feel nothing and do very little. But who would I tell and who would believe me?

A week later, I had a visit from Kerry, one of Joe's neighbours whom I had become friendly with and who did my hair for free. I confided in her, and she was appalled at the large bald patch on my head. I understated what had happened and never spoke about the tape. 'Come to my shop and we will get your hair sorted,' she offered. Gratefully, I accepted. I had no choice. I could not go out like this, as it was such a large bald patch that it could not be covered up. 'I think the police said they were charging him with assault,' she said. She had seen him and he had said nothing about the incident, but his brother, who was closer to Kerry, knew what had happened.

I tried so hard to be positive and upbeat, but even the thought of the hairdressing appointment that I had gratefully accepted did not erase or soothe my worries. Kerry had left with a promise to visit again and have a night out. 'Get him out of your system,' she had said.

That I tried, with fear as my protector, and as Craig was about to start school I struggled on. I passed the next few weeks scrubbing, cleaning and organising drawers, biting my fingernails, toenails and walking with Craig wearing a Claire Grogan-style French beret. Although Joe did not appear, I was terrified of every noise in the close and, in my isolation, afraid of the thoughts in my head. Fearing he would know my movements, I went to a different post office to collect my benefit money, as I was allowed to do this on two occasions per benefit book.

Several nights later, after I had become accustomed to sleeping with a kitchen chair lodging the front door shut, I heard glass breaking. I knew it was very close. Sitting up in my bed, afraid to breathe, I heard noises and glass cracking. As I sat there waiting, Joe appeared in the doorway of my bedroom. Slowly he moved from the doorway to the bottom of the bed, talking away and asking inane questions: 'How are you?', 'What you been up to, man?' I just sat bolt upright, waiting.

My kitchen chair thankfully did not hold and once again my shaky door, not seen as a priority by the council to fix, burst open. Once again the police were in my bedroom. Once again similar cries came from Joe: 'What have I done, man? What I have done?' Some neighbour somewhere knew what he had done. A culture code had been broken: someone had 'grassed' and, worse, they had grassed to the polis. Someone had good sense, compassion and could see the vulnerability. I was 'lucky'. The police told me that he had been charged on the previous occasion and then released. I phoned them the next morning needing to know how safe I was. He had been let go with a caution.

21

Come on, Eileen

I had high hopes of learning to communicate with Craig; education, after all, had all the answers. While I busied myself with that mission, I soon found myself in court. The law was to be respected, but I was about to find out that by no means did this require it to be respectful in return. As I stood in the dock answering questions about that night's events, my mind rolled back over the years and I thought of having to face my father in court at the age of 14. He had been charged with neglect after our neighbours had eventually had enough and broke the no-grassing code. I still felt like I had betrayed him, particularly after he was found guilty and fined. I took it on board that it was my evidence and not that of the police or statements from the child safety officer that had sealed his fate.

Now, several years later, I stood in the witness box in a very similar position. As had happened in the line-up identity parade at the police station with Linda, I had to point out the accused face to face in order to secure a positive identification. As I did so, it occurred to my wandering philosophical mind that there seemed to be three types of identity: who you are visually, who you are legally and who you think you are.

Nerve-racked but with my back and shoulders straight and my chin up, I raised my hand and pointed at Joe, formally identifying him. He stood there with his hair cut, wearing a new suit, no make-up, looking every part the respectable guy – suited and booted for effect.

Like my father, Joe had pleaded not guilty, and I now understand that both were probably legally advised to do so. I had had no contact with the police or offers of support before, during or after the case. There was certainly no discussion about what would happen or a trip to see the inside of the courtroom to put me at ease. Kerry came with me, but we spoke about inane subjects such as the weather, avoiding my imminent appearance in the box, as if the mere mention of it would topple me over.

Everything seemed straightforward until I was cross-examined by Joe's lawyer. I waited uncomfortably as he paced up and down in front of me before beginning his questioning. It was no doubt a tactic to unsettle me. He asked how long I had been in a relationship with Joe and how long I had known him. The questions seemed fairly straightforward until, raising his voice, he boomed at me, 'My client ended the relationship so you decided to get even, didn't you?'

I was shocked and not quite sure what he meant. Surely he couldn't really think that was what had happened? But there he was, saying it in court. I had naively believed his lawyer would ask me what had happened, then, as I had police testimonies as to what they had found, I thought he would feel it immoral to pressurise a young girl who had clearly been terrified and assaulted. Now, in my fear, and with a history of not being valued and believed, I thought the court would believe the lawyer over me.

Quickly, most of my naivety disappeared, but I was severely rattled. After managing an astonished but simple 'No' in response to his question, I stared around like a rabbit in the proverbial headlights.

'Were you jealous he might have someone else?' He paused for effect once more before booming another direct accusation at me: 'Were you sleeping with his friend?' to which, again, I could only respond, 'No.' I have forgotten the wording of most of the other questions, but the general line taken was that I had pushed his client to breaking point due to my behaviour.

The tactic of suggesting that I had pushed him to it had the desired effect and made me feel that I was weak for getting myself into this position in the first place. Joe's lawyer's accusations (for that was what they had become, not questions) seemed to go on and on, but I felt that no one asked the really pertinent questions. I was never asked about the drugs or the plait he'd made from the hair he'd ripped out of my head, and I eventually left the dock feeling shattered. How could a person working in a respected profession behave in such a way? Naive! Naive! Naive!

As I left the court, I saw Jim, and we weakly smiled at each other. I never saw him again. I don't know what he said in his evidence, or if anybody else was there. I went home to spend another night alone, staring at the ceiling. Nothing had made much sense to me and I had no one to share it with or comfort me.

I eventually found out that Joe had been found guilty of assault and fined. Victims and witnesses did not then have the right to know the outcome of a case, like they are supposed to now. I found out from the local weekly paper. The guilty verdict made me feel relieved for one main reason: I had been believed, though I was left wondering what would have been the outcome if there had been no police witnesses. By then I had got my head around the idea that everyone had the right to be represented in court, but the theatricality of it all still shocked me. Joe's lawyer had been so convincing and intimidating even in the face of two independent police statements about the night Joe assaulted me. It served to reinforce my view about professionals – that there was a clear division between 'them' and 'us'.

22

Tightly wound coils

'Freedom's just another word for nothing left to lose' rang so true to me. I should have been forging forward with plans for the future, but I could not see a clear road to follow. I had my own flat with no files, no inane rules, no one to tell me what to do, no one to confide in and no one to call a doctor if I was ill. My vulnerability, though fiercely denied, should have been apparent to anyone with an ounce of compassion. Also, my physical health was becoming a real concern. After taking what I had thought was the sensible and well-informed decision to get the coil fitted, I was in constant abdominal pain. I wonder now if Joe's attack had exacerbated my problems.

Attending my doctor felt like an endurance test, particularly when I had to undergo the ever-uncomfortable internal gynaecological examination. Afterwards, my doctor advised me to get an appointment at the local family planning clinic to get the device removed. This I did, and during another theatrical knees-up internal I learned that clinics were paid for every device they fitted. At the time I remember thinking that this must have compromised the impartial nature of the advice given by the clinic, but I was in no position to do anything about it and I could not really equate the clinic with what I perceived on my soapbox as the corporate evils of capitalism. Instead, I began to take more painkillers: Feminax, a strong analgesic for premenstrual stomach cramps. They seemed to do the monthly trick for me.

After spending Christmas in Aunt Helen's busy household, it was miserable to return home to the unwelcoming damp-ridden flat, but Craig cheered me up. My hyper, happy boy bounced on the bed beside me as we got into our pyjamas, then he cooried in beside me. He had been thrilled with his new bigger bike and I was delighted with the gift of a necklace from my aunt and uncle – it made me feel special, my first real piece of jewellery. I watched it glinting on the dressing table as I waited for sleep.

The next morning saw us both getting ready to visit our cousin Helen for a party. I found that gatherings and parties had the strange effect of making you remember the past while trying to enjoy the moment. When we returned home the next day, some instinct made me stall as we approached the concrete steps to our close. From the top step, I could see splintered light wood from my door frame exposed. I had my keys in my hands as I walked up to the door, but I didn't need them. My front door was lying open; flakes of blue paint lay at my feet. I could see straight down the hallway into the living room.

As I stood there holding Craig's hand, afraid to enter, I heard a noise coming from the top of the stairwell. Quiet footsteps padded on the concrete. Terrified, I turned to look up. My neighbour Betty stood with her finger on her lips. She was gesturing to me to be quiet. She too was frightened. We darted into my hallway and pushed the door closed, though it would not lock. Once more, I had a shaky front door.

'It was them, Eileen, it was them,' she pointed straight at my front door.

'Who?' I asked.

'Them – them next door. I heard them and saw them,' she said. Recently, the boarded-up flat next door had been occupied by two older single men. They were known local hard men.

I walked into the living room. My second-hand black-and-white TV was gone as were my iron and my twin tub with its broken spinner. I couldn't believe that two grown men would do this. They seemed to have money. It might have come from dubious origins, but they always seemed to be wearing the latest clothes. Surely this was too low for them? In my bedroom, the space where my new gold necklace had lain was empty.

Craig's bike was also gone, though his smaller presents remained.

'Why?' I asked Betty. 'Why would they do this?' Near to tears, I added, 'Why did they not take everything?' There was no answer to this question.

Shrugging her shoulders and with a pained expression Betty whispered, 'A van arrived and I watched them take your stuff away. Eileen, they're into serious violence and drugs. I can't give a police statement.'

As I wandered cautiously around the flat, I now saw that my electric fire had gone and clothes from the wardrobe lay on the bed, the covers of which had been disturbed.

'I just canny, Eileen,' Betty said again.

Minutes later, I stood alone and listened to Betty padding quietly up the stairs and closing her door as silently as she possibly could.

In the freezing cold, Craig and I walked to the nearby red telephone box I occasionally used. 'I'd like to report a break-in,' I said. The voice on the other end took my details and told me they would send someone out.

We took the long way home so I could get milk and bread. On my return, I found my kettle was gone too. It was not even a modern electric one. The kitchen chair became my security again, and I placed it against the door, lodging it under the handle. Craig played with his new bricks and other toys; I stared out the window, holding a cup of warm tea made from water from a boiled pot. Burning within me was fear and a cold rage.

Some time later, two plain-clothes officers arrived. They informed me that they were Criminal Investigation Detectives, otherwise known as CID. I told them what I had arrived home to. While one detective questioned me further, the other played around with Craig on the floor.

'One of my neighbours saw it happen,' I said, 'but they won't talk to you.'

Both of the detectives wore trench coats. The older one now opened his coat after questioning me about my new neighbours next door. He produced a card from an inside pocket and while handing it to me he said, 'Phone me when they are in. There is a warrant out for one of them.'

I stared at him. Did he know what he was asking me to do? The risk he was asking me to take? He obviously did, as he then said, 'He is a dangerous man.'

As they left, the other detective said to me, 'I suppose you have no house insurance?'

Was he joking? No one in this area had house insurance. I shook my head, confirming he supposed right.

'Well, phone me,' the other detective said. 'See it as one for the underdog.'

I sat alone reading that night as Craig slept, distracted many times by the empty space where my necklace should have been and remembering how I had saved up for Craig's bike. I had been so excited about giving it to him and had taken it to my aunt's house before Christmas instead of keeping it at the flat, to make sure it was a surprise.

In the early hours of the morning, still lying awake, I heard the screech of car wheels and then car doors thudding shut. The sound of footsteps, muffled cries and dragging noises had me sitting bolt upright in bed. Then the communal close became a battlefield. 'Fuck you, ya bastard, Ah'm gonna kill you,' a male voice was shouting. Bodies were hitting off the concrete walls and I could hear glass smashing off my door as I sat terrified, hoping and willing that my kitchen chair would hold. It didn't. I heard my door burst open and then someone smashed against the wall. Still the male voices raged. 'Get his troosers aff,' one voice bawled. I stood at my bedroom door. A body was being dragged from my hallway back out of my now obliterated door. There was the sound of steel slashing the close walls. 'Get them aff. Ah'm gonnae cut his balls aff.'

Another male voice began to scream from the back of the close, pleading with his assailants. I took my opportunity and ran to Craig's bedroom. I sat at his bedside like a child myself, knees up at my chin, stroking his hair and rocking myself. Wretchedly, I have to admit to thinking that at least he couldn't hear this. There was no escape route. Only one useless door in and one useless door out.

Finally, with a piercing scream after a fruitless plea of, 'Naw, please don't,' I heard footsteps running away. With my hands over my ears, I rocked harder. I knew everyone in my close, in their own wee flat, lay in bed frozen. It felt like the whole building was traumatised.

Next came a shuffling sound from the back of the close and then silence. I got up from my bed and crept to the door. The close was splattered in blood; there were pools and drips on the filthy concrete floor and sprays up the walls. Glass mixed with blood lay in mounds. A belt lay on the stairway. I stood in my doorway staring. There were blue flakes from my door in amongst the battlefield debris. Eventually, I lifted my door, which was hanging on one hinge, and fitted it into its frame, placed the kitchen chair against it, hoping it would hold till I brought another one from the kitchen. I then picked Craig up from his bed and placed him in mine. I did not sleep, though I took some painkillers. I just stared at the ceiling, thinking of the bed in the room above me. Were they still awake? Sleep just would not come.

The next day, I did not need to leave the flat. The council joiner arrived first thing; quickly he put a new frame on, banged in a few nails and fitted a new lock. He made a few mutterings of 'lousy bastards' and 'the time of the year', before he hurried back to his festivities. I had envisaged having to go to phone the council for an emergency joiner, but some other neighbour had done it for me. Though I knew not one of my neighbours would talk about what had happened, I was grateful that someone had been kind enough to place a phone call for me.

As I swept the landing clear of sawdust, splinters and screws, a car pulled up. I stopped and watched it. Somehow I knew it was the police. The same two detectives from the day before arrived, but this time they knocked on everyone's door. I watched the opening of garden gates and front doors being knocked from behind my curtains. I feared the implications of reporting the break-in and what might result from it. Betty must have too, as she came to see me. She also had been awake all night. She had decided to go away for the New Year. 'I have to get away from here,' she said. She told me two other sets of neighbours she had spoken to were going away too. People were too afraid to talk to me about it, though I knew because of the phone call placed to an emergency council joiner that they felt for me. I did not tell Betty that the CID had again asked me to phone them. As I locked my door, I heard the wood split. The emergency joiner had said, 'That'll hold it for now.' I knew different.

During that night, I heard footsteps. My heart began to race. It had done this when I feared it was Joe's footsteps. It banged so hard inside my chest I felt that the noise was deafening. Voices hung outside my door, swearing, laughing and whispering. Craig lay sleeping and as still as I sat. It was just me and them in this building. Their door opened and closed, and music and singing began. I was still in the sitting position when I heard their door open then close again. I heard the feet cross the few steps to my door. I knew this man was standing at my door about to break in. No kitchen chair or makeshift repair to a shaky door would save me. I stared at the wall straight in front of me and froze in anticipation of what would happen next.

Their front door opened again. 'Aw, cum oan,' a voice from the flat said. I heard a slight shuffle. 'Don't dae that. Leave it. Cum oan.' The feet shuffled and the music grew louder. Then the owner of the shuffling feet walked back into the other flat and the door closed. I let go of my breath.

Within five minutes, I was up and running around my room, pulling my clothes on on top of my pyjamas. I kept watching Craig while muttering away rabidly to myself. I could not stop. Visiting the toilet before I went into the kitchen, I was gagging but could not be sick. Fight-or-flight adrenalin was coursing through my body like a runaway toboggan. The cold air from the kitchen window hit me as I opened it and jumped out. I flew to the red phone box and called the number on the card the CID had given me.

'Hamilton Police Station, Q division,' the voice on the other end of the line said.

'A message for CID: he is at home,' I said as I gave them the address. 'It's for Detective Macdonald,' I added. Before I hung up, the voice asked me if I wanted to leave my name. In response, I slammed the black receiver onto its hook and burst out of the phone box. Running home, I willed myself to be invisible and hoped that no one would see me at this time of night. Pressing my back against the outside kitchen wall, I slid along to the slightly open window, then, taking a few breaths, I launched myself into the sink.

Throwing my clothes off, I went to the toilet and was now sick. There was a cold sweat between me and my pyjamas. Just as I had got into bed, I thought I heard a car door. Drawing too hard on my Ventolin inhaler, I crawled to the bottom of the bed. Sliding off the bottom and moving towards the window, I watched through a gap in the bedroom curtains. I could see there were no cars in the street. Suddenly a black figure shot underneath my window and pounding footsteps echoed through the close. I jumped back and just stood there listening. Swiftly, my neighbours' front door was burst open and inside their flat other doors got the same treatment. Within minutes, I heard a voice that I now recognised shouting, 'I'll get the fucking bastard that did this.' Through the gap in the curtains, I saw him getting dragged away in handcuffs. The street was now filled with cars and black figures. I was frightened but not as frightened as I had been when the shuffling footsteps had reached my door earlier. I wondered about the consequences and breaking the code against grassing. Hours of distractive cleaning would sort that out. Merry Christmas indeed!

23

Blood out of a stone

As the New Year holidays came to an end, many events evolved around me in a hurricane concurrence. Traditionally at the festive period, benefits are paid fortnightly instead of weekly. This usually meant that people were looking for a 'tap', 'a sub' or a 'wee lenny' – in other words a loan of some money to tide them over. As I had barely left the flat since that night which I told no one about, I offered to give Betty some money. She had a part-time cleaning job and could give it back to me before I cashed my benefit book on the Monday. Before Monday arrived, however, I realised I could not find my book. I searched my flat, under beds, under mattresses, emptied bins and drawers. I even frantically repeated the pointless process all over again and ransacked the outside bins. It was not to be found.

With a heavy heart, I headed off to the local DHSS office and reported my book missing. Craig and I sat in the smoke-filled office for hours. I had filled in a form with my claim and was sent back to my seat. The room was crowded and huddles of people stood outside, most waiting for promised giro cheques that had not arrived in the post.

We had been sitting for more than three hours when my name was called and I made my way to a booth. 'You have to come back tomorrow for a formal interview,' the desk clerk told me. Hungry and thirsty, we headed home, and I popped into my aunt's on the way. My cousin Lena was there. After the usual chat, I told her what had happened at the DHSS. She offered to come back with me. Ever grateful for any support I could get, I agreed.

The next day, with Craig left at my aunt's, Lena and I took the bus down to the DHSS. We waited for an hour, me in my smartest clothes. Waiting too were many of the same faces from the day before. Ashtrays overflowed, cans of juice lay spilled and babies in buggies were crying. Anxious people jiggled their legs, drummed their fingers, bit their nails or stood outside away from the oppressive atmosphere in the waiting room. It really was a smoke-hazed desperate room.

I knew Lena was not used to this and was glad when a shout came with my name. Instead of going into one of the usual booths, we were both escorted up the stairs. Suddenly it felt serious. We were led into a room, and I remember staring at the many grey venetian blinds. The whole room seemed grey: grey filing cabinets, grey plastic chairs and grey tables. The white walls around us even looked grey among all the greyness. Three men in what I would like to imagine were grey suits appeared. The mood was very sombre. They announced themselves as detectives from the DHSS fraud department.

'Right, who did you sell your benefit book to?' one grey suit said.

I was stunned. 'Sell?' I replied.

'Come on, we know you did,' another grey suit said.

'I don't know what you mean,' I said. I felt frightened but kept steady and polite.

A file was slammed down on the table. 'Do you ever cash your book at another post office?' the first grey suit asked.

'No,' I said. Then in my panic I stupidly stuttered, 'A while ago, I cashed it elsewhere.' The memory came to me of going to another post office after Joe's assault. Of course, it was too long ago to be connected in any way, but I just blurted it out, trying to convince them of my innocence, thinking they might already have a record from the other post office on file. I thought that the more information I gave them would convince them I was telling the truth. It didn't.

'How much did you get for it? Just tell us,' the questioning continued.

I rambled on, saying, 'I think I must have thrown it out while cleaning.' At one point I felt so desperate – I needed this money to feed me and Craig – that I thought of telling them to contact the CID and giving them Detective Macdonald's name. Maybe he could explain the bad situation I had been in and they would see that, due to the stress I had been under, throwing it out could have been more than possible. But I was too scared to say this as Lena was there and would hear. Maybe one of the grey suits was related to my neighbour! I could not reveal that. As nerve-racking as this situation was, someone knowing what I had done was too dangerous.

I protested further, 'I might have thrown it out with Christmas wrapping paper and boxes.' Feeling exasperated and tired, I finally asked, 'Has it been cashed anywhere?'

The grey suits stopped circling for a moment and looked at each other. They would not answer me, so I asked the question again, more emphatically this time. 'Has it been cashed anywhere?' They didn't answer.

Shortly after that, we were escorted out of the room and down the stairs after I was told that I would have to come back tomorrow. Breathing in the fresh air, Lena and I looked at each other. She was visibly shocked. 'How can they treat you like that?' she said.

'I know,' I said. I felt ashamed and sad. For her, this was out of the ordinary. For me, it was not. It was a reminder of my inferior position in society. I still see it today: a society that employs inferior people who use their position to elevate themselves by humiliating and demeaning others. Lena apologised that she could not come with me the next day as she was working.

Craig and I walked down to the offices the next morning and approached a booth, giving my name. As I sat back down, I noticed familiar faces mingling in with new ones. As we waited, I watched a woman in a well-tailored trouser suit flinch as a baby's dummy fell from its mouth. The flinch came when the mother picked it up, swirled it about it in her own mouth to clean it before placing back in the baby's mouth.

Betty had given me the money back that she owed me, with a promise to lend me some if I didn't get a benefit book. I didn't. On hearing my name being called, I stood up and was led into a private room. There I was asked for a statement and then had to sign it. As I did, I was told a book would be sent out in the post.

Monday arrived and no book appeared in the post. The money that Betty had repaid me had run out, as had the tobacco she had given me. Thankfully, as promised, she gave me a few pounds. I was almost out of food for Craig and had no bread or pasta left for myself.

Craig and I headed back down to the DHSS office. We again sat all afternoon only to be told it was definitely in the post. I would receive it tomorrow. After buying bread, milk and cheese, we headed home on foot to a plate piled high of roasted cheese with pepper. I sat up in bed the next morning and held my breath as I heard the familiar shuffle of the postman. I waited for the noise of paper coming through my door but it never came. My book did not arrive. We set off on foot again and again sat for hours in the DHSS office. I had read all the graffiti in the room by now and watched more being written. Eventually we left at closing time, finally holding an emergency giro cheque. Grateful but humiliated, I haughtily asked if there was any proof of my benefit book being cashed. 'No,' was the reply. Turning on my heel, I tried to claw back some dignity.

We dashed straight to the central post office in Hamilton to cash the cheque and then went food shopping. After we got off the bus, the short journey from the bus stop to our flat left my arms and shoulders aching due to the weight of the shopping bags. Craig proudly carried a loaf of bread for me. I could not explain to him why we had no money, what the DHSS was, never mind why we were there. We had jam on bread as we waited for water to boil in the pot on the cooker – I still had not got a replacement kettle.

It's a good feeling to be able to put food in the cupboard and for your child to have a luxury like real strawberry jam. I hated having to rely on benefits, but with no after-school care or support from grandparents I could not work, as I needed to be there when Craig got home, and he finished school earlier than other children. I promised myself that when he went to school full time I would get back into education so I could find a job with prospects and a better future for us. My benefit book arrived a week later.

At night, I still slept with the kitchen chair against my door. All had been quiet next door to me, though the house remained furnished. A neighbour had given me a Hoover; he worked for a charity and was on the lookout for a twin-tub washing machine for me. Until he found one, I used the bath to wash our clothes, as I had done before. It broke my back, especially doing the sheets. It took all my strength to wrap them round the taps and twist them to wring out the excess water. I was by now taking painkillers almost daily and awaiting an appointment to see a gynaecologist.

The bathroom in the flat was damp, which I tackled with bleach and vinegar. I wanted to give us a nice home and raise my spirits, so I decided to redecorate it. Asda in Blantyre again supplied me with wallpaper. It was a Laura Ashley print and cost £1.99 a roll in the bargain bin. I had snapped up three rolls. One night when I could not sleep, I got up and began to decorate the bathroom. I worked right through the night. The paper was self-pasting and I was delighted at my find. I filled the bath with enough water to submerge the paper and to activate the paste, then hung each strip, taking ages to match the tiny print with the next strip. The only tools I had were scissors and a knife.

The next morning, after Craig was fed and off on the bus to school, I slept for a few hours. When I got up, I boiled my pot for a cup of tea, then went to admire my night's work. I stood in the small bathroom, smiling at my achievement till I noticed that every single strip of wallpaper had been hung upside down! The pretty little flowers all pointed down the way and stems upwards. This was becoming a habit.

There was damp in the kitchen as well as the bathroom, which I was also tackling with bleach. I was by now having to use my Ventolin inhaler almost nightly, as the dampness was aggravating my asthma. I never considered that the stress I was under could also have been having an effect. I had never heard of the word stress used in relation to health. Stress was a word used only in association with mechanics and metals, such as applying pressure and stress to manipulate different materials.

There were also other problems affecting my health. I had attended my hospital appointment and after suffering the obligatory internal I was told by the gynaecologist that I had probably suffered damage due to the coil and would need exploratory surgery called a laparoscopy. I would be sent a letter with an appointment in due course.

My weight as always remained low, and I was incredibly thin. Diagnosed with anaemia, I was also taking iron tablets. As I stood at the kitchen sink, looking outside while I swallowed a tablet, Craig belted into the kitchen and banged into the corner of the table. The chair that would have normally have been there had remained permanently in the hall. He fell flat on his back with his beautiful blue eyes out on stalks and his curls bouncing. Before I had time to bend down and pick him up, he was on his feet and running round the living room.

The next morning, I woke to get him up for school and pulled back the covers. Immediately, I felt a sense of déjà vu. The side of his head was grossly enlarged. He just looked at me. Feeling sick with a combination of guilt and fright, I ran to a neighbour's and phoned an ambulance. As he had hit the corner of the table, it had been a nerve that had been damaged and caused the swelling. Craig looked such a sorry sight – his eye was curtained by the swelling – and the guilt I felt was dreadful. In the hospital, he just carried on regardless. The nurses laughed at him; I could not. It took weeks to disappear and I feared a visit from a social worker, which thankfully did not materialise.

24

Miss Ellaneous

Aside from my money worries, the other thing weighing heavily on my mind at this time was the lack of information about my background. During a visit to Fernlea, I brought the issue up with my aunt Elspeth, and she interjected with a question.

'Would you not like to know who you are?' she asked.

It was almost challenging. Or perhaps it was me that felt challenged. My response would normally have been to say, 'No.' Admitting to needing and wanting was a weakness. However, the significance to my son's as well as my own future of knowing information about my birth family was clear. 'Yes, I would,' was my simple reply. Having a particular purpose meant I could disguise any longings for a family behind a genuine and imperative cause: to have facts.

After a few phone calls, my aunt Elspeth scribbled what turned out to be an address and handed it to me. The address was that of the Sheriff Clerk, Miscellaneous Department, Ingram Street, Glasgow. 'Write to them for an appointment, and I will come with you,' she said.

'OK, I will,' I said.

It was the beginning of June 1982 when I wrote that first letter. I know this as I saw the date I had written on the corner of the letter when I set eyes on it again 27 years later in 2009. I was surprised to find it again because it was indicative of someone doing an unusually good job of record keeping. Though I have traced some of my records, many are still missing.

Instantly recognisable was my handwriting, giving details of my name at birth, date of adoption, adopted name and my adoptive parents' names. Sombrely, I had included the fact that my mother was deceased. How I knew some of these details is a puzzle to me – like many memories I have but can't anchor. For example, I really don't have a concrete memory as to how I knew my birth name. I have a very grey and vague memory of being somewhere in a building with a social worker and seeing a single piece of paper that revealed my birth name and a medical check I had on my eyes. I don't have the answer as to why I did not see my original birth certificate or why I had access to only this information.

Apart from enquiring about any information on my adoption, also requested in the letter was a copy of my original birth certificate. After it was posted away, with only the knowledge of my aunt Elspeth and me, somewhere in a dream box within my brain hope was nursed and eventually rewarded in the shape of a response in the post. I had an appointment at the Sheriff Clerk's offices in Glasgow to see my adoption papers.

My aunt Elspeth fulfilled her promise to come with me and we decided to take the train into Glasgow, arranging to meet at the station. It would have been too much for her to pick me and Craig up from my house, as it was not a pleasant area. She never visited, and I knew she would worry about parking her car. She described these places as 'like Beirut'.

It was a glorious sunny day, and I took it as an omen, a sign that it was going to be one of those days where something good is going to happen and change your life. As we stood on the platform, the blue train pulled into Hamilton West Station and once we were on board the sun continued to shine its personal presence just for me, flickering like a silent movie as we passed lines of trees. I began to feel anxious, or was it mounting excitement? Maybe I felt both; I really could not tell the difference.

I had not told my aunt Helen about the appointment. I know now it is common for children who were adopted to find it difficult to seek out their birth parents in case of offending or hurting their adoptive family. Back then, however, I felt deceitful. When Aunt Elspeth asked me if I had said anything to my aunt, I said, 'No, but I will.' She seemed to understand, but I did not understand what she understood about – all I knew was that she thought it was OK not to speak about it yet. It pacified me.

'You will tell her when you're ready,' she said.

Perhaps I was also afraid of what I would find and would not want to share it. Another deep and possibly horrific secret I was keeping had been uncovered as I trawled the library shelves. I had found a book on serial killers, and in one of the passages I read that one female killer had had a baby daughter who had been put up for adoption in 1963. When I read this, I remembered that a transient friend I now forget had made a throwaway comment about a black-and-white passport photo I had taken in my Punk days. She laughingly stated I was the 'spitting image' of Myra Hindley, which added to my identity crisis and fears about where I had come from. That comment had hounded and frightened me.

The drive to know who I was, for all the reasons I have stated, was almost primeval. During the journey, Aunt Elspeth and I chatted away in general about families and children brought up in children's homes. She said, 'You can always tell the kids from children's homes,' without backing up how, and added a few more social-work clichés that filtered in and out of my ears like the sun through the windows. 'Further rejection' was still her favourite phrase for me. From my time in Fernlea, Aunt Elspeth had been a real paradox to me. At times she would seem supportive and empathetic, only for me to discover that she had an agenda, like information she wanted me to get for her. But with so little in my life, the support she did give was much craved and precious to me, so the confused feelings about whom I was sharing this momentous experience with soon disappeared; after all, my choices were few.

After we reached Central Station, Craig was put in his buggy and we headed to Ingram Street, near George Square, where the courthouse was. The grey sandstone building was impressive and looked fit for its legal purpose. I had passed it on many occasions and all this time my personal information had been stored here. The plaque stating Glasgow

Sheriff Courthouse on the side of the doorway confirmed to me that this was serious business and I was embarking on a very important mission.

We bumped the buggy up the stairs and into the building. Though I was not sure of what I would find out, I was convinced that this day would have implications for both me and Craig. Maybe something about my family's medical history might be recorded or something else might lead me there, like a mystery just waiting to be discovered from dusty shelves. I realise now just how much I craved answers for Craig's sake.

We reached the reception desk, and Aunt Elspeth stood back to allow me to speak for myself. I felt very self-conscious, perhaps because I was getting nervous. Shoulders back, chin up, polite voice and show cheerfulness – this stance disguised my anxiety. That nice carriage that Aunt Elspeth had once been proud of saw me glide over to the official who was busy behind the desk. I showed him the letter that I had received and he asked if I had any proof of identity. If I had not been so nervous, I might have laughed and said, 'That's what I am here to find out!'

As I did not have a passport or driving licence, my proof of identity was my birth certificate. This piece of paper, which I had had to use at various times in my life, had 'Adopted' stamped on it, meaning that this personal information was available to whoever needed proof of my identity, and it always brought a comment. Now, however, I was going to find out information that very few people knew, and I hoped it would change my life.

'That will be three pounds,' the official said to me. Three pounds was the charge for me to see my own personal documents. I paid up and was told to take a seat. Fleeting fantasies began to fly randomly in and out my mind. What if I was related to the singer Andy Williams, like the children in one of the homes had said because I had a similar haircut to his children? What if that serial killer was my mother? Or what if my mother was rich and pining away for me, and could help us both? What if she had died? What if she had left instruction I was never to contact her? What if there was a terrible disease in the family? . . . The 'what ifs' began breeding like rabbits in my head. These random rabbits bounced around as I sat outwardly unruffled and busied myself with Craig, playing peek-a-boo, and chatting to Aunt Elspeth.

'Eileen Cooke,' the official called me. After leading us through two heavy doors, he pointed to steep concrete stairs, saying, 'It's downstairs in the miscellaneous department; someone will meet you there.'

As we descended, with a fanfare heralding in my head, I heard my aunt Elspeth muttering under her breath something I could not quite catch, but I was too nervous and intent on my mission to ask what it was she had said. We reached a door in the very bowels of the building on which there was a notice that read 'Miscellaneous'. As I pushed the door open, I felt a sense of slight disappointment. The room we entered was tiny, just slightly larger than that of a cloakroom attendant in a public toilet. We sat on an austere bench, in an austere room, waiting for someone to appear at the counter with information that could change my life.

Eventually, an official appeared and placed a sheet of paper on the counter. As if reading items off a shopping list, he asked me for my name, age and proof of identity. He was as cheerless as the room itself. After a while, he appeared again with another sheet of paper and said, 'That's all we've got.'

The piece of paper had my birth name, my birth mother's name, her birth date, her employment at the time of her pregnancy – she had been a machinist – the address of the Salvation Army Home in Great Western Road she had lived in whilst pregnant and the name of the hospital used by the home. The only other information it contained was a statement that my health had seemed acceptable for adoption. There was no record or mention of the details of my birth, how it had gone, who had been present, if there were any complications, or details of other relatives or contacts.

'Do you want to copy any information down, Eileen?' Aunt Elspeth asked me.

'Yes,' I replied, nodding to her. I could see she felt deflated and was trying to get something from the situation for me.

The official said he would have to get me a pencil, as pens were not allowed. After he handed me a pencil, I jotted down some information, mainly dates and addresses. The whole process must have been over in 20 minutes, after which we headed up the steep stairs again.

The whole experience had been an anticlimax and certainly sobered up my hopes and fantasies, but although disappointed about the lack of information I still felt relieved to have achieved something. Determined not to be downhearted, I clung on to optimism. Surely the details I had managed to gather would lead to other pieces of the jigsaw? Aunt Elspeth, however, was apparently horrified by the whole experience and as soon as we got back on the train she could not hold back what was on her mind.

'Miscellaneous! What a terrible label and environment for a child to find out personal information,' she said. That's what I had missed her saying under her breath as we descended into the bowels of the building. 'That was awful,' she continued, and she could not let it go. 'How must it feel, to be filed under Miscellaneous?' she repeated.

By the time I got home, I had been social worked. I felt worthless, uncared for and unwanted. I decided not to pursue my search any further. Aunt Elspeth's indignation made me feel worse than the reality of what had happened. I can still see us walking to and from the courthouse, her in tightly bridled Marks & Spencer country clothing, and me in clean but obviously not high-quality clothes. In my eyes, we looked every bit the sensible caring social worker and the poor wee ignoramus lassie of a client. Yet it had been me who had tried to be optimistic and see the positives in the situation. It's of these occasions that I now reflect on the professional caring more about the profession than the person they are supposed to be caring for.

In my flat alone, miserable and with no one to talk to, I began to go over and over the day in my head. The romantic fantasy of finding a home, a family and a mother had not been realised, and I thought of my mother, who had been roughly the same age as me when giving birth. How must she have felt at having to give her child up for adoption? My sense of my birth mother became sentimental, and I visualised her as a distraught, tortured girl with no options. I related and felt connected to this woman – the mother that I had never met. We had walked a similar path, only I had kept my child. Though times were very different, it remained illegal to have the father's name on the birth certificate and this, in my romantic and lonely mind, united me and my mother. Had she felt the same shame at signing a birth certificate with no father's name on it?

At least, I reflected, one of the questions about my identity had been answered. Although not really any closer to finding out who I was or getting answers that might help Craig, I knew who I wasn't. I was not the birth child of Myra Hindley! She was not my mother. The black-and-white Punk photograph showing my dark roots and typical dark-eyed make-up stared out at me. So who was I? Placing the photo back in my purse was symbolic, as it was to be a few years until I had enough confidence to begin my search again. In the real world in which I felt I had no place, the film *ET* had been released and he was phoning home. Eileen Cooke still had a long way to go.

25

Can't cry if I want to

After a low-key Christmas, I was looking forward to a night out with Kerry, the beautician, and her friends for my 20th birthday. I was getting ready to go out when Dana turned up at the door. In the past few weeks, I had got friendly with her. She was several years older than me and had just moved into the area. Certainly not local, her clothes were second-hand, like mine. Unlike me, Dana was a hippy in terms of both fashion and her lifestyle. Instead of carpets, her house had pieces of rugs overlapping. Joss sticks burned continually and she was concerned about 'the bomb'. She was considered weird in this poverty-stricken run-down area; alcohol, drugs and violence were more acceptable. Like me, she had no ties within the area and had a different accent. Hers was definitely not Scottish, and this mattered. Just like what team or school you went to, your accent identified your religion, allegiance and loyalties, defining your place and treatment within the community. The cuckoo in the nest, as she was also dubbed, experienced much ridicule. 'Weirdo' and 'nutter' were among some of the words cast at her by the local children and adults.

Dana would turn up at mine with books on the Dalai Lama, and this time she had brought the text of a speech about 'The Healing Power of Hash' and some fruit. As I rushed around getting ready to go out with Kerry, she said, 'Next time, can I maybe come out with you?'

'Yes, of course,' I replied, recognising loneliness. She had brought me a birthday card and I felt guilty as I left her. Craig and I walked quickly along the road to my cousin Helen's, who was going to look after Craig while I was out. Helen had been in the latter stages of pregnancy with her son Michael when I was concealing my pregnancy. Her son and Craig had a close relationship. This had been emphasised one time during a walk from my aunt's to their house. As the two boys ran fast along the street together, Michael suddenly began to panic. 'Craig, Craig,' he shouted as his wee cousin raced ahead. It was, of course, futile. Turning to his mother and me, he was bawling that Craig would get knocked down. Craig reached the end of the street and turned with a grin, unaware of the panic he had caused. Michael's fear had perhaps been intensified by the lack of language. I knew how he felt as I lived every day like that.

Although it was February, it was a bright evening. Leaving Helen's, I shouted, 'See you later,' then clocked up more miles by walking to Hamilton. My feet were aching and then my back and stomach by the time I met up with Kerry and her friends. I went to the toilet, doubled up in private and took a painkiller. Kerry bought me a birthday drink, strangers and known faces said 'Happy Birthday' to me and the night began. Dressed in black skintight leggings, and a black leather and cloth jacket I had bought from Oxfam, I felt good. I had finished my look off with a lace remnant wrapped round my head. Kerry had cut and dyed my hair: it was platinum, with a little quiff at the front. A black second-hand bag from a local jumble sale and I was sorted.

We visited two bars in Hamilton before arriving at my aunt's pub. In the corner sat all the Punks, the new emerging Indies and any other sort that was not mainstream. Hair either stood high, dyed and solid, or short cropped and gelled. The rest of the pub, it seemed, wore leg warmers and jeans. The chat in the corner was all about music. Some were getting a band together, if they had not done so already. The soundtrack to this time included Yazoo's Punk/Electro/Bluesy 'Only You' or 'Nobody's Diary' and Erasure's high-pitched 'Sometimes', as well as the (uncool to our corner) Pop tunes like Kajagoogoo's 'Too Shy', the cheesy 'Save Your Love', by Rene and Renato and Phil Collins' 'You Can't Hurry Love'. It was a time of no clear trends, many existed side by side, and there was something for everyone. Gone were the days when the argument was about Donny, Marc or David, T. Rex or the Jacksons.

As the evening wore on, it became clear that the pain was not going to disappear as I'd hoped. Usually it waned after I took the painkillers, but not this time. After being secretly sick in the toilets, I decided to go home to my cousin's. After making my excuses to Kerry, I left unnoticed by anyone else. Or so I thought. As I walked out of the pub, out of the corner of my eye I saw a hand wave. Faltering, I stared and felt as though I vaguely recognised the face, but nothing certain. No penny dropped and no name came to mind, so I continued out of the top door of the pub. As I walked quickly from Hamilton's Bottom Cross up Quarry Street towards the bus station and taxi rank, my feet cold in my cloth paddy sandals, I heard footsteps behind me.

'Hiya, Eileen,' the face from the pub said.

Immediately, my shoulders hunched; I felt uneasy. 'Hiya,' I said back. I tried to avoid eye contact and smiled as I forged too quickly on. I had reacted as the prey he saw me as: frightened, nervy and half cowering. My anxious smile was like a puppy's eyes pleading, 'Don't hurt me.' He did.

What seemed like five minutes later, a close door in one of the tenements in Townhead Street banged shut and created a blast of icy air. I lay in the close on the cold concrete ground. He had raped me. I still don't know who he was.

Picking myself up, I searched for my bag. My hands were filthy. Sorting my clothes, I opened the door. I walked out of the close and began my walk up the rest of Townhead Street. Ahead, I saw his figure in the distance. I waited and waited till I thought he no longer existed. I walked past Campbell Street, where the police station could clearly be seen. I walked alone for miles up Almada Street, by the County Buildings and the fountains, past Peacock Cross, straight up round the streets till I got to my flat. I could not deviate from this route, I could not stop a taxi, and I could not go to the police station. I certainly could not go home to my cousin Helen's.

As I approached my flat, I stopped outside Dana's, seeing a light in her room glowing orange. She was still up. At the time, and for many years, I could not explain why I decided to do what I did, why I chose not to scream, why I chose not to go to the nearby police station, why I was afraid to go to Helen's and finally why I did not knock on Dana's door.

Automatic pilot and my homing device got me into my flat. I ran a shallow bath. As the hot water immersion was not switched on, I had very little hot water. As the bath was running, I stood at the kitchen window and cleaned two tea-stained cups with salt till the stains had gone and they gleamed.

The bath was lukewarm and I began to shiver violently as I sat in it. Stepping from the bath, I grabbed a towel and kept rubbing till I was more than dry. My cheap paddy sandals were worn through at the toes and one buckle had snapped. I remember hearing it hitting the streets on the walk home. The stripy men's pyjamas I had rummaged from a jumble sale enveloped me as I crawled under my quilt. I could not stop shaking and felt exhausted. I could think of nothing other than how cold I was. My mind was full of noises of discomfort. It contained no words or streams of thought. Eventually, I got up and ran the hot water tap – it was still tepid – and swallowed more painkillers. Lighting a candle beside my bed, I spent some time shaking and placing my hand in and out of the flame. A few times I kept my hand there to see how long I could bear it. The heat did not burn. Eventually, I fell asleep.

I know I was in terrible shock and exhausted. My modus operandi was true to form: *Never reveal. Go into hiding. Don't share. Nothing in, nothing out. It will keep your mind intact,* I still could not place his face and I was too burned out to move or care what Helen would say to me the next day for not turning up. I had resigned myself hours ago to take what was coming to me.

26

Soap opera

When I turned up at her house the next day, Helen was naturally annoyed with me and must have been more so when I came up with some cock-and-bull story about a party and not being able to get home. My cuts and bruises as easily hidden as the non-physical injuries, I managed to reduce the incident to a picture and a smell. I felt a gutting guilt about the lie, but for me it was still better than the truth. My interpretation of those feminist books had been right: men did hate me, and it was my fault. No other explanation had come my way.

Terrified to confide in anyone and having no one I could trust, I shut down. I have no other recollections of how I felt about that night; I only remember having one of my talks to myself sitting at the bottom of my bed. A picture, as though I am watching myself, appears in my head. I am sitting at the bottom of the bed, smoking, telling myself not to burden someone with this situation of my own making. I believed it to be my fault, my irresponsibility of being out on my own. I was unwittingly becoming even more remote from myself, shrinking from my own thoughts and unable to feel any connections to the few people around me.

Soap watchers were revelling in the affair of Deirdre Barlow and Mike Baldwin at the time. There was no escaping the story, as all the media covered it. On the buses, it was the focus of gossip. 'Aye, she'd be better off wae Baldwin,' some would say. However, in my wee corner of the world an act like that by a woman would have landed you a black eye or, worse, a life of misery before finally divorce. No glamour there. It was a man's world. I watched in my aunt's house, uninterested. I would read papers and immediately forget what I had just read. Alone at night, I came alive and plunged myself into more history books about the two world wars and the Holocaust from the library's shelves. I was unknowingly searching for something that would make me feel, anything that would allow me to understand myself. Starved of answers, I devoured everything I could.

Plays, I now discovered, were for me the bridge between a poem and a book. I read Arthur Miller's *Death of a Salesman* again, but it was *The Crucible* that had the most impact on me. It frightened me, but I only knew at the time that I did not know why. I realised it was based on the famous witchcraft trials of Salem and an allegory about the McCarthy witch-hunts, but at a fundamental level it suggested to me that I had a hidden dark streak and would always be a danger and in danger. It was a play that we had studied at school, but my interpretations of it were very different from the discussions we had had there. Abigail, the niece, had been described as a whore, a Lolita and spiteful, but I saw a changeling, a cuckoo in the nest with a traumatic past. I perceived Proctor as being opportunistic and using motherless, underage Abigail, while during our debates at school Proctor was portrayed as her victim. I did not agree but was afraid to say anything that might give myself away. When I revisited it, it seemed the answers were further away than before, probably because I now felt I had more to lose.

Another pressure came my way. One of Joe's pot-smoking friends, Gazza, who was a social worker in a children's home, began to show a sudden interest in me. I met him just after I had got my nose pierced. After leaving the jewellery shop where the facial adornment had taken place, I walked up Hamilton's Quarry Street. Holding my hand to my now throbbing nose, proud of myself for not flinching while the piercing gun attacked my left nostril, I bumped into Gazza. He looked at my nose stud and was impressed. 'I would buy you a diamond for that, Eileen,' he said.

I did not reply to that offer, hoping he understood my uncomfortable silence as a rebuff. I was to be disappointed. For the next few weeks, he would turn up unannounced at my flat. As we sat drinking tea, I stupidly tried to deflect him with friendly chit-chat. I had never heard of the word stalking before and could not work out why he made me feel so uncomfortable. After all, I was in my own home, my own territory, and he was a social worker.

The most unsettling incident between us happened one day when Kerry popped in on the way home from visiting someone else. I had casually told her about him, without really explaining how uncomfortable I felt as I didn't want to exaggerate what was going on. It would have felt arrogant to suggest he had taken such an interest in me. Alarm bells would nowadays be deafening me and anyone else around.

As Kerry and I blethered away, mostly about what she had been doing, we both heard the distinctive sound of a black hackney taxi door shutting. Edging to the front window of the flat, just out of full view from the street, I saw Gazza walking from the taxi towards my flat. 'Oh no!' I groaned.

Kerry looked and saw him getting closer. 'Right, hide,' she said. 'I'll get rid of him.'

I ran into my bedroom and then in a panic ran back out again. 'What if he comes looking for me?' I said.

'He won't,' she hissed at me.

'Please lock me in my wardrobe,' I pleaded.

My fear must have been clear. After she agreed to my request, I sat in my wardrobe, as I had done as a child in my Narnia wardrobe at home, and disappeared. It was only when I heard the key turn and knew I was locked in that I was able to exhale and begin to breathe. The feral child in me nestled down into a corner as I heard my letterbox being rattled. Kerry's long legs strode down the hall and I heard her opening the door. 'She's not here,' Kerry said.

'I'll wait,' Gazza replied. I pictured his long legs and shoulder-length straggly hair less than a foot away from me as he strode up the hall.

An hour passed before Kerry could release me from the second-hand, damp-smelling wardrobe. It had seemed longer and with no Christmas savings hamper to munch on, as I had had as a child in my parents' wardrobe, I was tired and hungry and my bum was numb.

Kerry was furious and released a stream of anger. 'I can't believe him. He just would not go. He is a bloody creepy nutter.' She continually tucked her escaping curly fringe behind her ear as she related to me what he had said to her.

'He would not stop asking questions about you,' she said. 'Where is she? Who is she with? What time will she be back?' he had asked, demanding answers from Kerry. 'Three bloody cups of coffee and still he sat,' she continued.

Pacing nervously, I said to her, 'I need to do something about this.' But I never did. His attentions turned elsewhere and soon I was to find out just how right we were to think he was creepy.

27

Out of touch

Craig became ill. Late nights, coughing and a visit to the doctor left us with a diagnosis of whooping cough. 'Nothing you can do, it will take its course,' the doctor said. It was terrifying, and for nearly six weeks Craig slept in beside me. I sat up night after night, rocking him in my arms as he began his fits of frightening coughing. Watching him struggling to breathe and hearing the whooping noise at the end of each cough exhausted us both. I gave him junior disprins, anything I knew was safe that might at least offer him some comfort. I took him back to the doctor only to be sent away with the same sentiment: 'Nothing you can do, it will pass.' One night his coughing was so hard and prolific that in the early hours of the morning the neighbour from upstairs came to the door. 'Do you want me to get a doctor, Eileen?' she asked. I told her I had been twice already and thanked her.

In those weeks, I found my frustrated arms rocking my wee boy hard with tears silently running down my cheeks. I now realise that the events of the night out with Kerry began a spiral that other happenings, such as Craig's whooping cough, escalated.

My only day out now was a Monday, and this was because I was forced to go out. I had to cash my benefits book in order to feed us and pay bills. I went to the library straight from the shops and then home till the next Monday. There was nothing in the library on whooping cough. During these excursions, I wore jeans and an old ski jacket I had got from a jumble sale to wear when it was my turn to clean the close. People did not recognise me. I combed my hair, but that was that – no make-up, no boiled sugar to make my hair stick up.

During our wakeful hours at night, Craig and I would look through the second-hand books and the encyclopaedia collection I had bought. Dinosaur pictures were an obvious favourite, but I would also point out the pictures of the constellations in the book and we would search the sky for them, nodding or shaking our heads to acknowledge what we thought. We did this by candlelight to keep the electricity bill down. I had just received a huge bill. Even though it was a winter bill, it was extortionate and it was swallowing up most of our benefits.

I wonder what Craig thought back then in his wee wordless world. I had heard a story of a deaf child who had learned to sign. At the dinner table one day, the child asked his mother, 'What did the dog say, Mum?' The mother signed back, 'The dog can't talk.' The child simply said, 'Then why do you talk to him?' He believed animals could talk because no one had told him they didn't. I wonder if Craig thought that dinosaurs existed somewhere on the planet in the present day. Today, those memories move me to tears.

Physically and emotionally I was done, exhausted, though I did not know it. Deep depression had set in, but no one told me and no one saw it. My memories were drowning me – those of Urquhart, my violent alcoholic parents, sitting with the body of my dead mother, the children's homes, the shower lady, the handyman, and many more, including the recent birthday night out. I had spoken to no one about anything. Living like an aged hermit, I was just surviving. I lived in near isolation, connecting to no other social support or group. I made no effort to phone anyone, and I had few visitors. Betty, my neighbour, had got a boyfriend and was getting married; I rarely saw her. Dana, I had found out through a last visit from Barbara – who was a friend of Dana's cousin – had been sleeping with Joe, and we decided that perhaps Dana had begun to visit me because she had fancied Joe. After her visit, I slept a good part of the rest of that day and woke tired. As soon as Craig was bathed and settled, I crawled back into bed. My tiredness was drenching and I was in a lot of physical pain too. The painkillers were no longer working.

In August that year, after finally getting rid of the whooping cough, Craig started school at the age of three. This is a special occasion for any child, but in Craig's case it was accompanied by the enormous hope that it would open the doors of communication. Feeling nervous for both of us, I tried to shut out thoughts of disappointment that Craig had no grandparents around to buy him his first uniform, which was a practice written in stone in our area. With so much at stake, I told myself that there were more important things to worry about.

I knew that the school catered for children with special needs, but there had been no prior visits to meet the teachers or other parents and their deaf children, which I thought would have been helpful for us both. Indeed, the day itself passed with little or no fanfare. A bus simply arrived at the door in the morning to pick him up and he was dropped off again in the afternoon. As Craig couldn't tell me, I learned little about how he had spent his day but he seemed happy enough.

I knew that the current research suggested that deaf children start school early and that the head teacher at his school did not believe in the use of sign language. This was frustrating for me, as the only information readily available to me in the library related to sign language. Craig had now been fitted with a hearing aid and, as I understood it, the aim was for him to communicate through spoken language. I would learn later that he and the other children were made to sit on their hands in an attempt to force them to speak when they needed to communicate.

This made me uneasy and all the hopes I had had about Craig's entry into education now seemed to have been overly optimistic. Overall, I felt less than happy about the school's regime, and this stance brought me into direct confrontation with the headmistress, Ms Stanley. I had asked one of Craig's teachers if there were any classes for sign language or for parents of deaf children. Shortly after this, I was summoned to the headmistress's office. 'Miss Cooke,' she said, 'we are professionals here at what we do and know what is best for your child.'

As she sat there, I knew she was a good churchgoer, another God-fearing woman, a respectable member of Presbyterian society. She wore all the symbols: sensible square-toed shoes, heavy girdle and frilly blouse. She was a perfect mixture of Aunt Elspeth, Mrs Woods and Mrs Linn, and she next told me, 'It's not really in Craig's interest that his mother dyes her hair.'

I was partly too intimidated and partly aware that talking back would cause trouble in the future for me and Craig to ask what difference that would make to him, so I just sat silent as she continued to talk down to me. It quickly became clear that parents just did not have any input here at all.

I listened as she told me that there were plans to separate the deaf part of the school, as all the pupils met in the playground and the deaf children were mimicking the other children with different disabilities. This was deemed to be detrimental to the development of the deaf children and a site for a separate school was being looked at. Ms Stanley stated that she would then become the headmistress of the new school.

I went home via Hamilton town centre and bought sticky labels from WHSmith in the precinct. Determined to have some kind of input to my son's life, I began posting these labels all over the house, naming the furniture and anything else I could think of. Perhaps, I thought, we could write to each other if he learned to read. I also went into Oxfam and, in reaction to being told I was to have nothing to do with my son's educational development, bought more books for us to share.

Shortly after he started school, Craig fell off the red-and-yellow dumper truck I had bought him. I heard the crash as I stood at the kitchen window doing the dishes. Craig was out the back door, pedalling round and round the small patch of communal grass. He had crashed into the rubbish bins. Running out through the close, I picked him up in one arm and trailed the truck behind me in the other. There were no tears, just a wee curly head snuggling into me. As I bathed him, he was more subdued than usual, which was not hard to spot as Craig was normally a curly-headed swooshing whirlwind, so much so that I had stopped all fizzy juice and most sweets after reading something about a possible link between hyperactive children and food additives.

The next morning, I went into his room to get him up for school, which was unusual in itself as he was normally up first, bounding into my bed and then into the kitchen, pouring cornflakes everywhere but into the bowl awaiting him on the table. (It was a habit I had picked up from the homes, setting tables the night before for breakfast, that and tucking bedsheets in an envelope style.) He was lying awake. As I looked into his eyes, they told me all I needed to know. When I pulled back his Transformers quilt cover, he flinched. One hand covered his other arm, and I set about getting enough clothes on him to get him to Casualty. In true Craig fashion, after the X-ray showed he had broken his arm, he began to bound around the Casualty department. Back at home with a 'stookie', otherwise known as a plaster cast, on his arm, he continued to bounce around, climbing over the back of the couch. There we were: a livewire with endless amounts of energy and a mother riddled with guilt at bathing and sending a child to sleep with a broken arm.

Two days later, a health visitor arrived at my door. Apologetically she said she had had a report from the hospital and had to follow it up. We chatted and she acknowledged Craig's endless amount of energy. 'You really should be trying for a different housing situation,' she said. 'Do you know it's council policy not to house single parents in ground-floor flats?' I had never heard of this and promised I would look into it.

Within the week, Craig was back at school, his curly hair and plaster cast disappearing onto the school bus in the morning. I renewed my efforts to improve his diet and mentioned food additives to his teacher. Her reply stung me, perhaps more so as I was secretly trying to impress her and develop a positive relationship for the benefit of Craig's education. 'We have found that children born to young single mothers have peculiar agitations about them,' she said.

It felt like my son did not belong to me. I had no influence or say in his education and no way of communicating to him in the way they proposed they had. Also, it was clear I had no value as a person or Craig's mother in her eyes.

Just as another Christmas was approaching, I had arranged to pick Craig up from school as we had another appointment at Yorkhill Hospital. It was for the results of the multitude of tests Craig had previously had. When he saw me, he ran towards me from his little class seat. This obvious display of pleasure was welcome in what was becoming a hostile environment. Closing the classroom door and with Craig on my hip, I bumped into Ms Stanley in the long, cabbage-smelling school corridor.

'Where are you going?' she asked.

On edge but obedient, I replied, 'Yorkhill, for the results of Craig's tests.'

Her cruel response only shows how much she disliked me as I stood there with my short dyed-blonde hair, with Craig balanced on a protruding hip. With her hair set like the Queen's, wearing a twinset and pearls, she retorted, 'Well, if it turns out to be rubella, be aware of the possibility of blindness and brain damage.' After that, she turned away and her heels clacked in the frozen silence.

As I walked the length of the corridor and out of the school grounds, I refused to cry. I refused to do anything but keep going with my shoulders back and chin up, straight forward. Another way I found of keeping tears at bay apart from counting external objects was to run my tongue round my mouth and note the ridges, the bumps, the jagged edges, unhinging jaw and squinty teeth, and it was this tactic that I now employed.

After the visit to Yorkhill, during which I was told that the test results had been inconclusive – his records simply stating: 'With no signs of any other effects on his eyes, brain or significant organs' – I visited my aunt Helen and told her about my encounter with Ms Stanley. As I waited for her response, Aunt Helen's face looked as though it could combust. I realise now that I was so accustomed to cruelty in many shapes and forms, and in particular by professionals in situations where I was on my own with them, that I had become desensitised to a large degree. With no strong family ties and a poker face that could be read as defiant, I was easy prey. However, my aunt Helen's actions astounded me. It seemed like she catapulted herself from her fireside chair, her teacup was banged down, her cigarette placed in the ashtray and into the hallway she went. I heard her talking to directory enquiries and the paper rustling as she scribbled a number down. The phone was banged down on its receiver and promptly picked up again to be banged down.

'Bloody party line,' she shouted as she thumped her way up the stairs and slammed the bathroom door shut. My aunt shared a telephone line with her next-door neighbours and she'd heard a conversation when she'd lifted the phone. A few minutes passed before she came back down the stairs and got straight back on the phone, her fury not tempered any. Within minutes, she was on the phone to Ms Stanley. 'I'll be down there. What are you trying to do to her, destroy her?' was all that I overheard.

It felt wonderful to have someone stick up for me and be my ally. Particularly because it was my aunt in my corner, I could pretend for a while it was or would always be like that.

The demons were kept at bay during the day with my obsessive cleaning, but they slipped into my nightmares.

28

Another settlement

As I sank deeper into myself, gaining no satisfaction from music or people, the arrival of the school bus at our door in the morning and then again in the afternoon when it dropped Craig off was my only connection to the outside world. But one Monday saw a last-gasp flicker in my heart. As I returned from the post office, I noticed familiar splintered light wood as my front door had been burst open again. The door hung there like a painted piece of corrugated cardboard. Betty had returned home on a rare visit and came down the stairs. We did not say much to each other. We were friends because of circumstances, it seemed. However, she did say, 'Eileen, I have been told that them next door have been tapping into your electricity.'

Within hours, I was on the phone to my cousin Bernadette. I actually broke down and told her about the break-in and the information I'd been given concerning the electricity. She arrived and looked around my flat. 'Get your bags packed and come and live with me,' she said.

I packed what I could for Craig and then returned the next day and panic-packed all I could carry into a taxi. The front door of the flat would no longer lock. I left it as it was. I still have nightmares about my life there. It was a dark period where I felt constantly under threat and vulnerable. My memories hang loosely in an unstitched tapestry, like patches that do not know their position. Similar things happened to others, too. I know I was not the only one.

I phoned my aunt Elspeth the next day to tell her my news and give her Bernadette's phone number. Aunt Elspeth had news of her own. One of the social workers in a nearby children's home had lost his job. I felt sick when she revealed it had been Gazza, the man I had hidden in the wardrobe to avoid and who had been harassing me.

The box room Craig and I shared at Bernadette's contained us like two stowaways on a ship. This ship thankfully was free of the flotsam and jetsam of violence and drugs. The only wreckage was me.

Bernadette had got the marital home back as part of her divorce settlement and had finished college, securing a place at university. She had two young boys and a cock-eyed tiger-striped dog called Ben to look after. Bernadette worked nights in a pub and I watched the boys. Initially, organising our benefits so that Bernadette would not be out of pocket for taking us in proved to be difficult. The DHSS rules stated I could not apply for help with rent as I was a family member. I was terrified and desperate. I could not go back there to a flat with a broken door. The relentless anxiety about my tenuous security just seemed to continue wherever I went. I could not break free. However, my older cousin was knowledgeable about our rights, knew whom to speak to and was able to put across our case, so in fact there was little resistance. The relief I felt was immense. No one treated me with anything other than professional courtesy. This time there was no DHSS man groping around, enquiring about sexual positions.

Soon after moving in, I inadvertently gave Bernadette a huge shock. One night as I stood half-naked, getting ready for bed while chatting to her, I turned to see a horrified look on her face. She was looking me up and down. I turned away and continued chatting. My body was so thin that I had a soft down of hair on it and my bones jutted out. I had also taken to scratching my skin with a hard hairbrush. The crawling, itching feeling that constantly plagued me was not relieved by nail-less fingers. Long scratches covered my legs.

Was I anorexic? To look at me you would have said yes without a doubt. However, I ate any dinner that was put down in front of me. I enjoyed food, though sometimes it was difficult to keep it down.

Neglect, extreme stress and poverty were killing me. Tenacity – what I thought had been my strength, my backbone – had become a weakness. The tenacity born out of terror, the terror born out of experience, had kept me from relaxing, trusting or flourishing – and no wonder. I do not ever remember feeling relaxed, except when exhausted and forced to be. All my life I had lived with heightened anxiety, I just did not know it.

Bernadette's multitude of earrings became a focal point for me again. No sooner had I tidied up, found singular ones, sought out their partners and paired them off, than she had another set lying apart. I do not know if she ever noticed my compulsion; if she did, she never said.

The house, though chaotic, had two doors that locked and decent neighbours. Evening would sometimes see us walking up the nearby country back roads, often returning with a tiger-striped Ben stinking of green-coloured animal shit. He did this every chance he could. It would be chaos in the house as we tried to bathe him: there would be lather and water everywhere, with flecks of green splattered up the bathroom walls and Ben escaping from the towels as quickly as he could.

One evening saw Angus, Bernadette's eldest son, doing an errand for me. He skipped to the post box at the end of the street to post a letter for me and as a treat he was allowed to buy some chips for supper. He took so long to return that I wondered if he was growing the potatoes. On his eventual arrival, he related a story of falling down a hole that had been dug in the road by the council. He had been stuck there, shouting, he said, for help and had skinned his knees while crawling out to go to the chip shop. 'It's all your fault, you sent me to post the letter,' he grinned. I'm not sure to this day if I believe his story about falling down the hole, but he milked the situation for all it was worth, applying the guilt thickly. 'It would not have happened if you had not sent me.' Still grinning, he said, 'What if I had not been able to get out, how would you have felt?'

'Terrible,' I bluntly replied with a grin.

As I dished out the chips and buttered bread, Angus continued. He liked to do that: relentlessly wind you up till you responded. Usually by that point it was in the negative, such as, 'Well, if you'd broken your neck we would have peace.' I considered asking him how his friends were, as I suspected the truth of the matter was that he had spent the time dilly-dallying with them.

Another incident that stays seared by embarrassment in my memory happened around this time. I had a doctor's appointment. As Bernadette was working, all three boys had to trundle along with me. After bussing it from our house to the bus station, we then wandered up several miles on the tree-lined road until we reached the surgery at Hamilton's Peacock Cross. Before we arrived, I noticed that I had snagged my tights, and the rip continued up my leg faster than a knitted jumper unravelling in a cartoon. The newsagent across from the doctor's surgery saved my embarrassment as I was able to purchase a pair of tights. The four of us then crossed the road and got comfy in the surgery before I told the boys to wait and behave as I was going to the toilet.

After removing my holey snagged tights, I dropped them into the bin at the side of the toilet bowl. My name was called as I unlocked the toilet door, and as I dashed into the reception to collect my medical card, which gave the doctors back then some brief information and a rough idea of the last few visits, I told the boys again to behave. After closing the door of the doctor's room, through a glass slat in the door I could see the boys jingling around. I wondered how many patients they had annoyed or had laughing. When my appointment concluded, I went back into the waiting room and said, 'Right, time to go.'

'Aunty Eileen, Aunty Eileen,' Angus's voice implored, but I knew better, as he only called me 'Aunty' for fun.

I turned, and as I stood there in the middle of the surgery, with all the other patients sitting patiently in their chairs, he held up in his hands my holey tights! 'You left these in the toilet, Aunty Eileen.' I snatched the offending tights that Angus had seen fit to rescue from the bin and bustled the boys out the door. I did not glance back. Feigning innocence, he grinned at me. I did not say anything back to him. I decided that would only add to his pleasure. That was Angus and his preoccupation with the perversity of humour.

Craig loved the company of the boys, and there were plenty of their friends and other people around to keep up with his hyperness. Across the road was a small park with a chute. Lena came to visit me; she had been away nursing in the States at a summer school and had written to me at Bernadette's. She had been homesick and missing her boyfriend Calum. We chatted over Craig's head as we pushed him on the swing between each other. She told me all about her time there, and I asked many questions. It sounded wonderful, an adventure.

Suddenly, Craig half jumped, half fell off his swing and ran towards the chute. Before we could get there, he was up the steps and down the steel chute and had sliced open his arm on a broken glass bottle. Another visit to the hospital resulted in butterfly stitches and an unfazed Craig adding to his catalogue of injuries.

I watched this buzzing child run rings round people; he was exhausting to watch sometimes but incredibly funny, his face contorting at everything he saw, expressive in the extreme. Sometimes it was a joy to watch: his eyes pooling wide at the sight of something new or desired. Sometimes it was heartbreaking: always having to explain on a daily basis when people spoke to him that he was deaf, hence him not replying. Watching the boys and their friends communicate in an exaggerated fashion with him was like watching a street full of Rowan Atkinson's Mr Beans – all arms and facial gymnastics. I knew then, though, as he grew up and became more aware it would not be as fascinating or easy for him to mingle with others.

In our busy, full house, our time passed quickly. It was a novelty to use an automatic washing machine every day and to sit round a table for Sunday dinner. It was only sometimes in the wee small hours or in my sleep that visions continued to be my secret and unwelcome companions.

But I'd learned by now that nothing lasts for ever and after her graduation Bernadette found a job in another region of Scotland. As the removal van left the street with Ben the dog, her kids and herself, I found myself alone with Craig and another fight on my hands. The council rules stated that I had no legal right to the house as I had not lived there for the statutory one year required to claim permanent residence. Heartbroken, I began to pack up our belongings and made a visit to the council homeless department. For the remainder of the time, I slept on the old couch.

Two weeks later, I found myself walking back through the doors of Hove House, where Mrs Woods was waiting for me. Yet another chapter closed and an old one was to be revisited.

29

Prodigal

Over three years had passed since I had lived there, and the sweet memory of the day I had walked triumphantly away from the humiliating Dickensian rules and regulations only reminded me of how vulnerable and stupid I had been. I had got myself right back in the same situation. I was turning 21, a stigmatised unmarried mother of a 'handicapped child'. I had no mother, no father I could rely on and no siblings. To top it off I came from a 'troubled background', with no support from my legal guardians or the social work department. I was on my own. My descent into homelessness had left me without friends. About the few I had had, I wonder now whether they deserted me or I them, embarrassed by my situation. Kerry kept loosely in touch, as did a male friend, Derek, I had met through her. I was to find out his agenda in a few months' time. For now, I was once more in the position of feeling grateful. His phone calls and letters were to be appreciated.

What would Hove House hold for me this time, after the rungs on my ladder of dreams had splintered and broken beneath my feet? I thought it served me right for hoping and dreaming. With my shoulders back and chin up, I pretended, like a child, it was a test of my endurance for some better purpose, though I felt sick and was full of dread about what lay ahead. Pretence was like antiseptic, it kept the rot from setting into sores.

I knew it was pretence; it was my way of avoiding awkward social moments. A sad example was my 21st. Kerry was going to see a band, Prefab Sprout, in Glasgow and asked if I wanted to go. I would pretend then and later that this was another birthday outing just for me. Whenever people reminisced about their 21st birthdays, I would recite vaguely about my evening of going to see a band in Glasgow. It wasn't an outing for my birthday, though, and I had never had a birthday party or outing since one memorable one I had had as child, where I had cried.

Feeling unlovable and a bit sorry for myself, I arrived at Hove House as I had triumphantly left – by taxi. There, standing at the imposing oak-panelled double doors, Mac-Mac was waiting in the same checked overall. I talked myself out of shedding a tear.

Mac-Mac hugged me as soon as she had ushered me into my room – the same room I had occupied years before. She kindly closed the door before acknowledging the situation. 'What happened, Eileen?' she asked. Her habit of taking hankies from her overall pockets and dabbing her face had remained with her, I noticed. I briefly told her the story, not wanting to get emotional. Sensing that she should leave me alone, she said, 'Better get settled before her ladyship comes to see you.'

I sighed and sank onto the same old bed in the same old room. Mac-Mac's statement and the familiar sound of heels on the wooden stairs signified the music I was about to face. The dreaded meeting with Mrs Woods finally took place. 'Well, well, what brings you back here?' she asked.

My reply was curt and straight to the point in order to stop myself from breaking down. 'I am homeless,' I said.

What else she said I cannot remember. Did my reply make the warden of a homeless unit feel stupid? Was she wary of me because of the manner in which I had left and the support I had had last time I had resided here? Did she have any pangs of conscience regarding her ridiculing me over my concerns about my son's hearing? (I had obviously been vindicated in this as Craig was attending a special school and wore two hearing aids as evidence.) I can't really say. It never occurred to me that perhaps she had some fears about me; my own anxiety levels were far too high to detect anything.

Craig's school bus had to be notified of a change of address, and Mac-Mac informed Mrs Woods about this. The phone box rules remained, and the short run of the women being able to access the phone had stopped when BT received a request from Mrs Woods for a new number. The grey steel payphone in the porch hung on the wall behind the same locked door. To me, it became a thorny symbol of Hove House's hold on the misfortunate, reminding us it was all our own fault. Sometimes it would ring as we women went about our daily duties. Our inability to silence the ring and the phone's inaccessibility became a constant taunt to us.

Mrs Woods' heavily girdled appearance, like Mac-Mac's overall, remained unchanged, as did the rest of Hove House. Nothing was different other than the residents. In the austere kitchen, I was allotted the same cooker, and memories of melted shoes and frying eggs sifted back to me. The large painted number above the electric-ringed cookers corresponded with the room numbers. I cannot remember mine. Knowing myself, this is probably deliberate – I am not a number!

As I got to know people, I naturally asked Mac-Mac about the previous residents I had known. Everyone had been re-housed in different areas. I was sad when she informed me that the nearly-there woman, Annie, had died. Lifting her hand up and down to her mouth in a cupped shape, she indicated it was alcohol related. I still carried the woman's writings with me, along with the mink brooch and watercolour that had belonged to my mother.

One of the residents, Janey, who was particularly vocal and cursed like a trooper, became my friend. Probably because she was single, after office hours her door remained open, unlike the married couples whose lives were closed off to us, like the kitchen door after teatime.

Janey would dye and perm her own hair, get weekend passes and party. She reminded me of a drinking friend of my mother's who always stank of eye-watering perm lotion and had pipe cleaners as rollers for her hair. Though the perm lotion was not as eye watering and the pipe-cleaner rollers were now different-sized blue and pink plastic tubes with rubber bands, the attention she paid to painting her nails was also evocative. In contrast, my hair was platinum blonde, short and spiky.

My nails remained unpainted, as I didn't want to draw attention to their bitten state and bleeding skin. Inwardly, I marvelled at the final result that a small brush stroking a long, well-shaped nail produced.

Naturally, as comrades in misery do, Janey shared her story with me. I would tiptoe up the dark stairway, past Annie's old room and creak open Janey's door. We sat at the table positioned by the window and watched the world go by as we talked.

She was about ten years older than me and had been married with children, both of whom were with her here in Hove House. Janey had lived in a far-flung rural village on the outskirts of Hamilton. Having married a local man, she had generally lived like everyone else around her. Her bombshell had come in the shape of accusations that her husband had 'interfered' with boys. It seemed that swiftly following these accusations – about which on the odd occasion she would mutter that she thought they were true – she had discovered the marital home was in rent arrears. Having separated from her husband, she had tried to negotiate with the council to pay off these newly discovered debts. Her front door had been splattered in paint and obscenities, the council refused to negotiate, and she and the two children were evicted. It took just under two months after the allegations became public for her to find herself here in Hove House. Incredibly, not only did she suffer the punishment of becoming homeless with her children, she had to stay in Hove House and pay the arrears off before she got re-housed. She had argued and tried to negotiate payment while remaining in the family home up until the day the council workmen had arrived and boarded it up.

I never got an answer to my questions about whether her husband had faced any criminal charges. In my fearful mind, the story was a loud warning, a red beacon flashing. Her ex-husband was living with family in a nearby village and had access to his children. She lived here in humiliation and was paying for more than just the monetary debts. She had been made to pay for her husband's crime. People whispered about her behind her back and sometimes did not hide it or bother to whisper, she told me. Often, her door, like mine, was locked shut, indicating her need to be alone. The sound of depression and anxiety resonated through the solid doors. I would lie in my bed, hers directly above me, the ceiling dividing and separating our personal darkness, powerless to do anything but let it pass. A day or so would go by and we would regroup around the chip pans and numbered cookers, chit-chatting about nothing.

Craig and I settled into a routine. With no language to tell me how he felt, or for me to explain what had happened, Craig just had to accept the change in his life. He was no longer running free with the boys and their friends or playing with the dog in a home environment. How he must have missed the company. It was home from school and locked in a room with me till teatime, with the occasional walk to the park. Cheap rolls of lining paper from the nearby Asda and crayons kept him amused for short periods. Only after Mrs Woods had finished her work and gone home could the children of Hove House congregate in the hallway and occasionally play marbles or other games. This didn't happen very often, as they mostly remained in their rooms, their parents too afraid of the wrath of Mrs Woods should they be caught.

By now, I knew the only way to deal with difficult situations: keep busy, get organised, show no weakness and cry in private. I would clean every day after Craig got picked up by the school bus. An old hand at the vinegar and newspaper window cleaning, I got into it with gusto. Habits like holding my breath while scrubbing the communal toilets came back instantly.

On one occasion, I was allowed to babysit for Janey. That was something we were not supposed to do – look after each other's children. Only husbands were allowed to take on that responsibility, which left Janey and me pretty much up the proverbial creek without a paddle. I don't know how she did it, but somehow Janey persuaded Mrs Woods to let me babysit so she could go to a wedding. The reality was that there was no wedding. She simply wanted a night out. It did make me laugh, and I admired her spirit and determination. She either had balls or felt she had nothing left to lose!

Mrs Woods left early on the Friday, entering Janey's room beforehand to say, 'Have a nice time at the wedding.' My heart was thumping as I waited for her to leave. Trusting no one, I feared one of the other residents – a pet – would tittle-tattle. Thoughts about where we could go if we were made homeless from a homeless unit rattled about my mind. Finally, Mrs Woods' car disappeared through the open steel gates and songs from Janey's radio could be heard as she got ready to go to her imaginary wedding.

Soon, I watched from upstairs in Janey's room as she too disappeared through the gates. Her black-and-white stripy batwing top swamped the short skirt she wore. It looked like she was wearing just a long jumper as her funny-shaped calves with tiny disproportionate ankles skedaddled into the distance. Sarah, Janey's daughter, and I sat watching the hired television in their room. I didn't have one, though Derek, Kerry's friend, had promised to track one down for me. Craig and Janey's son Mark slept as the screen flickered. Sarah and I talked in whispers; her hero was Boy George. Other company included tea and painkillers.

Janey had been given an adult pass for the imaginary wedding till the late hour of ten o'clock! Needless to say, she did not adhere to it. Mac-Mac checked in at ten. Opening Janey's door as I sat there, she popped her head in. 'I was not in here, Eileen,' she said.

'OK, Mac-Mac,' I replied.

'The door was locked and Janey sleeping, I assume,' she said.

I smiled at her. 'OK,' I said.

Our conniving was complete – the official story was to be that Janey's door was locked and Mac-Mac reported she had returned and appeared to be in bed. If questioned, I would need to conspire with that story. I was more afraid of betraying Janey than the establishment of Hove House, so it was no contest. Sarah climbed onto the top bunk and fell asleep. This was in the days before mobile phones and with no access to the porch phone I waited quietly for Janey to return.

Not long after midnight, half asleep with head in hand, I heard gravel showering the window beside me. Prising open the heavy sash window as quietly as I could, I hung my head out. Janey stood below with two other people. 'Psst! Eileen, come down and open your window,' she whispered up.

Heart thumping, I sneaked downstairs, checking to see if any lights shone from beneath the doors of the other residents' rooms. Only one was on. After creeping into my room, I closed my heavy door and ran to the window. As I pulled back the heavy, damp-scented curtains, I saw Janey's company was two males. She signalled frantically to me to lift the window, her arms jutting up and down like a Russian weightlifter.

Five minutes later, after the window had been opened, we sat around my table with a bottle of wine. Mick and Franny were the guests Janey had brought home with her. 'Portmahomack, that's where I am from,' Franny said. His hand extended and shook mine. Fascination silenced me; what a strange place name, I thought.

Janey's toes peeked through a rip in her black tights from her brown sandals. She had complained before she left she did not have another pair of shoes, never mind a black pair to match her bag. My feet were a size four to her bunioned eights. I did not own a brown bag either. However, coordinating seemed furthest from her mind; she was in full flow and unaware of my anxiety about anyone finding them in my room.

Mick, with his wild hair topping a long, battered, swinging leather trench coat, sang songs that much older men would sing, such as 'Please Release Me' by Engelbert Humperdinck. Memories of home lurked in the corner of my room. It was my mother's era.

From that night on, an unspoken deal was cemented between me and Janey. Once a week or fortnight, Craig and I would spend the night in Janey's room while she entertained in mine from after ten at night till six in the morning. Her depression door was shut less. We were both getting one over on the Establishment, our secret perhaps a source of medicinal defiance against the septic salt of humiliation of Hove House.

30

ILLumination

It was the end of 1984. No Orwellian coup had happened, although the miners' strike did bring passages from the book to mind. There was plenty to sympathise with elsewhere as well. Hunger and disaster had struck in Ethiopia. Everyone knew the words to Band Aid's single 'Do They Know It's Christmas', as it had become the fastest-selling record in UK history. The government had unbelievably refused to waive the VAT on the sales of the record-breaking single but public fervour, already angered by the strike, rose and they were forced to recant. It gave me a bit of hope that my despairing dystopian view of the future might not happen. There were unprecedented scenes of starving and dying children on our screens night after night. Who, indeed, was I to complain about my life? Voices from my own childhood whispered in my ear: '*Eat all your dinner, there's starving weans in Africa that would be thankful for that.*' Bob Geldof's iconic rant: 'Give us your money' was in stark contrast to Margaret Thatcher's battle cry of 'The lady's not for turning.' There seemed to be despair and anger everywhere, which made me feel that mine was insignificant.

Halfway through another mostly forgotten festive season, a surprise event came my way. Derek, the friend I had met through Kerry, had suggested a trip to Blackpool. 'You and Craig could do with the break,' he said. Slightly concerned that accepting this offer would mean I was

195

covertly agreeing to sex, I hummed and hawed till eventually I heard the words, 'I mean as friends; we can go just as friends.'

I liked Derek and did not want to hurt him or give him the wrong idea. Trusting no one was too exhausting and I remained optimistic about humanity. His proclamation of friendship was the green light I needed. Everyone always said what a lovely guy he was. Derek epitomised suburban middle-class geek chic before the stereotype even existed. Physically, he was gangly, bony and pale, his movements limp and gentle, with a smile larger than his face, which was round and framed with lank dark curls. '*Yes*,' I convinced my lonely self, '*what a generous and lovely offer. There are good guys in this world after all.*'

With the dreaded New Year just round the corner it was something positive to look forward to. The opportunity to enjoy company and have some time away from Hove House was certainly too good to turn down. Someone cared enough to ask me, want my company and respect my wishes. He didn't make me feel embarrassed.

We left on 28 December. Since he had dropped me off previously, and was well aware of my homeless situation, I allowed Derek to pick me up from Hove House. I had secured an official pass to go from Mrs Woods, and she had strangely approved. 'A good family,' she had said.

Considering she had only met Derek once to my knowledge, when he brought me an old record player, I wondered how she could make such a precise judgement. But I felt comfortable with my decision to go – everyone who mattered knew that we were going, so I felt a certain sense of safety.

We drove down to Blackpool in his father's borrowed Volvo. The Smiths – both of us having seen them at Barrowland's Ballroom – blasted from the cassette player. We discussed Morrissey, Spear of Destiny, Billy Bragg and many others. As we pulled into Coronation Street, where we were to stay, I saw Blackpool Tower for the first time. Looming over us, it was very close by and lit up the surrounding skyline. As we arrived in the dark, everything looked magical, with the lights and carnival-type noises.

Our self-catering apartment was a few streets away from the beachfront. It was on the second floor. Once we got upstairs, I put our luggage into one room and Derek took the other. We went out that night and wandered the streets, looking at the lights. Craig was tired but he stared saucer-eyed, stared and pointed at the sights around him. The smell of vinegar-splashed fish and chips wafted out of many a fast-food shop door. There were Kiss-Me-Quick hats and Blackpool rock in abundance. The stories I had heard were all true: these icons of the British seaside resort really existed. Breathing out hot air into the cold night, I felt tired but alive. Having arrived late, we settled for chips with sauce and agreed to return to the apartment for an early bed.

The next morning when I got up I found that Derek had been out and brought back breakfast. Craig had been very quiet the night before and had slept for most of the drive down. On our walk along the beach promenade he had seemed listless. I thought maybe he was dazzled by his surroundings and the lights. However, when he woke he was limp and tearful. Alarmed, as this was very unlike him, I told Derek that I wanted to phone a doctor. Craig lay in bed and stared blankly from red-rimmed eyes. A pale rash had appeared on his body. His nose was running and his forehead was hot.

Miles away from home, I was more than worried. Again, I asked Derek to call a doctor, but he was reluctant. 'It's probably just a cold,' he said with an unconvincing smile. I knew he thought I was being over-protective, but I also knew he was desperate to have a good weekend. I did wonder whether I was overreacting, but I persisted anyway. Eventually, just after three o'clock in the afternoon, the emergency doctor appeared. After examining Craig, he diagnosed measles. Given my knowledge of measles, I was frightened and upset. I knew it could cause more than deafness. The doctor left me a prescription for medicine that would reduce his discomfort and told me not to worry too much.

I apologised to Derek for the loss of the weekend. He bravely said it was OK. As always when I was worried or anxious, I wanted my own space. Derek had tried to comfort me, but he had become too touchy-feely and I shrank back from him. This had the opposite effect to what I desired. He became more tactile. I asked that he go to collect the prescription for Craig. I would not leave Craig with him or go out myself. I had tucked him up on the couch in the living area. Eventually,

Derek did go out for a while, returning with not only the prescription but several bottles of red wine and a video.

Craig fell asleep and I moved him into his bed. Guilt saw me chatter away to Derek and attempt to ease the situation by way of being good company. I had some wine, and we chatted as the video played in the background. Satisfied he had forgiven me, I kissed him on the cheek, thanked him and said goodnight. The atmosphere as I organised the empty bottles and glasses into the sink began to feel awkward, and I felt uneasy. Relieved to be in my room and breathing freely, I crawled into bed with Craig to soothe and comfort him. But there was also another reason I would not admit to myself. Admission would make it real.

Then it happened. The bedroom door opened after about half an hour. Derek crept over to the side of the bed and snuggled down beside us. He stroked Craig's curls and took my hand in his. I was tensing up but remained polite. 'Please come into bed with me, Eileen,' he begged. 'Please.'

My anxiety disappeared and in its place seeped anger that gave rise to a sense of revulsion and contempt.

'Please, please,' he begged, and then he began to cry.

'Derek,' I said coldly, refusing to look at him. 'We agreed and Craig is ill.'

He left the room and I could hear him weeping in the next room. An age-old anger and sense of disappointment kept me awake.

The next day, we travelled home early in a polite silence. Hove House for once had a sense of sanctuary. In my room with Craig in bed, I sank into my borrowed space and bed.

New Year passed with the same memories plus more. I never heard from Derek again. Weeks later in Hamilton town centre, I met his younger brother. 'That was not very nice what you did to Derek,' he said, chastising me. Speechless, I could not reply. '*What's the point,*' I thought, partly because I was so dumbfounded and partly because I thought it would not matter what I said. After all, he was a nice, gentle guy from a lovely, respectable family. I stood no chance!

31

Tell-tale heart

Our daily routine in Hove House continued as before. The years had not changed the institution or seen any updating of its principles or practices. On Tuesdays, my vinegar-soaked cloth wrapped round the wooden barleycorn twists on the hall dresser as if I had never left. Wednesday was my allocated washing day. On Thursdays, I scrubbed the toilets. We all had a pail, brush and mop that sat obediently in the corner of our rooms. The tools of our trade! We also had a cardboard can of Vim with a metal lid peppered with holes like a large salt shaker. This powdered cleaning material filled all the toilets and mop pails. Vinegar and Vim was the anaesthetising antiseptic for Hove House's humiliation.

My physical pain was anaesthetised by painkillers. My emotional pain, though unacknowledged, was also being controlled by the numbing of the painkillers and keeping busy. My nail biting continued, despite many adults over the years slapping my hands down from my mouth. Now when I see someone doing the same, I want to stop them by slapping them as I was taught. I can understand how others find the gnawing irritating. I had reverted to scratching myself, as my weight was dropping again. My heart would thump at night like the guilty murderer in Edgar Allan Poe's short story 'The Tell-Tale Heart', and I was certainly, as the protagonist in the story describes himself, suffering from 'an over-acuteness of the senses'. Unlike him, though, I *did* think

I was going mad, perhaps because he knew he was guilty of committing a crime and I felt I was guilty of allowing crimes.

Unaware of my pounding heart, Craig would sleep soundly in the dark room while his mother lay racked with anxiety and confusion. When the phone rang in the porch, it was a mocking reminder of our position. Although emancipation sounded like a condition, for me it was a condition I wanted to suffer from, and it was on these quiet nights alone in the dark that the unreachable ringing phone served to act as a trigger for me to make plans for escape.

I had learned that I could only rely on myself. I had to break myself free of this vicious cycle. I continued to hanker after a proper education and the pursuit of this became my focus. Revitalised with resentment and frustration, I secretly made an appointment with the local college while Craig was in school. Sneaking out to make phone calls from the red phone box at the end of the street and having a hidden joy alerted the ever-astute Mac-Mac that I was up to something. She would appear in my room and hoover, while taking the opportunity to question me. 'What you up to?' she asked, eventually giving in after dancing round the issue with me.

As devious and guilty as I felt, I was too scared to part with this information. I was terrified the magical plans I was making would somehow be ruined just by revealing them or, worse, Mrs Woods would be informed, I would be ridiculed and a phone call would stop me gaining entry. To ease the pressure of my guilt and to appease Mac-Mac, I promised I would tell her when the time was right. Fearing that she might inform Mrs Woods that something was afoot if I kept her at arm's length, I had to try to keep her sweet.

Mac-Mac's reaction to the situation floored me. She was the good cop in the good cop–bad cop scenario. She mulled over what I had said as I gathered up mine and Craig's dirty washing, then finally announced that the new family residing next door needed today, my wash day, to do washing as they were just 'settling in'. 'You don't mind, do you, Eileen?' she said, holding my gaze.

I knew she was challenging me and if I was in any doubt she followed up by provoking me further: 'I mean, her upstairs wouldn't want to hear you have said no.'

My heart skipped a beat and stupidly I reacted. Incensed and hurting, I threw my wicker washing basket to the floor, which resulted in my peg bag opening and the coloured pegs flying like plastic butterflies everywhere. Mac-Mac stormed out of the room and I stood and listened to her heels stomping up the stairs to the office.

Heartsick, I collected the red, green, blue and yellow plastic butterflies and dropped washing, then sat staring into space till my name was shouted from above. In the office, I stood like a guilty squaddie, legs slightly apart and hands behind my back. My chin was out to steady my trembling as I was briefly told that the council would be informed of my behaviour and that Mac-Mac was in shock after being hit by the flying pegs. Turning on my heel, I closed the door civilly and walked falsely confidently and purposefully down the stairs to my room. Back straight, shoulders back and no facial response. I passed two of the other female residents, whose heads fell down, afraid to meet my gaze. *Nothing in, nothing out.* I closed my door and plotted.

As I waited on the payback for my behaviour to arrive, my plans strengthened. I went 'food shopping'; the trip was really my college interview, which had been arranged on the phone. Pale faced with make-up as I walked up the avenue to the college, my strolling almost went to strutting in bright red brogues matching my lipstick. My tartan skirt and blazer from Oxfam and the piece of lace in my platinum hair like a cherry on an iced cake finished off my look. At the time, I thought how original I was, how un-'80s I looked. Of course, I looked typical Indie '80s, minus the shoulder pads. I began to feel a sense of something unknown to me, but it felt good. On poignant reflection, I realise it was that elusive sense of self and hope of a future I was feeling.

The interview went well. It was a course with five Highers – English (of course), Art (of course), Modern Studies (of course), Psychology and Geography. They would send me a letter to confirm if I had been accepted. It was embarrassing to have to explain to them as I was leaving that I lived in a homeless unit, but, as I had done when younger and in a children's home, I was upfront and blasé about it on the surface. I asked if I could phone to confirm instead of a letter being sent to my address. Noises of sympathy were made, but the interviewer convinced me to receive the confirmation by post, as I would need the letter as proof for a grant. Accepting this, I soon let my frustrations fade away as I headed home positive with plans and a future.

My punishment for the flying plastic pegs was to be dealt on the following Monday. On arriving home, I was informed by Mac-Mac, 'She's told me to tell you Mr Johnston will be coming in to see you on Monday.' Her eyes rolled upwards as she indicated her boss. Mac-Mac never apologised to me about the peg incident or the upcoming repercussions, but what she did next went some way to making up for it. She had obviously guessed that I was somewhere other than food shopping due to my attire. In a pre-peg conversation, she and I had been having a collusive talk about Hove House, Mr Johnston and her boss, Mrs Woods. I had my usual rant about how demoralised the women and families were living here. I mentioned all the money we handed over and questioned why we could not have our own bank accounts. I had unwittingly stumbled onto something.

'Remember that conversation we had about bank accounts, Eileen?' Mac-Mac now said.

'Yes,' I replied. Though I was very wary, afraid I was about to be set up, I knew I had to engage in this conversation.

'Perhaps someone should investigate the "bank account",' she said.

Turning to look her straight in the eyes, I didn't know then what she was implying, but I knew that whatever it was, it was serious. Mac-Mac was aware of the circumstances in which I had left the last time, so maybe she thought my mysterious behaviour and reluctance to share with her meant I was getting outside help and I still had contacts. I wished I did.

She became agitated. 'I will speak to you tonight, don't want to spend too much time in your room,' she said. After she left, I could hear her voice, louder than normal, talking purposefully to another woman.

Why would someone get you into trouble and betray you, then take you into their confidence again? Beggars can't be choosers, though, and while I could sense that Mac-Mac was using me, I needed to get out of here.

I didn't even know why I was still at the hostel, as I didn't have any rent arrears. Restless about the college letter I was waiting for, I felt desperate for my own address where I could receive private mail and pursue my dreams of a new start for me and Craig. My dreams consisted of getting off benefits and buying Craig clothes, toys and perhaps taking him on holiday – the joy of being self-sufficient. Material possessions aside, I also wanted to get some respect for myself, maybe get to university and build a career as a writer or a designer, anything in which I could be creative. The desire to never have to set foot in an establishment like Hove House again made the hunger in me almost a starvation.

Later that night, I lay on my bed turning unread pages as I waited for Mac-Mac to do her ten o'clock round. I had avoided Janey, afraid she would guess I was up to something. The more you feel you have to lose, the less you trust. Footsteps on the tiles indicated Mac-Mac was in the building. I listened as she went to each door and knocked, waiting for an answer to make sure people were in for the night. Locks on doors opened, murmured voices were heard, doors shut and the knock came closer, finally arriving at my door. 'Come in,' I said. I had not locked it.

The old heavy oak door opened. Mac-Mac came in rather than standing outside and closed the door behind her. Her habit of putting her hands in and out of her uniform began as she talked. Swinging my legs off the bed and standing up, I listened. As she was leaving, she put her hands in her pocket and drew out a piece of paper. 'You'll need this,' she said. Unfolding the piece of white paper, I saw a local phone number. 'It's the porch number,' she said. 'I'll "forget" to lock the porch door and call tonight as soon as I get home. Then the residents can say you got the number that way.'

I did not fully understand, and my look told her this.

'If you get caught, you can say you knew I had not locked the door because your room is next door to the porch,' she finished.

I was still puzzled and perhaps preoccupied by the information she had told me.

Exasperated, she said, 'You can say, or another resident can confirm, you asked the caller what number they had dialled and that's how you got the number.'

'Ah,' I said, as the proverbial penny dropped. The risk was that if I got caught, I stood alone, and I was already in trouble because of the same woman who was standing in front of me. I also knew she knew I would give the other women the phone number when I left, as I had last time. She was protecting herself. I did not give much thought to this behaviour; I was more than used to it. Outraged by the story she had just shared with me, I agreed and Mac-Mac left my room.

I bit my nails as frantically as my heart raced. Sitting by my window in the late summer light, I watched her heavy figure waddle out of sight. Lying on the bed, I waited, turning the pages of my book again. Within half an hour, the phone in the porch rang. Not hesitating, I stomped up the stairs in order to be heard, opened the glass door and answered. Anticipation tingled through me. 'Speak as though you don't know me,' Mac-Mac's voice instructed. I did so. When I replaced the receiver, I repeated the stomping back to my room, hopeful I was not overplaying it.

The next morning as the children were hushed and hurried out to school, Shona, one of the women, stood in her pinny and stared at me. It was evident that she knew I had answered the phone. I only hoped she would not say anything at least until I had utilised the phone for what I needed.

Monday morning saw me hand over part of my benefits for savings to Mrs Woods in the office; however, this time it was in the presence of Mr Johnston. Mrs Wood sat with the triangular-cut sandwiches that reminded me of the snobbery at Fernlea – today, I cut them that way myself. She left the room at his indication, after he had firmly stated that he had received a complaint about my behaviour.

I dreaded being left alone with him. Even the presence of Mrs Woods would have pacified me. I stood, fixated on the window catch. Like a Victorian patriarch, he said, 'What do you have to say for yourself, girl?'

'Nothing,' I replied. It was a stupid thing to say, but I did that often. My response to fear often made me dumb. People mistook it for arrogance. It was as if I was preserving energy to ward off an attack that took the power away from my voice box.

He stood up and moved beside me, stopping at my ear. 'Nothing,' he said. My ear tickled and my jaw set. He circled me, muttering. The phone rang, and he answered it and had a conversation. I did not hear a word he said. Mrs Woods knocking at the door was the next noise I remember. I was promptly dismissed. Although I felt a strong compulsion just to up and run, I had Craig to take care of and I was stuck in Hove House.

In the media, articles were beginning to appear about a horrific new deadly disease contracted through sex. The adverts showing gigantic icebergs with RIP etched into them scared me witless, what with my relationship with Joe, his drug taking and the event in Townhead Street. My worry would turn to anger and I tuned in to the hostility surrounding Margaret Thatcher being re-elected for a second term. It was easier to attach my fear and confusion to anything in the external world than to deal with what was really going on, even if I had a clue what that was, which I didn't. The miners' strike was in full swing. It was safer to attach my rage to their anger than to talk about my fears of AIDS, or, more profoundly, of death. Elsewhere I had read that, unbeknown to the miners, the government had learned from the '70s strike and stockpiled coal and petroleum in case the railwaymen came out in support of the miners. It was clever but underhand. This divide between the powerful and powerless resonated with me, particularly after the meeting I had just had with Mr Johnston. My rage fuelled my fight.

In the haven of my local library, I had found the phone number for Shelter, the charity set up to campaign for homeless people and better housing conditions. Mac-Mac had pointed me in their direction.

The first call took place when Mrs Woods was out at an afternoon meeting. Mac-Mac kept the other women busy as I sneaked into the porch and made the call. They were very sympathetic and angry about our phone situation and agreed to phone back only at arranged times. I organised these times with Mac-Mac.

The act of relating the story that Mac-Mac had told me incensed me further, as the reality began to hit me. I heard my voice steely and hurried as I told them of years and years of money going into a bank account which only two people, Mrs Woods and Mr Johnston, had access to. When the person from Shelter asked me, 'What happens to the interest on these savings?' the penny dropped about what Mac-Mac was implying. None of the residents had ever received any interest on their savings or the banked arrears money. I had asked the others privately and in an apparently innocent way to confirm the situation.

As I relayed the conditions in the home, such as up to six people living in one room, the way we were often humiliated while scrubbing toilets by Mrs Woods standing over us when we were on our knees, telling us, 'You have missed a bit,' and the paper slips required as passes to leave the building at night and weekends, I was panting with fear. The cat was really out of the bag and I had let it out.

In the phone calls that followed, I told them that we were only allowed to cook at certain times and that furniture came in and was stored and then taken away by Mrs Woods' husband. Mac-Mac had told me they distributed it to people connected to their church – Shelter was appalled. So was I when they asked if I would I speak to the newspapers. The adviser I was in touch with from Shelter informed me they had received several complaints over the years about the conditions and treatment in Hove House. From this I concluded that Mac-Mac had possibly set this situation up before.

Like a caged or cornered rat, I instinctively fought back and agreed to speak to the press. Shelter had promised to make sure I was protected. 'What can the council really do to you?' the man asked. 'We would find you a nicer place if anything happened.'

He, being on the outside and more experienced in these matters than me, remained calm and steady about the situation. Distress was my reaction, but it was mainly internalised. My vomiting returned, and I was a young woman with too many secrets. I was under a lot of psychological pressure and it was affecting my health. My diet largely consisted of prescribed painkillers. I had no idea that mental stress increased pain and that the two were connected.

The mood seemed to change in Hove House. No one spoke as easily. Perhaps it was my awareness of what might be happening that made me less willing to talk. Mac-Mac's nightly check-in visit was the only time we spoke in private. Our conversations were always interspersed with, 'And did you tell them that?', 'What about such and such?' She was hoping for early retirement, and I really began to fear for myself and Craig.

Mr Johnston appeared within a week of me making the first call. It was unusual for him to visit again so soon, and I vowed I would not go into the office while he was in the building. My door remained locked.

Less than two weeks after my initial contact with Shelter, Mrs Woods called me to the office. 'We have a nice flat for you, Eileen,' she said.

Picking at my nails and with my heart racing, I asked, 'Where is it?'

'Hamilton,' she replied. 'Get your coat, I'm taking you there myself after lunch.'

As I stood in the room that had become living room, dining room and bedroom for both myself and Craig, I was astonished by what seemed to be happening, and my thoughts were airborne like a juggler's balls.

When we pulled away from Hove House, I sensed the other women whispering in the kitchen. Mac-Mac would be there with them. Did they know what was going on?

Trees seemed to drive by me as I sat still in Mrs Woods' black-and-chrome saloon car. I was getting away and was not sure why. Mrs Woods remained tight-lipped about the flat but was overly pleasant, putting on the radio for me and asking if I was warm enough. The tension and unknown territory had the effect of making me scared. Where was she really taking me?

Eventually, we reached a scheme at Peacock Cross, near my old doctor's surgery. At least I would know these doctors, I comforted myself, while still questioning why this was happening so quickly. We drove round a maze of similar-looking streets. I was not aware they existed, tucked away behind main streets. Finally, one of Mrs Woods' shiny, black-patent square-heeled shoes covered the brake and we stopped. As she removed the keys from the ignition, she reached into her pocket and produced another set of keys. Two keys and a brown piece of card attached with string dangled in her hands. 'Well, come on then. Let's go and see.'

We had stopped at a traditional four-in-a-block flat. They were like the steel house I had lived in with my adoptive parents. I noticed the top left one had no curtains. I assumed correctly that this was the flat on offer to me. Unlike my childhood home, it was upstairs. The door was a side entrance, unlike the back and front doors of the bottom flats. There was an expanse of green lawn at the back. That pleased me. Each door I pushed open in the two-bedroom flat uncovered clean rooms. The flat was spotless. No signs of dampness or mould could be seen. As I went from room to room inspecting, I began to smile. There was no ripped wallpaper, broken tiles, cracked windows or stinking leftover carpets. Water-tight and windproof, it was basic but clean and in good repair.

We both walked into the middle of the living room, our feet clomping on the bare floorboards. 'Well?' she said.

Nodding my head, I looked around and back at Mrs Woods. 'Yeah,' I replied. 'I like it.'

She began to pass the flat keys from one hand to another before saying, 'You can't talk to the papers.'

Thinking I had misheard her, or maybe hoping, I stood silent and confused.

'No journalists or talking to Shelter,' she said.

Thinking on my feet at this unsurprising in retrospect yet at the time to me unforeseen order, I replied, 'OK.'

My meek agreement to this arrangement led to me being rewarded with the keys. 'You can move in as soon as you like,' she said.

As I locked *my* front door and returned to her car, she added, 'This week if you want.'

As I belted up to begin the journey back to Hove House, Mrs Woods handed me an envelope. It had been opened. Across the front was 'Motherwell College'. I pulled the letter from the envelope. Contained within the brief letter was the word 'Acceptance'. I had got on the course.

'Why did you not tell me?' Mrs Woods asked.

I did not reply.

'Were you afraid you would not get on the course?' she added. She had given me a ready-made answer to her own question. I nodded, though it was not the truth. I wondered if she would have given me the letter if I had refused the tenancy of the flat. The fact that my private letter had been opened before I received it was not mentioned. I was in no position to challenge that. Yet!

I sat quietly, picking my nails on the journey back to Hove House, but the words, phrases and thoughts in my head were clashing and drowning each other out. On one side I could hear '*Bribery, blackmail, and corruption*' and '*buying my silence*', while on the other side I could hear, '*Don't be a fool, you have Craig and yourself to think about.*'

I had already accepted the bribe. After arriving home and preparing dinner for Craig and me, my mind continued to race with confusion and guilt sweetened by the thought of escape from Hove House and the excitement of having a nice flat. By the end of the week, I was packing the little we had. My savings had bought carpets for all but the hall stairs from a local dealer. Two second-hand beds from the Hove House storeroom had been delivered, as well as a cooker. A small grant fast-tracked by Mrs Woods allowed a social security strings-pulled cheque to be sent to a second-hand furniture dealer who supplied and delivered a twin-tub washing machine.

On my leaving day the next week, I went to say goodbye to the other women and children. They had been avoiding me and I them. As far as they were concerned, I had jumped the queue, sold out and got lucky. Janey had kept her distance, though I had taken her into confidence about what had happened on my trip out with Mrs Woods. She would not be able to leave until she had cleared the family debts, and there was inevitably a sense of resentment that I had managed to get away. Although I understood that, the cold shoulder really hurt. However, there is no doubt now in my adult mind that any one of those women would have done the same without a second thought.

As we said our goodbyes and muted good lucks were shared, I slipped into each woman's hand a piece of paper. On it was the precious porch phone number. As my getaway taxi full of plastic bags, a mop pail full of plastic butterflies and cleaning material drove away from Hove House, I did the unadvisable. I turned my face to the back window. As I looked back, I saw a few hands still in the air waving. Guilt weighed me down, though the thought of privacy and a clean flat for me and Craig lifted me up.

Two weeks later, the local paper ran a story on Hove House. Shelter had sent secret cameras in to investigate and the issue of the bank accounts was strongly highlighted. My name appeared in the newspaper interview, as did my address, and my heart, like the tell-tale heart, continued beating loudly owing to unnecessary guilt. I had spoken to journalists and to Shelter. There was a certain sense of liberation in realising Mrs Woods and the others no longer had a grip on me and that they could not threaten me any more.

It was not long after the article appeared that all the residents were re-housed and Hove House was closed down. I thought that maybe some day I would bump into some of the women, but I hoped I would not see Mrs Woods or Mr Johnston again. I imagined him in a council office somewhere trying to explain himself. A sense of poetic justice being done placated my fear somewhat. At least I knew I would not be returning a third time!

32

Tools for Life

As we settled into our flat, I once again went on a cheap-wallpaper hunt at Asda. A pair of scissors, a dinner knife along with a kitchen table and chairs were my tools of the trade for wallpapering – necessity definitely being the mother of invention. A green branch pattern covered my bedroom walls. Pots from Oxfam with plants from Asda sat on my green carpet. Two brightly coloured garden pictures cut from a book and inserted into clip frames finalised my attempts at interior design. I fixed a brush pole from a hardware store in the bedroom cupboard to create an instant wardrobe and was feeling rather pleased with myself at my resourcefulness. Years later, I found an old notepad with the ditty I had originally pencilled on the wall before papering over.

Skimming
Stick plasters to cover all
Crumbling flakes from a wall
Suffering a condition really needing a bandage
The depth no doctor could possibly gauge
Plaster upon plaster, it will eventually fall.

This was me at one of my happiest periods. I felt self-sufficient. Kitchen knives doubled up as Stanley blades for cutting paper and tucking it into skirting boards, and as a screwdriver for putting in and taking out screws. Heels of shoes or any ornament that came to hand became a hammer. A multifunctional toolbox existed all around me. Craig's room was easy. Blue carpet, blue and white emulsion over the woodchip and a few Transformers and football posters cheaply turned it into a boy's room. A plastic dumper truck filled with toy cars sat in the corner making it 'his' room.

I took a risk and bought a second-hand black-and-white television from a local church jumble sale. With the metal-coat-hanger-as-an-aerial-trick, it worked. Two cheap black-and-red pull-out beds doubled as my living-room suite. Wobbly metal-framed shelving held several books and looked the part as long as you did not touch them. After having the luxury of using an automatic washing machine in many of the establishments and Bernadette's, I was now back to relying on a trusty twin tub; however, at least I did not need to use the bath and my feet. '*See the upside and get on with it,*' and I did. As the twin tub tucked away nicely under the bunker in the kitchen, it also filled an otherwise gaping hole.

What I could not source, make or magically materialise was a family – brothers and sisters, and in particular a mother. Home life seemed many, many years away. It was a memory that seemed not to belong to me. I could never admit to myself that I missed my mother, but I ached unwillingly for motherly love. To acknowledge this would be fatal. An emotional weakness I could ill afford. Neediness was scorned, something so human was deemed diseased, contagious and a flaw in one's character, at least that's how I felt, that's what I had learned. The saying '*Better to die on your feet than to live on your knees*' exemplifies this mindset. It fitted me perfectly. My search for my biological mother and a genetic understanding for Craig and myself had been put on hold till I could feel I would appear normal and make her feel proud of me. My fear of rejection and shame overruling the natural response to want to know, I promised myself I would finish college and resume my search.

Not surprisingly, my attempts at gelling relationships with others always seemed to fail. I initially thought that was down to me, but as I have grown older I realise this is not always the case. People unconsciously and sometimes consciously shy away from difficulties, they move on or your use runs out. Never being able to convey how I felt or not knowing how I felt exacerbated insecurities on both sides. One guy told me I was impenetrable, while another one said I was deep. I took these comments as slights against my character, and though they certainly weren't meant as compliments I know now they were the result of frustration. However, it never occurred to me to consider it might be them and not me who was at fault, if indeed there was a fault. Today, I would have retorted back and traded the words, 'So shallow and transparent.'

I started dating Mark, a guy I met through Kerry. However, when things moved on and it came to the crunch, as usual I felt dead inside. Like many woman I have spoken to since, I did the worst possible thing: I pretended and dug myself in deeper. There was no going back from that lie. The pleasure of adult sexual love was still lost to me. Although comforting, the final act itself remained mechanical and without resolve.

From another suitor, I acquired a kitten, to which I found it easy to show affection. Pebbles was the name I gave her. Being half Burmese, she was vocal and affectionate in nature. Animals like my aunt Helen's numerous dogs were easy to love. I borrowed them from time to time, even sending postcards on their behalf when my aunt and uncle went away – 'On holiday with Aunty Eileen' was the message I wrote. It reminded me of home and the love of animals that my adoptive mother and I had shared. It was as if I was trying to keep something alive of her, of a home – my fantasy rather than reality. Apart from the odd angry references made by my aunt now and again, my mother existed only in that unique filing cabinet called my memories. It was a filing cabinet full of frightful information, disorganised and dysfunctional, because no one wished to bear witness to it, and I in my aloneness did not have the capacity.

As August 1985 began, my hospital appointment arrived. On 3 August, I underwent a surgical procedure called a laparotomy. Craig had to go into overnight foster care, which wounded me more than the post-operative pain. I made it a condition it was only to be an overnight stay. The surgeon agreed.

On waking from the procedure, the surgeon told me I had adhesions and scar tissue. He asked me if I had ever had the coil fitted and I told him that I had. Nothing more was said. I wanted to go home.

'If you remain in pain, we may need to do a further operation,' he said.

'OK,' I replied. The discussions were brief and stiff. Privately, I made a mental note to check out any information at a library.

I left the hospital having signed a consent form to be let out early and, armed with more prescribed painkillers, I went home to wait on Craig's arrival from foster care. Only after he was home and my door closed did my hunched-up body relax. My anxiety at my young son having been in care resulted in us both snuggling up at night, back to watching stars from my window. I felt an incredible sense of shame: shame because I had no mother to care for him. I felt embarrassed that the doctors and nurses would feel sorry for me having no familial support for, as far as I was concerned, I didn't deserve their sympathy. I blamed myself for not getting help and saving her.

Cold steel clips held my surgical wound together. They pinched and hurt. It seemed that patients were no longer stitched together like an old teddy or rag dolly but clipped to fit like flat-pack furniture. It led to less scarring, the nurse had informed me.

After a few days of painkillers, I began to straighten up and stopped shuffling around like an old woman missing a Zimmer frame. I could now attend to education for both myself and Craig. Our lack of language to communicate and express our feelings was becoming increasingly distressing.

My own education was proving not to be without its problems. I could not go to college until Craig had been picked up for school, and I had to be back in time for him coming home. Thankfully, the college was sympathetic about my situation and allowed my incomplete attendance with a pledge from me that I was looking around for a sitter for Craig. Eventually, I discovered a partially deaf mother of two hearing children who agreed to take Craig after school hours. I paid her from my college grant.

With that hurdle bounded over, I found I was dealing with Ms Stanley again. Craig had been transferred to the new deaf unit and, as she had predicted, she had been appointed head of the unit, which was attached to the local secondary school. It was the result of new attitudes towards deaf children and their education. It was now deemed forward thinking for deaf children to be educated at a solely deaf primary that ensured no copycat behaviour of other 'handicaps', then integrated into a mainstream secondary. However, the old regime of Ms Stanley now ran the new progressive system, so only the surroundings had really changed. It was more of the same.

Craig's hyperactive behaviour was becoming a problem. His tiny sinewy frame could often be found racing around the secondary school playground, his blond curls bouncing free in all that space. The hearing aids he had been fitted with were discarded and flung across the playground. On one occasion, I was called to the office at college. Craig's school had phoned asking me to come as he had run away from school. Immediately, I ran from the college, apologising to my art lecturer as I grabbed my bag from class and went to the nearest bank. Extracting some money, I hailed a taxi and headed straight to the school.

The black cab sped past Strathclyde Park up through the centre of Hamilton and past my old school, Hamilton Grammar. Turning left at Peacock Cross, we headed along that long road with the familiar Philips Lighting factory. The secondary school towered in the skyline as my fingers fumbled for the money to pay the taxi. I slammed the door behind me, and it was barely closed before I was halfway across the playground. Mr Millar, the headmaster of the secondary school, was walking towards me with Craig by his side, his trousers covered in mud. 'Hello, Eileen,' he said. He smiled sympathetically at me, which relieved my tension. 'He is quite the sprinter, is Craig,' he said.

Nervously, I laughed. My relief and astonishment was brought to heel by Ms Stanley's voice, which sarcastically spat at him, 'This child needs a good smacking.' Then Craig began to indicate by slapping his buttocks and pointing to her that she had smacked him.

Nobody said anything. I did not understand that the politics of school territory and pupil possession gave Ms Stanley the educational authority over Mr Millar. Taking Craig's hand, I said, 'We should just cancel his seat today on the school bus. I will walk home with him.'

On the long but contemplative walk home, Craig swung his free arm as if he did not have a care in the world, but without a doubt I knew different. He had started biting his nails and wetting the bed. What could I do? His sitter had begun to gently complain to me about his hyperactivity and I'd had my own frights with him. The weekend before, I had been doing our washing in the twin tub, tongs in hand pushing the washed clothes into the spinner part of the machine, with steam from the boiling water dripping from my nose, when I noticed he had disappeared from the back garden. Just as I was drying my hands and panicking, I heard the front door. Standing there as I opened it was a young dark-haired boy just older than Craig, who panted to me, 'You need to come and get Craig.' The pair of us dashed down the street together. His pants continued: 'He won't come down. We have tried to get him down.'

Just at the end of my street, I saw a small gathering of people. Scaffolding surrounded the four-in-a-block building. Craig was at the very top and no workmen were to be seen. My downstairs neighbour, Pearl, was there, shouting and gesturing up at Craig. 'Get doon here, boy, or I will skud yer arse,' was one of the more polite statements she was making.

Terrified, I looked up at Craig; he beamed a smile and waved to me. He continued to climb, hanging on to the large rusty joints, which resembled arthritic ochre finger knuckles. I gestured frantically to him to come down, as I was used to not being vocal. Pearl's voice boomed upwards, 'Ya wee bugger ye, get doon here.' Flinging her cigarette on the street, she skelped her hand across her buttocks and pointed at Craig, beginning to laugh. 'That's a toe rag and a half.'

As Craig was encouraged by the attention he was getting, I knew it would be a job and a half to get him down. Ingenuity was needed, I realised, as the small horde of people stood around laughing and signing up to him. The other children danced about the front gardens, lapping up the event. Squeals of, 'He's gonna climb higher,' and, 'He's mental,' came from them.

Making eye contact with Craig, I lunged forward and began to climb. As I pulled myself up to the first set of wooden planks that was used as a walkway, Craig stopped dead in his tracks and his eyes expanded in disbelief. My puffing and panting, screwing my face up and scraping the wood with my fingers, pretending to struggle more than I actually was, had the desired effect. His head was shaking, indicating a no to me. His slender figure came down, I imagine, much faster than he got up.

As everybody clapped, Craig stood grinning at them before I whisked him sharply up the street to the safety and privacy of home. Once indoors, my attempts to relay my concerns to Craig were limited to our homemade signs, and I banged my heart with my hand and wrinkled my face to show fear and worry. His large curls sprang around as he bent his head sideways and then reached his arms out and pursed his lips to offer me a kiss and cuddle. As we hugged intensely, with his head buried into my breast, I wiped away a tortured tear that had escaped. A knot of complete frustration born through love left me with a heavy feeling of impotence as his mother. On reflection, I am relieved my mother was spared the sight of my own escapades of climbing trees, running over garage roofs and 'dreeping' out of windows and down walls.

The school incident coupled with the scaffolding antics led me to seek out information on sign language. Craig had indicated to me that he still had to sit on his hands at school. 'It encourages their voice development,' was Ms Stanley's response when I challenged her about this. Very few parents at that time would question their child's school or teachers. It was the same syndrome that protected doctors and other professionals. Their word was Law, and they closed ranks. I found this doubly hard because of the hostility she obviously harboured for me and also as it was a specialist education unit. Who the hell did I think I was, challenging this? I had ideas above my station surely? I knew that in their eyes I was an upstart.

In the local library, I had seen a poster giving details of a deaf club for adults in Hamilton, so I attended in the search for information.

As I sat and watched pool being played, cards and conversations all intertwined with rapid hand signs, I felt hope. It was truly fascinating and inspiring. Though I had no idea of anything that was being said, I could see the communication flowing freely and easily. One of the women there was employed to oversee that the club ran smoothly and to liaise with the authorities. She was hearing. Her name was Sonia. Her father was deaf. After asking her several questions about education and deaf communication, she told me about a school in Edinburgh. 'Donaldson's, it's called. Total communication is the system they use,' she said.

Total communication, it seemed, was a system that aimed to utilise all the non-oral faculties we use to communicate, such as facial expressions, hand signals and body movement. She said it was known as 'non-manual communication'. British Sign Language or signed English was used. I devoured this information. I told her that Craig had indicated to me that he had to sit on his hands and about Ms Stanley's response.

She gestured to a young man to come over and join us. While she was signing to him, she also spoke for my benefit: 'This lady's son is deaf; he is attending the Deaf Unit.' The lad looked quickly at me and back to Sonia. I noticed how he watched her hands, face and lips, while flicking his gaze back and forward between us both. That's what Craig did: visually vacuuming up the information being imparted, gaining tone and inflection by the movement and nature in which it was imparted. His head nodded constantly as she spoke. He was obviously agreeing with her.

When it came his time to speak, Sonia interpreted for me. However, he made it so clear by his signs and facial expression that I picked up most of what he was saying. 'I hate Ms Stanley,' he said, twisting his face up. Then he placed his hands under his buttocks, quickly removed them then wagged his finger and sheepishly placed them back again. 'Ms Stanley made me do that for years, and we all got smacked,' he said. 'I learned sign language as a teenager in Glasgow,' he added.

As I thanked him, he read my lips and reached out to shake my hand and put his hand on my shoulder. He then rejoined his company and began rapidly telling them who I was. Heads nodded in agreement. I did not need to be a signer to know they were talking about their shared experience under Ms Stanley.

Sonia went to get me the phone number of the school as I watched their conversation, transfixed by both the ease of their communication and what they were saying. I left and walked home in the dark to my cousin's to pick up Craig, full of anger and resentment but with a new-found determination. Within a week, I had phoned Donaldson's, had an appointment to visit there and another appointment with the local education authority. I needed them to sanction and fund Craig's placement at Donaldson's.

Two weeks later, Craig and I went to visit. Craig was still in his sixth year, and looking at yet another move. The school was a huge stately building in Edinburgh's Haymarket area not far from where we got off the train. The school grounds were extensive and we later found out it had a swimming pool. The large black railings and wall ran the length of the street. We walked through the gates and up the long drive. As I sat in the office of the school psychologist, Dr Maloney, whose wife was a teacher at the school, Craig stretched up on his toes to look out of the window and watch the children who had appeared outside on one of the lawns. I watched him as he watched the children with intensity. The back of his head remained still as he watched.

Dr Maloney and I chatted for a while. I always felt that I was punching above my weight when dealing with authorities or professionals. Also, I mostly assumed that educated people were clever. They had power and I assumed I had none. That's what I feared most. Then as in later life, I realised I felt I was judged by my accent and the clothes I wore. More deeply, though, I felt and feared that they could detect my past crimes. Among these I included my violent alcoholic home life, the children's homes, lack of education and the dreaded crime of Urquhart. All my faults and failures! However, looking back I realise that I dealt mostly quite well with these situations, always doing my research, being well spoken and ready with questions.

'Let's take a walk outside with Craig, Eileen,' Dr Maloney said. The architecture of the building was beautiful, and as we walked through long corridors and past high windows I learned all about the place, its ghost stories and history. It had been gifted to Edinburgh with the stipulation that it was to be used only as a school for the deaf.

Dr Maloney signed to Craig. He opened his hands and spread them around to indicate the building. Then he banged his two closed fists side by side, giving the school its sign name. Craig nodded up at him, understanding instantly, and made the sign several times to himself as we ventured outside. He then stood unusually shyly at the side of the lawn as Dr Maloney and I chatted about the problems of lack of language at an early age. I forget most of what was said, other than his words, 'He will settle down once he has full communication and a community, I am sure.' These were the words I had longed to hear. I felt ashamed as I welled up and tears fell from my chin. As usual, my throat ached from trying to hold them back. Hope had elicited them.

One of the teachers had signed to Craig to join her and the other children. He looked back at me for reassurance, and I nodded. Tentatively, he walked towards them. I watched him as Dr Maloney patted my shoulder. I apologised for my tears. I was watching my wee son being vulnerable and overwhelmed by this occasion. Fifteen minutes later, he was running around, stopping every now and then to watch the conversations.

Dr Maloney and I shook hands when it was time to leave. 'I will put together a report for the education authority as soon as possible, presenting the case for Craig to attend here,' he said. He gave me a copy of a book he had written about the psychological research he had completed on deaf children. I was grateful and full of hope, but by now I was also exhausted and racked with abdominal pain.

My friends, the painkillers, took the edge off, and we headed for the train home. Craig sat making the Donaldson's sign on the train as it rattled on the line from east to west. I took it from this that he approved. Other passengers stared. People always did, fascinated by our signs. Although our conversations allowed for privacy, because no one knew what we were saying, sometimes it irked both of us to be constantly watched. For him, though, this would be his life-long experience.

'He is just touting for business,' Ms Stanley said. This was in reference to Dr Maloney and Donaldson's. How she found out, I don't know.

It was several days after the visit. Perhaps Craig had been signing Donaldson's and she recognised it. I had learned during my visit to Donaldson's that when Ms Stanley had started out as a teacher of the deaf she advocated sign language. I don't know what had happened to change her mind. The teachers at Donaldson's appeared to have a certain amount of disdain for her. That was about to be returned. Ms Stanley phoned me to ask what I thought I was playing at, saying, 'I'll bet the red carpet was out for you.' Her bitterness worked. I was on edge and had severe panic over my decision.

Within two weeks, I found myself in a meeting with social workers and educational authorities. Ms Stanley's disapproval was acknowledged and dismissed. It was agreed that Craig could start at Donaldson's as soon as possible. My joy was tethered somewhat by the fact that he would have to go initially as a boarder. This would be reassessed in six months' time. As I walked home from the meeting, I felt torn. '*You will be giving your son a good chance at education,*' numerous professional voices including Dr Maloney said in my head. The vision of the young deaf people at the club all nodding in unison to indicate their resentment of Ms Stanley reappeared too. But I did not want my son to go away from me, and the reassurances I'd been given about him getting a '*better education*', being among '*his own kind*' and coming home '*every weekend and for school holidays*' weren't enough.

Eventually, the inevitable decision was made when I managed to get the school to agree for me to come with Craig for the first week. I was so terrified about what might happen to him that I had to acknowledge it to myself. By going with him, I was trying to show Craig, or more importantly those who would be around him, that Craig had someone to protect him, unlike my own situation as a child both at home and in the children's homes. I had convinced myself if any Urquharts existed in the school, a child with a protective parent would warn them off. He would not be like me – a sitting target.

Full of positive plans for me and Craig, I decided to write a letter to the Salvation Army asking for any information they had on my birth.

As I posted the letter in the red post box, it dropped to the bottom with a quiet landing that told me finding my history had just gone from a 'to do' list in my head to a 'wait and see' pile.

My aunt had asked that Craig and I stay at our own home this Christmas. That we did, without question. On Christmas Eve, wrapping the presents up for Craig, I felt so alone. Superman pyjamas were among the gifts retrieved from the back of my makeshift wardrobe, also a wigwam and a Scotland football strip. He had hung his stocking on the handle of the cupboard that housed the electricity box in the living room. On our shaky bookshelf sat Santa's glass of milk and a carrot for the reindeer. After wrapping his presents, I stuffed the stocking with a Superman watch, gold-wrapped chocolate money and the obligatory fruit, which was an easily peeled satsuma and not the traditional orange. It took me back to all my own miserable childhood Christmases. Dropping all the change I had into the sock, I hung it back up. Sitting back, I smiled through my tears at the pile of presents that sat there awaiting Craig and cheered up at the thought of his face and the magic of his night dreams being of excitement and surprises. His expectations and joy were my King Canute: they held back the threatening tide for a while longer.

On Christmas morn, I lay awake in silence till eventually I got up and made a cup of tea, the colourfully wrapped presents still waiting patiently on the chaos that was Craig to descend on them. Twice I had to wake him from his sleep, and then I had to bathe him from his bed wetting before we entered the living room. The silence that ensued was broken only with the sound of ripping of paper and his expressive eyes and mouth. Together we built his wigwam, with him flinging poles in my direction while running around in a Superman pyjama top with a bow and arrow. The next memory I have is sitting with him at the table eating dinner.

That New Year I don't remember, perhaps it just passed me by, perhaps I slept through till 1986 and missed the dreaded bells of another Hogmanay.

With another festive season past, we were now facing Craig's start at his new school in Edinburgh. I went with him for the first week, which went well, and I hardly saw Craig. He slept in a small dorm with three other boys. From the steps of the large double entrance doors, I watched him play on the lawn, running free and splashing and dashing about the swimming pool. I read quietly in my room as he left to go on outings without me; I had conflicting feelings of hope for him and intense fear for myself of losing him. However, I was backed into a corner due to the situation with Ms Stanley and felt I had no choice.

When the week was up, we went home together. I dreaded the following Monday when the taxi would come and he would return to the school without me. I had received a book on basic sign language and a video. I did not have a video player at home but was too embarrassed to say so. We had learned the alphabet and spent the weekend writing words and spelling them out with our fingers. The excitement of having a language together was the sticking plaster on my grief. We wrote words on paper and stuck them on furniture, carpets, beds and anything else we could. Then I would gather them all up and hand them back to Craig one by one as he spelt them out and put them in their right place correctly almost every time.

I lay awake watching him as he slept on the Sunday night. He had crawled into my bed with crayons and paper. I left him there. Unashamedly, I needed the comfort of his closeness. His little bag had been packed and sat at the top of the stairs; new socks, pants and T-shirts filled it. He had his uniform laid out on his bed. His bedroom door remained closed. I put a few of the drawings we had done together that weekend in the bag and a page that contained only a few words: 'Be good, I love you, from Mum'. Kisses in criss-cross fashion adorned the bottom of the page. I hid it inside a T-shirt, imagining how his face would light up when he found it.

That little black bag sat there like an unwanted guest in the house. Each time I passed it, it said to me, 'You are going to lose him.' As he slept, I ran my fingers gently through his hair, straightening out his curls for them to jump back into place again. My belly muscles ached, then my throat. Eventually, I cried. My weighty tears fell one after the other, my nose began to run and I sat up to rock myself. My pain was physical as much as anything else. I never knew if my mother had felt anything like this. I had never witnessed it if so. My pain was heightened by my aloneness. However, I would have been so ashamed if anyone had witnessed me in this state.

Craig left the next morning, with me smiling and waving. My heart had missed several beats when the horn from the taxi sounded. He clambered into the back of the car to sit next to the woman employed to care for him on his journeys. I felt I had lost my son to experts when he attended the deaf unit. Parental input was discouraged. They knew best. I felt angry he had to go away for a better education. I hated the deaf unit for not allowing sign language. He had to go away because he was deaf! I raged to myself. I had no one to share any of this with.

Through some basic signs, we had made a pact that every day at three o'clock when he finished class I would open the living room window, kiss my hand and blow the kiss eastwards. It was to reach Edinburgh and fly in a window to land on his cheek.

The deadness I felt anaesthetised my anger and sadness. The taxi disappeared round the corner with Craig waving and blowing kisses back to me. He was seven, full of love, hope and innocence.

33

One step forward, two steps back

With Craig away at school, I could attend college as I should have been. However, I was suffering from escalating exhaustion and in constant pain. Determined to see it through in the hope all would get better, I popped the pills, put my faith in the doctors, waited on hospital appointments and carried on.

I had made few friends at college. Throughout my life, I have always been able to walk into a room and chat with that wonderful facade face of 'I am all right', but I could never really make sincere close friends, shying away in case they discovered the truth. I have since discovered this is not uncommon for someone with my background. In fact, it's the norm. Most of the time, if not all, I was not aware of my self-protective behaviour. I had an old head on young shoulders and was vulnerable, perhaps more so because people either thought I was strong and coping or didn't care if I was. My dates or scarce relationships never seemed to fulfil me, though I was loyal and giving. Fear controlled how close I would get, yet a relationship was the one thing that could enrich my life now Craig was away most of the week. I still believe, given the way society was back then, had I spoken of what Urquhart had done to me, with no support round me, I would not have coped.

Over the course of the previous year, I had met several guys, but my relationships with the opposite sex remained very confusing and frightening for me when it moved up a level. This, though, you would never have guessed! To some of the outside world and my peers I seemed assertive, aware. I was almost the epitome of 'fake it to make it', though I never made it. Frozen fear, my protective backbone, plus a deflective sense of humour, set me apart. Sexual relations were never discussed with friends, though I did ascertain from conversations we had after a few drinks that several of our company saw sex as a pleasure. My experience always stopped short. In a fantasy it was pleasurable, romantic and exciting. In reality, though, my body would freeze – it was grubby, mostly painful and I was useless. I had never heard of a condition called vaginismus, and nor would I for many decades. Sadly, it seems neither had the gynaecological doctors or consultants. 'If I knew then what I knew now,' is my sad reflection on the benefits of hindsight and information.

My body was certainly paying the price of years of stress. Eventually, I had to go back to the doctor, as I had not heard from the hospital. He wrote to the hospital requesting an emergency appointment for me. I was a guilty queue jumper. By now, I was doubled up in pain and taking far too many painkillers each day. Pain was controlling my life, and I started to crush the pills up so they would get into my system sooner and bring some relief. It became a roller coaster of pain endurance, then relief.

I was in such a bad way again that the consultant at the hospital booked me in immediately. Devastatingly, I was halfway through my exams. I had sat my English exam high on painkillers; I don't even remember it. But I was past caring about college, as I had to organise for Craig to spend two days at the weekend with foster carers. Again this caused me a great deal of grief and anxiety.

Being in hospital did not frighten me; in fact, I enjoyed the company and camaraderie on the wards. I was in a six-bed ward in Monklands Hospital in Coatbridge. Still smoking, I got friendly with the smokers in the room, which included most of the other patients. Down the corridor there was a TV room that was also the smoking room. It's incredible now to think a communal place existed for shuffling slippered patients and addicted staff in a hospital. The room was always busy and thick with smoke. You never needed to ask where the room was in the sterile environment; even as a smoker I could smell its mix of stale and fresh nicotine. It was the hub of the wards. Every surgical war wound and medical condition was discussed – what doctor did it, when and where, and there would always be a horror story about an operation that had gone wrong. There commenced a no-holds-barred competition; no body part was off limits! The game was always won by the most horrific account.

As always, I asked what I thought were the right questions about my condition, hoping to appear sensible and of sound mind. It was explained to me that they would remove my right ovary, as it was stuck to the back of my womb, and other adhesions. The medical title of the procedure was salpingo-oophorectomy. Just pronouncing it in the smoking room won me brownie points.

That night, high on painkillers, I wrote a poem from my hospital bed. The consultant had informed me that I might eventually have to come in for a hysterectomy, as the operation I was currently scheduled to undergo was considered a minor procedure and might not be successful. The poem was called 'Fake Fur'. It was as much figurative as it was literal. Physically I would be different; however, the implication was clear: I would finally become the fake I already felt that I was. A cheat, an imitation! That was how I felt about myself. The poem was angry and revels in a loathing of victimhood, sounding almost triumphant that I felt my femininity was being destroyed. Having no idea what sexual pleasure felt like, I did not know what else to do or who to speak to. What was wrong with me?

Fake Fur
50/50 chance of success
Of the minor succeeding.
Failing that
It's a major
Wrench from my body.
My femininity tore out.
Surgically removed

My cave of protection
Cut out – my beginnings
And the chance of others
Scrapped shell like, empty.

The mannequin that is me
Will look complete
But there's more to the saying
'Empty feeling in the pit of your stomach.'
Origins of man, stripped
Of my womanhood
Preserved in a pickle jar
For medical use.
To be thrown away in a steel bucket
And incinerated
Like spoiled meat in a slaughterhouse.

The consultant I had seen several years ago when I started to have abdominal problems had apparently written in my files that I was suffering from pelvic inflammatory disease. PID, according to him, was caused by too much sexual activity in the lower classes. I was horrified and deeply, deeply ashamed when I discovered this. Reading medical books alone in the library should have been banned back then! The descriptions were dry and clinical with no room for sensitivity. However, the more I read, the more I wanted to read. I began to think of the possible hidden infections I could have caught from an old man like Urquhart.

The most committed smoker in the room, Alice, had befriended me. This was due to both of us having disturbed sleeping patterns. Two nights before our operations, we had talked into the small hours in the smokers' room about families and dissatisfaction with our lives. I remember her telling me she had wanted to travel and work abroad, but she had got pregnant and never left Coatbridge.

The next morning we all showered as ordered, regimentally took suppositories and had our pubic regions shaved. It was called 'prepping'.

Like Christmas turkeys, we lay there passive and bald, waiting to be surgically sliced. A blue tablet was dished out to each of us – a pre-op relaxant. By the time the uniformed orderlies had come to take me down to theatre, a paper hat and slippers had been slipped onto my sleepy body. All that was missing was the tinfoil.

My smoking friend Alice waved sleepily as I disappeared from the ward on the trolley. Waving back, I heard her say, 'Good luck, see ye when ye git back.' The rattle of the trolley, plus the checking of my name band on my wrist filled the time till we got to the theatre. My attempts to count all the lights on the ceiling were interrupted by crashing into lift doors and the chatter between the orderlies and from other passing trolleys. Double doors with round windows opened; waiting for me was the anaesthetist who had previously visited the ward.

'Hello there,' he said.

Smiling, I replied in a monotone, 'Hi.' I wanted to get up and leave but was sleepy and had gone beyond the point of no return.

'Just going to put this into the back of your hand,' he said.

I said nothing.

Ripping open a sterile bag containing a needle he said, 'You will feel a cold scratch.' He tapped the back of my limp hand. 'Count back from ten,' were the next words he said. I managed to get to seven as a cold liquid travelled like mercury and filled the vein in my arm.

'Give me my sandal back,' I heard my own voice as I came round. A vision flashed in my head of climbing up the heavy metal headboard of the hospital bed.

'Hi, Eileen, we were worried about you,' my smoker friend's voice came from the side of my bed.

I heard my own moaning and scream then blacked out. My next memory was rolling around the bed mumbling and drawing my knees up. I was in agony. A doctor appeared at the side of the bed with an injection; the pain quickly disappeared and Alice stood in pyjamas at my side. By now I was aware I was in a side room out of the communal ward and on my own. 'Why am I here?' I croakily asked Alice.

'Don't you remember?' she replied.

Shaking my head, I continued rolling and moaning in the bed.

'You were screaming and climbing up the bed frame,' she said, then coming closer to me she whispered, 'They had to remove you.' The vision of that and the bizarre words 'Give me back my sandal' came back to me. Then Alice bent over me, took my hand and said, 'I know what's wrong. I know by what else you were saying.'

Though I was engulfed in agony and the drugs were disconnecting me from feeling the full force of my surgical pain, I knew instantly that my behaviour had revealed to someone my Urquhart past. My terrified eyes met hers and I saw recognition in them. My heart did not beat. I passed out.

The sound of paper being rustled was the next noise I remember. My consultant stood reading my notes at the bottom of my bed. Tears slipped from my eyes. I could not stop them even though they were unwanted and made me feel ashamed. 'Why did you not tell me it would be as bad as this?' I cried.

'Because you would not have come in for the operation,' he replied.

It felt like someone had cut me open, attacked me with a cheese grater and stitched me back up again.

'That bloody coil, it should be bloody banned,' he said angrily, and he threw my notes down. They scattered onto the floor. As a nurse scurried around, picking them up, he asked me, 'When did you get it fitted?'

I told him.

'Did you ever have any problems?' he asked.

'Yes,' I replied.

'Do you know they get paid for every one they fit? Bloody wrecks women's insides and causes lasting internal problems,' were the lines of his continuing tirade.

All I managed to say was something like, 'I thought I was being sensible with all the media scares about the pill. I did talk to the people I was told to talk to. I did research.' I was still leaking the odd tear and wishing I could curl up. I lay flat and helpless.

'I am sorry,' he said. 'We removed the right ovary from the back of your womb and there was scar tissue everywhere, stuck onto your bladder.' He squeezed my arm as he left the room. His eyes still blazed.

I received pain relief throughout the night. Drugged, alone but still in pain, I never saw my smoker friend again. The next day she was gone, and I felt my secret was safe. How close I had come to revealing my crime, I did not really know, as I had been drowning in anaesthetic and driven by physical pain. My thoughts turned to the immediate situation and I began to feel the familiar stinging of metal clips in my wound.

Two days later, my hand had swollen up and the tissue had hardened around the area where the needle was inserted that fed the drip of saline and antibiotics into my weakened body. A phone call had been put through to the nurses' desk. It was Craig's foster parent. Craig, too, had been up all night complaining of toothache.

'Who is his dentist?' the nurse asked me.

I told her. When she left to pass the information on, I cried into my pillow, my shoulders heaving. I had failed my son. He needed me and I was not there; I could not comfort him. Visions of him crying during the night tortured me as I sobbed. I had also failed to get it right in my research of sensible family planning.

The next day, my cousin Lena came to visit me. She had trained as a nurse. As we discussed the situation clinically, I put my decision into action. At the end of visiting time, I announced I was signing myself out. 'Craig has toothache,' I said to Lena.

We walked together to the lift and along the maze of corridors then out to her car. I was hunched up, with her arm supporting me, and she carried my pain medication. We had been close as children. I missed that. My secrets, circumstances and guilt separated us now, but I was grateful for her visit and subsequent drive home. I wore a cardigan she had knitted me. It was beautiful: baby blue, like a dress I had worn on a night I had gone to the Charleston Disco in Bellshill. She had knitted a matching hat. Though I had thanked her, it was not enough. Perhaps the cardigan represented what we could not say to each other about the significant events that had occurred in our lives. Thanks was not enough, but I could say no more – I did not know how to – nor could she.

We collected Craig on the way home. As I entered the foster house in

Bellshill, the foster mother suggested it was OK for Craig to stay there a while longer. 'He is awfully boisterous, Eileen,' she said, putting her hand on my hunched shoulder. 'We will bring him over tomorrow if you want. Go home and sleep.'

I refused. Craig's arms were round my neck and kisses shared. I smelled the dentist from him and noticed a dark hole in his mouth where a tooth had been.

By the time I got home, I was nauseous, in great pain, but glad to be home safe with Craig. Fear had driven me to make that decision. That night, Craig told me he had been smacked at the foster home. As he slept, I knew I would have to make new decisions for us. My disappointment at not being able to do all my exams resurfaced, and I decided to contact the college and discuss next year, to see what could be salvaged. I would not give up! My education was important, probably more important now than it had been when I was attending many schools and dreaming of escaping the children's homes to become something, somebody. Craig's education was particularly important. As a deaf person, what did the future hold for him? I worried. I had to set an example. It would be harder for him than me, so I had to lead the way. I had to create something good for us. Also, our communication together and Craig's ability to interact with the world was a driving force in my quest. How could I get the best from our situation? First, I would have to strengthen my resolve and pull my socks up.

Craig would be away at school, so I did not need to slog away with the twin tub and do any clothes washing, which was just as well as I could barely stand for the first few days. Pearl, my next-door neighbour, brought me bread, milk and other basics for the first week; she worked on the local grocery van. Her oldest son did a weekend shop for me. It took me several painful shuffling and drugged weeks to recover.

34

Right under your nose

At some point during that summer, Pearl popped in. She would sometimes do that, bringing her 'wee bottle' with her. This time it was for another reason. 'Eileen, Eileen,' she called, her voice searching for me. 'Have you heard?'

I came out of the kitchen, having put the kettle on.

'What is it?' I asked.

'Walter has been found deid,' she replied.

'What?' I said. I ran to the window to see a black car outside. Walter was my downstairs neighbour who lived with his sister. According to Pearl, Walter and his sister had lived there since the four-in-a-blocks had been built. He only left the house to go to Pearl's grocery van. He would stand, his hair long and greasy, not speaking to anyone in the grocery queue. No one had apparently seen his sister for decades. I had never seen her.

Pearl sat her wee bottle on the kitchen table and sat down. I gave her a small glass. 'Oh shite,' she said. 'I have left my fags in the hoose, be right back.' She disappeared to get them. It was over an hour till she clumped back up my stairs, returning with them. 'You'll never believe this,' she said, screwing the wee bottle top off. 'The sister's bowdie is in there. She hus been deid for years.'

'What?!' I said.

'Aye, been deid fer years, that's how nay bowdie hus seen her.' Pearl sat

233

there, her yellow hair showing several weeks of overgrown roots, striped like a skunk. When she left, she took a tumble down my hall stairs. She was mumbling about her own mother being in her 70s, living in the street all her life and never knowing about the dead sister. With Pearl up from the heap she had fallen into at the door, I began to become anxious. With my life, my movements and behaviour subject to the scrutiny of the social work microscope, either by being recorded or discussed, I found this news incredible. That night, lying in bed alone, sleep would not come. My thoughts kept creeping to the vision of the female body that had been possibly in the room directly below me all this time.

Pearl's son Terry came visiting the next day. He often brought records of the latest Punk band to show me. Being of the second-generation Punk era, it was Thrash Metal bands such as Slayer, Metallica and Megadeth he had proceeded onto. Though this was not the era or music that I enjoyed, the company filled my emptiness.

'Did you hear the news?' he said, as he walked towards my record player with a new record. 'Wait till you hear this.'

With my travel money refund from the college, I had managed to buy a stereo encased in black wood with a glass door. With a plan in mind, I picked up a second set of speakers from a charity shop and wire from the ironmongers in Hamilton. By the end of that night and with a pair of scissors and Sellotape, I had wired up the second set of speakers in my bedroom. This meant I did not need to lie awake listening to the chaos in my head or the silence outside it. Falling asleep to music was a comfort.

'Yeah, the news,' I said. 'Your mum told me last night about Walter's sister.'

'The sister is going into a home; she's no right in the heid,' he said.

'What?!' I replied.

It turned out that Walter had lived there with two of his sisters. One had died many years ago. They informed no one of her death and kept her body in her bedroom.

As the gossip raced and raged in the street, I felt frightened. It seemed like I was living in a Bates four-in-a-block motel. Within a week, the gossip had moved on, but I still lay afraid of my nightmares.

The repugnant thought that I had been only separated from a dead body by wood and plasterboard ate away at me. People could live their life surreptitiously in society, I realised. It never occurred to me that this was how I was living with my past secrets, for they were as yet unrevealed. Perhaps that's what was scaring me most – the echoes of how easily people go missing, disappearing into the night and their absence going unreported.

Then it came, coincidentally as I was to discover on my birth mother's birthday, the awaited letter from the Salvation Army. My mother's name and date of birth, which I already knew from the copy of my birth certificate I had seen, was about all they could give me. Only her home address in Possilpark at the time of my birth and my exact place of birth was news to me. The Fraser of Allander Home in Cleveland Road in Glasgow's west end was where she had lived for the last four weeks of her pregnancy till she gave birth at a hospital called Homelands, also in the west end. All secrets ultimately come to light.

The news of a possible grandmother for Craig was far too complex to explain to him, even if I had had the language to express it. It would also have been premature of me to discuss it. I put the letter away, not yet ready to take action on it. How could I explain all that background to a child anyway? But I knew I would have to one day. My sister Cathleen had grown up with no knowledge of being adopted. Yet we all knew and assumed she knew. Life seemed like a patchwork quilt: threads connected us together, but not necessarily the same threads, and how could we know what we did not know?

I was not ready to rock that boat. Craig was just settling down to his new school routine. For the first time, he was getting homework and I had put an alphabet poster on his wall, which we would both go round signing the alphabet and the objects contained within the 26 pictures. All news was good from the school. He was popular and enjoyed sports they said, though he hated his hearing aids. I had so many questions to ask, but received only a few lines explaining how he was doing. In order to get my son a good education and find a means by which I could communicate with him, I had to send him further away from me. It seemed contradictory because it was.

35

Goodwill to all men

My father visited Craig and me in sporadic bursts. When one of these sprees happened, he usually appeared on a fortnightly basis. He was still on the wagon, sober and attending the AA. I would know this by the language he used. Our otherwise inane conversations would be peppered with statements like, 'One day at a time' and 'Drink is a cunning master'. Through a perfect row of false teeth he would laugh, hale and hearty.

On the occasions he visited, we always had dinner together. We continued the same conversations we had been having for years. My father never knew I had been in hospital, never knew about Craig's schooling or the meetings I had attended. We never discussed books, films or life. He spoke about his sisters in Ireland, farms and the countryside. It was always nostalgic in tone, even when describing, with his clenched fist shaking in the air, that his father would 'leather' him with a belt. That was the only fact I ever gleaned about my adoptive grandfather.

My father and I never once discussed my mother or the events that led up to her death. We never discussed the children's homes, the violence, the drinking and my shaming of his family in becoming pregnant. In all my years as his daughter, I had never received any Christmas cards or birthday cards for either me or Craig from his family. Once, I made the effort and sent over Christmas cards, the arrival of which was acknowledged in a letter my father received in his yearly Christmas card from them. We were never acknowledged by them as part of his family – except for the shame I had brought on their good name.

We lived in the moment, my father and I, replaying the same conversations. Perhaps I was replacing my mother, his mother, the lead female role in his life. It was a role I certainly was not fully equipped for, just as he was not equipped to be a father, although he never forgot Craig's birthday or mine – embarrassing memories of a squashed birthday cake delivered by a drunken father in the children's home remain with me. Our birthdays he kept written down in a small beige notebook with a British Railway logo on the front, evidence of his previous employment. All his important addresses were contained in it. Once, he showed me his sister Eileen's new address and some photos she had sent him, all adults with Orange Lodge sashes on, reminding him of his commitment to 'the cause'.

My father had also found himself homeless at one point, though the reasons remained unknown to me. References to Bell Street and the Great Eastern Hotel in the city's east end appeared in our conversation. Grim and squalid would fairly describe the conditions within the Great Eastern. My father said he had his own cubicle and got breakfast. As I had lived in a hostel for young women in Dennistoun, I had passed by the Eastern doss house many times. Situated on Duke Street, with two Corinthian-style columns topped with an art deco facing, at one time it had been an impressive mill house. My only memories are of seeing the steps of the building housing a congregation of drunks, smokers and lost men. He had been quickly re-housed in the south side of Glasgow – 18 flights up in a concrete skyscraper known locally as Suicide Tower.

His play fighting with his grandson had very little similarity to the 'play' fighting he had performed with me as a child. The restrained blows never made contact, but he still laughed unreservedly, the sound bordering on manic and cruel. Though no longer doing manual work on the railways, his hands remained large and solid like shovels. For Craig, this was fun, as was the receiving of a few pounds of pocket money every time he saw his grandfather. However, as with most people, that's where the interaction stopped. It was not so much a language barrier – more of no language to literally speak of.

I was the only constant family my father had, though I did not realise this or recognise his loneliness. It felt like a duty or habit between the two of us, and neither of us questioned it. Perhaps he had been encouraged by the AA to make amends. I accepted the situation out of obligation and guilt; somehow I still felt I had let him down and that it was a daughter's duty. I would be bad if I did not acknowledge this man who had adopted me and given me a home. It was a relationship borne out of a shadow of Stockholm syndrome that had never been discouraged. Also, though I never knew it at the time, I hoped for answers from him.

Only once in this era did I mention the name Urquhart to him. I remember he sat at my bench table in the kitchen eating the dinner I had just made for him. With the fake pine panelling on the walls behind him, he noisily scraped the plate with his knife. 'Do you know what happened to William Urquhart?' I asked. My heart was thumping. It had taken me years to ask that question. A brief glance and ramblings about something totally unrelated was the deafening response. It was as if he had not heard me. I could not ask again.

That winter, the snow fell extensively. It was a white-out everywhere. Beautiful as it was, it brought the area to a standstill. The normally white elongated bars on the wall-hung electric fire radiated red. They remained on constantly throughout the freezing day. It took me nearly two hours to plough through the snow to the shops. It reached my knees. Crunching my way back through the packed snow, I carried bread and milk from the queues I had waited in. Baker vans were at a standstill and very few essentials were getting through. One loaf per person was the ration.

Craig was not coming home that weekend. All taxis were off the road for such a long distance. The school had phoned me to inform me he also had the flu. Years later, I would learn it was glandular fever he had been suffering from. I was sad and frustrated not to be able to comfort him in any way. I could only hope that my phone message of 'I love you' would be passed on.

The following weekend, Craig made it home. Pale but excited, he ran towards me, leaving the taxi door lying open. We squeezed each other's separation anxiety away and built a snowman from the deep snow in the back garden.

My father came to stay for several days over Christmas. We had spoken on the phone briefly, and he said, 'I'm not going anywhere for Christmas, just me and the Alexander Brothers.' Within seconds, I had invited him. It was one of the only times I heard a loneliness in his voice. Perhaps that and the guilty thought of him singing 'Nobody's Child', 'Underneath the Stairs' and 'Here's to the Castle' on his own provoked my sympathy. It also meant I didn't need to burden my aunt and uncle with my presence. I was making decisions and getting on with it.

He brought his usual Christmas gifts of selection boxes wrapped up, and cards containing money for both of us and one for Cathleen. 'A woman needs her own money,' he would say frequently. He had said that several times to me over the years. It sounded like a phrase he had digested and learned in the AA. His dress remained smart, and he was suited and booted, always with tie. This time, though, he wore a fake fur hat. 'Just like a Russian,' he said. He would laugh at his swarthy reflection in my mirror that hung on the artexed wall.

My father seemed unquestioning, childish and one dimensional to me. I could not find any way to get under his manic surface for us to be able to connect. Though he had taken to wearing a matching hat and scarf that were no longer in football colours, my father remained loyal to and passionate about Ireland, Rangers Football Club and the Orange Order. I never saw him fervent or steadfast with anything else.

Out of the blue, my father offered his services for babysitting. I knew Kerry and her friends would most definitely be out and about, dressed up to the 'nines' in new Christmas clothes and full of seasonal cheer before even walking through the door of the pubs and clubs, and I would now have the chance to go with them. I was stunned, as babysitting had never been on our agenda or an accepted part of his role in our life. Although I was cautious about his abilities, as he had never been the ideal father, the offer did please me. As I sensed that my father was perhaps trying to make amends of some kind, I agreed. Terry, Pearl's son, had already offered to let me out one night, but it felt good to be able to say that Craig's grandfather was babysitting. I was looking forward to going out and I also quite enjoyed feeling that my father was doing something family-orientated. Although it was an irregular occurrence, it felt normal. That in itself was strange.

So, it was looking like it would be a happy few days. On the first night, Craig got out his cards and placed them face down on the burgundy carpet. We all played at pairs. Later, when Craig was in bed and I had gone to mine, I lay awake. My father had settled down on the couch in his pyjamas. It was obvious to me he had thought this out and had planned to be of use. Confused, but also slightly pleased, I fell happily asleep. At least, I thought, he had tried.

The next day, I phoned Kerry at her work, to find out her arrangements. My phone rang several hours later; it was Stella, a girl from college. Eagerly I arranged to meet up with her too. The meeting place was in my aunt's pub around seven thirty that evening. The day passed with me ironing clothes for my night out and cleaning the house with enthusiasm. In the late afternoon I went on a short walk to the shops with my father and Craig for the purpose of buying some treats and goodies for him to enjoy that night. This made it seem even more like a normal event – that's what grandparents do. Craig pointed to packets of Love Hearts and the bags of colourful Rainbow Drops.

As I later rattled about the kitchen making the evening dinner for us, my father suddenly announced that he was off to the shops again. He waved his hand towards Craig to indicate for him to go with him. Again I felt anxious, but Craig was out the door with him as quick as my anxiety rose. I didn't question my father about why he wanted to return to the shops. We never questioned each other about anything. Pacing between the kitchen and living room window to watch for their safe return, I gnawed intensely on my nails. Just under an hour had passed when on the horizon of my street two figures came into view: one small one dancing circles up the street as though running round invisible poles, the other larger one my father with a swagger that could dry the washing on the next-door line.

Craig with his escapee noises that deaf children produce, which seemed to propel him up our stairs, burst into the kitchen red cheeked and laden down with a bottle of Irn Bru, crisps and a football magazine with free stickers. My father appeared some time behind him, out of puff. He had bought me cigarettes and a cake. His swagger, it seemed, was one of pride, but I watched for tell-tale signs such as occasional visits to the toilet, and though guilt was with me then, fear was stronger, stronger than even the worry about a heavy-handed whack from him. The deceit of alcoholism leaves a heavy imprint. I checked his inside overcoat pocket for a bottle. There was none. My father watched the TV, never taking his suit jacket off as I gratefully organised myself to go out.

My preparation began as I boiled sugar water, leaving it to cool before pouring it over my head onto my short platinum hair. The sassy short quiff sat above my forehead stiff like cardboard, unbendable in any wind, but it would collapse and taste like cheap syrup in the rain. I wore three earrings: a huge glass one hung from my right ear like a chandelier, one was star shaped and the other was a stud – a match for the one in my nose. Pale faced with red lipstick, I headed for the bus into Hamilton town centre.

Travelling in on the bus, I felt like an Annie Lennox lookalike, though I probably looked like a groupie attending a Spear of Destiny/Cyndi Lauper concert. My father had given me extra money on the premise that I would get a taxi home. As I was leaving, he said, 'You will not be drinking.' It was not an enquiry but more of a request and expectation. It made me feel like a daughter. Maybe it made him feel like a father and a grandfather.

The town centre was heaving with people. The dress code was extra sparkly and glittery as it was the Christmas silly season. For some, dresses would be bought and worn for one time only then placed at the back of a wardrobe and brought out to be laughed at or sent to a charity shop the next year. The Housemartins' version of 'Caravan of Love' video played on every wall. It seemed like brewers had put up massive video screens wherever there was space. Wherever you were in a pub you could watch music, not just listen. When there was not a screen, the space was mirrored. Blue-and-red neon strip lights glowed in the dark. The atmosphere was electric.

The diehards of the Punk clientele still sat in their corner; beside them the Goths, New Wave Romantics and Indie crowd expanded the pub's diversity. The reality was, of course, everyone was posing. At another corner were the frilly blouses and flick fringes inspired by Princess Diana. I knew most of the customers by sight. My aunt had told me once that she enjoyed the diversity of her pub clientele. I had made her more open minded, she said.

Almost immediately, I met Kerry, and then I saw Stella sitting on her own in a corner. Kerry knew everyone and would chat while circulating. Kerry was to designer clothes and hairdressing what Stella was to Paddy's market and backcombing. Stella dyed her hair pink and still wore Punkera bondage. She would sit in the same place and only speak to people who spoke to her.

It was while sitting with Stella that two young guys our age struck up a conversation with us. One was called James. He was to become an integral part of my life. At that point, however, it was Christmas, everyone was in a great mood and living for the moment. As Europe played the 'Final Countdown' on the screens and last orders were being shouted, everyone was deciding what nightclub to go to. I had to go home. My babysitting hours only covered pub time, not club time. My father would have been horrified if he had known I was meeting my friends in the pub, even though he knew it was my aunt's pub. At least there had been no repetition of him screaming at me and scrubbing off my lipstick, as he had done when I was younger.

The lights came up and the crowd began to spill onto the street, singing either the conventional Slade's 'Merry Christmas Everybody' or Wizard's 'I Wish It Could Be Christmas Every Day'. As I stood up to leave, I drank a Pernod and blackcurrant James's friend Lonny had bought me, then James suddenly asked to walk me home. Smiling, I replied, 'I am going to get a taxi.'

Not taking no for an answer, he continued, 'Can I walk you to the rank?'

His persistence paid off. 'Yes, OK,' I laughed.

Outside the pub, as we stood in the doorway, he began kissing me. In an attempt to be romantic and impress me, he clumsily whispered in my ear some basic Spanish. I laughed. I thought he was fooling around, but it was meant to impress, which only made me laugh more. We both laughed. As we walked through the freezing night, there was an atmosphere of good cheer.

I noticed two gold chains round his neck. They seemed out of place, more akin to the accessories and attire the 'squares' wore. Catalogue gold, it was snobbishly referred to as. I had my own idiosyncratic dislikes like slip-on shoes, popular with waiters, sandals with white socks, and my pet hate was jackets with the sleeves too short. However, the gold chains did not put me off. It had been a good night, and I had enjoyed the company and being out. For some reason, probably to prolong the evening, we decided to walk along Townhead Street and stop a taxi when one of us decided the night was at an end. We squealed and ran, chasing each other, but this was hardly noticed amongst the many others walking the streets in a festive mood. Distracted by this happiness, the walk home from this area remained less contaminated by a dark shadow in my memory. That camouflaged haversack called baggage I was carrying on my back was so well concealed I did not know it was there myself. External symptoms such as my thinness and well-bitten nails went unnoticed and seemed unconnected.

Eventually, laughing and chatting, we reached Almada Street, stopping on the way several times to kiss in the cold air. Several other couples were following suit. Doorways housed a few of them. At the towering County Buildings with the fountains and Christmas decorations, we paused for a while. As a backdrop, it felt as romantic a setting as any. The clear sky, white frost, Christmas hope and expectation made it feel special.

Soon I was in a taxi on my way home with the promise of a phone call. I travelled past Peacock Cross and down Burnbank Road in the black cab and arrived at my door. Freezing, I locked the main door and ran upstairs. My father began bawling and shouting at me as soon as I entered the living room. 'Ah canny deal with him. He got up and would not settle,' he repeated furiously.

Craig was sitting on one of my couches, smiling. 'OK, OK,' I anxiously replied.

As I tucked Craig into bed, I could hear my father's Irish brogue raging through the doors. 'Ah will no be back.' I was still very much afraid of my father's volatile nature and being alone here with him brought that home to me. 'You've been drinking,' he spat at me in disgust several times.

I lied. 'Aunty Helen gave me a Christmas drink.' I hoped her name would sanction the alcohol and bring him to heel. It did. Making him tea, I chatted away nervously, like you do when trying to ignore a situation. My avoidance tactic worked. I asked him about his childhood Christmases in Donegal. 'We'd get a stocking with an orange in it and a penny,' he grinned. As always, he splattered his Donegal conversations with stories about receiving the strap, working in the fields and ended by saying, 'I am an Irishman.' Only when he was drunk did this quote change to 'I am an Orangeman.' His attempts to affirm and identify who he was always puzzled me. I realise now that my father's early life must have been very emotionally and financially impoverished, brutal and full of hardship. His bullying and violence were perhaps partly the result of his own unknown fears and fragility, and partly an immaturity and unwillingness to do anything about them. Though this did not explain why one man from this background would become a loving father and resolve to be different while another carried on the terrible tradition.

My bubble completely burst, I lay in bed staring at the ceiling, hoping he would not kick off. I had smiled and placated him as best as I could and left him to settle. My thoughts turned to Craig and how I was going to help him and deal with his behaviour. His hyperactivity and random, frantic runarounds were exhausting. Of course, on this occasion my father must have wound him up with play fighting then expected him to settle. But that's what most people did. Due to problems with communication, they engaged with him in an animated fashion that they soon tired of but which left him like an overwound clock. But when he slept, he slept soundly.

I screwed myself inside like a wrung-out tea towel. I had begun to read all the books I could find on psychology. Apart from the academic book Dr Maloney had given me, there was very little in the way of psychology of the deaf on the library shelves. I needed material that was applicable, information that would help from day to day. A practical solution!

Several days later, I received a call from James's friend Lonny. He was inviting Kerry and me to a party. I knew I would not be able to go but coolly said I might turn up. I knew James was listening in the background.

Next came the dreaded New Year. As usual, I went to my aunt's. The tension always built up in me for several days with relief coming only after the ringing of the bells. At Aunt Helen's, the coming and going, and the singing and west-coast humour continued into the wee hours. Then it was all over. Till the next year. As I rode that raging roundabout of mother memories, it seemed I could never get off.

After receiving another call from Lonny well into January 1987, I agreed to meet up with them along with Kerry at the weekend, but I never did. With no money, and feeling despondent, I felt like I had nothing to offer.

Weeks passed without me seeing anyone after Craig went back to school, and I began to make further enquiries about signing and communication. My hopes were lifted when I heard about signing classes that might be getting set up for parents or anyone interested. I began to make plans. Reluctantly, I contacted my old social worker Rebecca Mower for more information. She came to see me. Wandering about my flat, she commented on my bedroom. 'It's like a garden,' she said. This was the effect I had tried to create – nature! I accepted all her compliments, despite the fact I was extremely wary of her. The comments she had made when I was younger about her Down's syndrome client having sex with her uncle and cousin sat like a billboard in my skull. 'She was enjoying it. Why should she not be allowed to have sex?' Was this liberal philosophy, I wondered, horrified if it was. Or was it a certain type of feminism? If it was, her warped ideology certainly didn't fit with my interpretation of liberalism and feminism.

The practical solution Rebecca now came up with was to transfer me to the local social work department. 'I mean, it's not as if you are going to come back to Glasgow now, is it?'

I had to agree. But irrationally I felt like this move meant I was severing my only connection with my past, my mother and the only home I had known. Or, more to the point, as it was not my choice to make this split, Rebecca was severing the connection for me. No one knew how I felt, no one asked, and I certainly wasn't aware. I had been silent too long to know. My nightmares and other symptoms of the traumas I'd suffered, such as excessive nail biting, scratching and vomiting, now seemed normal. On a sleepless night, I allowed myself to consider why I behaved as I did, but I thought that surely after so many years this behaviour could not be connected to anything that had happened in the past. I was still gripped by fear of death at the hands of Urquhart or being locked up because of my association with him. The nightmares persisted, with visions full of monsters, blood, running on the spot and feelings of impending death. They left me tired and depressed in the morning. Often, I would go back to sleep and straight into another nightmarish landscape of fear and running. Deep down, I knew something was wrong but had no way of knowing what to do about it. I had never faced or discussed these sleeping dogs, therefore they lay under the surface, secretly gnawing away and always returning to haunt me at night on my seamless roundabout ride.

Another social worker came to visit me. I recognised her from school. She had been in the year above me. She had always dressed like a Sunday-school teacher and was considered a snob. But life had taught me that people could be full of surprises and that I should never be hasty or judge a book by its cover. Hoping I would be granted the same courtesy, I was pleasant, chatty and asked about signing classes. I also spoke about having Craig's transport reassessed and discussed the living arrangements at his school. I mentioned that the boarding situation was always supposed to be temporary and that I wished he could travel there on a daily basis.

Nodding her head and appearing to appreciate what I was saying, she wrote notes. While chatting to her, I was organising clothes. In order to utilise the time while I waited in for her visit, I had spent the day clearing my drawers and wardrobe. The clothes were to be bagged and returned to the second-hand shops they had originally come from.

Speaking mostly in a high-pitched voice and constantly rubbing her right pinkie, she agreed to do what she could to find out information for me. I never saw her again. It was decades later that I read what she had written in her notes: 'Eileen had obviously had a party the night before, as clothes were strewn everywhere.' It demonstrated to me that the combination of power and stupidity can be dangerous, especially when, like me, you felt helpless to do anything about it. Challenging these situations only led to me being given more labels like 'hostile' or 'defensive'.

The college had agreed to look at what they could offer me and suggested that perhaps a few night classes might be better suited to my situation. My art tutor spoke of his disappointment at me not attending my exam. 'Stella did not turn up either,' he sighed. I had not known that. Nor had I seen her for over a month. I enquired if he taught art at night school – desperate to make him feel better. 'No,' he sighed again and finished by telling me, 'They're letting me go. Apparently I don't have the right qualification to teach art.' I left with a new prospectus for the college and renewed hope, a plan and determination.

Walking through Motherwell's town centre, I found myself in the local record shop and sifted through new and second-hand records. Out of character, I made an impulse buy of a love song. It was the love song that was out of character more than the impulse buy. I was a young woman bursting with hope, needing a dream and something to fill the emotional void in my life. I bought Jennifer Rush's 'Power of Love' in the format of a 12-inch single. Grinning, I held the cover close like a secret, a delightful dream I was afraid to lose.

Next, I headed into the centre of Hamilton to do my food shopping. The red single-decker bus trundled down Windmill Hill Street and past leafy Strathclyde Park. My destination reached, I got off at the bus station and headed into the public toilets. Once inside, I gasped. The record! I had left it on the bus. 'You all right, hen?' one of the toilet attendants asked me.

With my eyes wide in disbelief, I said, 'I have just left a new record on the bus.' Trotting back out of the toilet, the attendant followed in my footsteps as I strained at the large windows to see if the bus had left the station. It had, and was nowhere to be seen.

'Go next door to the inspector's office and see if anybody has handed it in,' she offered.

Not needing to be told twice, within seconds I was at the counter of the small office. As I waited till someone came to the glass partition, I cursed myself quietly and paced.

'Can I help you?' the woman on the other side asked.

Explaining the situation to her got me the immediate response that no one had handed anything in. My best bet, she said, was to phone the Motherwell depot in about an hour. She gave me the number.

Dejected, I made my way home on another bus after getting my shopping. Dumping my college bag in the hallway and taking my jacket off, I punched in the number she had given me on my house phone. The male voice on the other end laughed at me when I whined, 'I have left a 12-inch on your Motherwell to Hamilton bus, has it been handed in?' Instantly, I realised why he was laughing. After feigning mock horror at his joke, I later accepted that the record was gone, my embarrassment subsided and I sniggered quietly to myself. His crudeness, though funny, took the edge off the loss of my token, which had outwardly indicated my desire to love and be loved.

During my food-shopping venture, a voice had shouted my name as I packed my shopping into plastic bags. Scanning the aisles, I saw a familiar face. The voice belonged to Alison, a girl with whom I had shared a few adventures while I had lived in Fernlea, the children's home. Alison had gone to England to escape her violent home life. Lifting the shopping bags, I walked towards her. She had three children with her, two girls and one boy. The youngest was only six months old and sat in her shopping trolley. She had married a wealthy guy from Birmingham and now had a lovely house on the outskirts of Hamilton. 'I had a rough time in England,' she said, and it showed in her face.

She invited me up to her house the next night. 'I am getting divorced, and it would be great to catch up with you,' she said, grappling with the kids. I agreed to phone her that night. Our call lasted for an hour as she told me the grim details of her first year in London. Listening was all I did on that call. 'I have got a few people coming round tomorrow night, one of them's a local guy I met, Punky guy,' she said, telling me his name. I knew him. 'We are just friends, it's company,' she added.

The next night I was in a taxi paid for by Alison and walking through her door. There in her drawing room sat Dave, with his shaved head displaying one frontal spike like an unkempt unicorn, and the friend he had brought along. The friend was James! Alison lived in a lovely new-build house with large well-furnished rooms. The kitchen had all mod cons, including a dishwasher, tumble dryer, food blender and coffee maker. She had two large bathrooms and the gardens were well maintained but austere. A couple of high chairs and buggies gave the house the air of being a family home. In contrast, my mod cons were a telephone, a stereo and a twin tub, so this was a proverbial palace with grounds.

At school, Alison's home life and background had been well known. However, now, as the saying goes, 'she had done well for herself'. As we all chatted away, it was acknowledged that James and I already knew each other, though we did not reveal the details. Alison was enjoying being the hostess and produced bottles of wine from a collection in the kitchen. Having one bottle in the house would have been a luxury for me, but her supply seemed endless.

A comment from Dave changed the mood of the evening. In response to a now-forgotten remark, he retorted, 'It's been a hard time for him.' He was referring to James.

Looking from James then to Dave, I asked the obvious question, 'Why?'

Dave solemnly supplied us with the information that James's mother had died. 'It was just last month,' he stated.

As we looked at James, the room was temporarily silent.

'So sorry,' I said, and Alison followed suit.

The awkward silence was filled with a quiet 'Thanks' from James. Then Alison blustered in with, 'What happened and how are you?'

The answers were kept to a minimum: 'A brain haemorrhage', and the subject was purposefully changed and steered onto insignificant topics. For me, though, my heart was sinking and heavy with empathy. Another motherless human being! Memories flicked over in my head. Romantic visions conjured up secret soft feelings. I remembered our Christmas night through rose-tinted spectacles: sitting outside the twinkling county building lit up with festive lights and the blue-coloured water fountains. In my fantasy, it was akin to the opening scene from the '70s series *The Champions*, starring Alexandra Bastedo. She had stood protected and powerful in the opening scenes of each episode beside her main men in front of jetting fountains. In reality, the only commonality was that we were both slim and blonde!

As the wine dwindled, hunger hit. We phoned in an order for Chinese food. As the prawn crackers were ravenously used to scoop up the chicken and fried rice like dissolving spoons, Alison emerged with yet another bottle of wine and some taped music for the stereo. I had never heard the music before, but I liked it. It danced and entranced from the speakers in the corners of the room. The twangy fusion of mystic eastern sounds were created by a musician Alison had discovered in London called Ravi Shankar. The exotic notes that the sitar cheekily danced out evoked romantic notions and an atmosphere that even I, as someone who frequently missed obvious chat-up lines and moves, could not fail to detect. It was clear as James and I became locked into our own private chat that the initial attraction was still there and was being acted on. The food and wine had relaxed me, and my heart had already been won by way of empathy. A kindred spirit! Apart from in the children's home, I had never met anyone in my peer group who had suffered the loss of a parent. Of course, my conscious mind didn't work this out. I simply felt connected.

After much canoodling, kissing and talking, we agreed to meet up again and within a week I received a call. 'Hello, is this Eileen?' a female voice questioned me as I answered my phone.

'It is,' I replied, curious.

'OK, hold on. James would like to speak to you.' I could hear the chitchat in the salon where he worked as a trainee hairdresser. I quietly smiled to myself after I worked out he was trying to impress me by getting another trainee to act as his receptionist.

'How are you?' he enquired.

'I've got the flu,' I cheerfully replied.

The next night he arrived accompanied by the roar of a 125 cc. After parking the bike, he casually strolled to the front door with a bottle of Lucozade and a sympathetic smile. He stayed the night, despite not being sure of Pebbles the cat. His mother did not like cats, I discovered. Curiously, I thought to myself, the fear of cats reminded me of the superstition surrounding cats that was rampant in the east end where I came from. '*They steal the breath of babies*' and '*A witch's mate*' were some of the sayings I remembered. (That was how my life worked: triggers and flashbacks. It meant that in company I would often find myself jolting at the words, 'Hey, you!' with someone laughing, 'She's no aw there,' or asking with concern, 'Are you all right, Eileen?' I also learned how to wing it after missing out on half a conversation when something someone said triggered a memory.) However, as the cat scampered cutely around the flat, it didn't take long for him to unlearn that fear. Pebbles purred in his lap and followed us to bed. As I had been feeling low, lousy and alone, I appreciatively lapped up the sympathy and bodily comfort. In the morning, he left for work from mine. I thought the dark helmet and motorbike gear looked funny and would only admit to it being slightly sexy. As he rode off, the fear began and my nails were ravaged.

We had shared some stories the previous evening and into the early hours. His account of his mother's death moved me. As we sat together, I watched him unravel and speak more freely than any man I had ever met. I remained silent and listened intently as he told me how angry he felt about his mother's death. He felt that something might have been done to help her if she had received prompt medical attention, but his father hadn't seemed to realise how serious the situation was. I felt so angry for him. I didn't know what to say. I felt strangled by the years of stoic self-preservation of my own unrevealed history. The opposing arguments continued to collide in my head. '*Don't listen, Eileen, stop the feelings*' vied against another more optimistic voice: '*Maybe you could, just maybe you could do this.*' Maybe I could share! While this internal battle raged, I continued to nod and make sure it looked like I was listening carefully.

The internal fear and arguments continued as our relationship quickly developed. I felt very close to him and his situation, closer than I had ever felt to anyone. A month later, I introduced Craig and James. Anxious that they should get on, I watched them both carefully.

The motorbike did the trick; Craig was more than impressed and ran around with an oversized helmet wobbling on his small head. He was promised a 'backie' on safe terrain.

Like any mother or partner who was not a natural motorbike enthusiast, the thought of a road accident was prominent in my mind. Despite this, I did go out on the bike several times. The most epic adventure was a day out to Ayr, where I showed my true colours.

I found that there was something quite exhilarating about being on a motorbike. I had never been behind the wheel of anything other than the dodgems at the funfair, and the whole point of them was to crash! As we raced along coastal roads, I now found myself physically and emotionally wrapped around someone. Secretly, I loved every swoop and turn down the A71 to the west coast: perhaps it was allowing someone else to take the lead and me just going with the flow. We stopped at a lay-by near Prestwick airport and watched the planes flying overhead. Some flew so close that you could see the people through the windows. The planes symbolised freedom to me, a life that I so wanted to experience.

Back on board, I discovered that sticking my head out only got the helmet covered in fly splatter. Helmets should have wipers like cars! I clung on and moved my body in tune with his, accepting every bend and manoeuvre with natural ease. It was the beginnings of trust. Frightened and confused by the strength of my feelings, perhaps because of the years without them, the word 'love' swam about in my mixed-up mind, though I certainly couldn't tell him!

We turned onto the road to Croy and passed the infamous 'electric brae'. You could stop your car there, turn the engine off, take the handbrake off and the car would 'roll' uphill. For much of its history it was thought that it was mysterious electric forces at play, while it has now been established as an optical illusion, with the slope and outlying land configuring to give this visual false impression. It fascinated me, and I made a mental promise to return one day by car. The view over the sea was stunning; the castle and Heads of Ayr could be seen clearly on the horizon. We turned and ran out of coastal road, bumped down a dirt track road and landed on the beach at Croy Bay. Though my hands and legs were cold from the run, I was happy and excited. 'Can I have a shot?' I pleaded. I danced from one foot to the other, hamming it up like a child. 'Please, please.'

Once on the bike, I did a convincing job of listening and nodding at the instructions I was given. Our positions were reversed. James climbed on behind me, and, being over six foot, he easily leaned over and started the bike. Gloves on, our feet still on the sand and with Culzean Castle and the rugged coastal cliffs in my eyeline, we geared up to go. The sea lapped to my right as James kicked the stand up and gently we began to move. Under the helmet, my face was beaming with an elated grin. James was wrapped around me and with my feet on what I thought were pedals we gathered speed.

Down the beach we went, faster and faster, the thrill causing me to grip the handle bars tighter. James began to shout something inaudible to me; between the wind and helmets I couldn't make out one word he was saying. Having forgotten what I had been told about how to stop the speeding bike, I just continued, helpless as to what to do. We were running out of beach, and the small house and rocks at the bottom of the cliffs were coming closer. James's muffles grew louder. Suddenly, he straightened up behind me and leaned over, indicating with his hand for me to turn the bike handles. This spurred me into action. I turned the bike from twelve o'clock only to stop at three o'clock and was still heading straight for the sea! Frozen in panic, and aware of James's shouts and his body moving, I lifted my feet up and placed my legs out like helicopter blades. In my head, I had removed my feet from the pedals that powered the bike. However, the bike just got faster as I gripped the handles tighter and the cold grey sea came towards us.

As we sat waist high in seawater, we removed our helmets. 'Why would it not stop? My feet were up, I lifted my feet.' I was honestly perplexed.

'The gears are on the handles, Eileen!' he gasped at me.

The bike was thankfully new and had been in at Lloyds, a well-known motorbike shop at Peacock Cross in Hamilton, getting modifications, so the seals remained perfectly intact. We hauled the bike out of the waves and back onto the shore. I was extremely apologetic, embarrassed even, but the thought of me and my helicopter-blade legs plus the complete idiocy of gripping the handles in fear being the very action that sped us into the sea had us both laughing.

Kerry had told me she was spending the week down in Ayr at a relative's caravan. We had been asked for dinner and I had excitedly promised her the visit. Recounting the story to Kerry and her boyfriend took away any guilty angst I had. The laughter made me feel like part of something: a couple, a circle with a shared adventure. We ate and laughed as the steam rose from our clothes hanging over chairs in front of the caravan fire. Teased, my nickname for that event was 'Scampi Fry'. A TV advert for the snack showed a van driving into the sea.

Though it was natural for feelings to progress within a romantic relationship, my excitement and delight were tempered by fear. My emotions were beginning to resemble those I had read about in the pages of poetry, plays and books. It was sometimes too scary and I did not enjoy the heart-racing feeling. Overriding my joy and ever present was that lifelong companion – fear.

Out roaming free and happy for now, though, we drove home before the sun went down, and after twisting and turning in unison through the freezing rain in damp clothing and narrowly missing sliding under a bin lorry due to a corner skid I decided perhaps a car and a living boyfriend were more desirable. James had, it seemed, unequivocally forgiven me: no mean feat, as it seems some men see their bike as a brother. For my part, I had discovered that I wanted him to stay alive. It was 'the' pivotal moment. I had been frightened into realising my feelings and fear of loss. He never blinked an eyelid about the bike incident. Our relationship survived and became for me more overwhelming.

In April, as part of his recovery process in dealing with his mother's death, James had booked a flight to visit his friend Lonny for a week, the friend I had originally met him with that Christmas night. Lonny had gone to Lloret de Mar with his father and opened a classic Spanish/Brit bar. I found myself in that lovely bittersweet place of missing someone but enjoying it. The solitude was welcomed, giving me the privacy to revel in my feelings of hope, love and dreams of the future. Before, I had only been able to do this through the language of love in poems. Now I was experiencing it. I had made up a tape of music for James to play on his Walkman during the flight. 'Wild is the Wind' by David Bowie my favourite, I imagined him listening to it as I did at home.

He called every night from Spain to report on his day. That one short phone call became the highlight of my day. Our feelings for each other had remained unsaid. Only once had I almost been forced to put my cards on the table. A week or so before he went on holiday, on an evening out an acquaintance had let the cat meowing out of a half-open bag. Casually, as we sat at a table while music blasted, she shouted, 'Of course she loves you.' The normal reaction would be one of embarrassment and the retort of, 'Get away.' My response was an understated overreaction. I froze; my heart thudded to a standstill. The look that must have been on my face! Instead of just being a bit embarrassed and waiting for a response, I felt like I had been shamed. Everything went silent; James looked at me, smiling. I wanted to cry. Steadying myself, I got up with a poker face that just needed a prod for that house of cards to fall down. With my chin out, a stiff spine and not looking back I went to the toilet where I paced, frantically biting my nails and looking for a window to escape from, to jump out and run away. This revelation was too painful.

Eventually, I burned myself out, gathered myself together and with every piece of dignity I could muster I went back to our table and continued as if nothing had happened. The tension sat under the table, shaking like my knees. The love word was never mentioned again until his last few days in Spain. During one of the calls, he said the words 'I love you'. In the safety of a phone call and with the distance of several hundred miles between us I replied, 'I love you too.' The call ended, and I found myself cradling the handset against my heart, my action ensuring the moment was kept alive. Not sharing it with anyone, I savoured, wallowed and relived it all night and for days to come. Weeks later he told me he put the phone down in the club he was in and shouted to everyone, 'She loves me!'

Shortly after his return from Spain, James asked me to marry him. That tightly wound-up ball named 'belonging' began to unfurl and show its layers. Whilst not being overly open to emotional shows of affection or love apart from when it came to Craig, I allowed my excitement to shine through. I was in possession of a precarious happiness. The proposal came after a night out. We woke up hungover, and perhaps dizzy from the night before, he asked me. I grinned yes.

A date was plucked out of thin air. The month June was decided on, then the date of the 22nd. Without knowing it, we had unintentionally chosen the day after the longest night of the year. We had met originally in December 1986. Now here we were getting married in June 1987.

Announcing our plans predictably led to a mixed response. 'Marry in haste, repent at your leisure' was one saying cheekily used. For me, in my excitement and joy, the rose-coloured glasses were firmly on and I stamped my foot haughtily at the first whiff of fatalism. Again, it was my aunt who spoke of caution, like she had when discovering my pregnancy – advising me I did not need to get married. 'I thought you'd never get married,' she said, almost with a hint of disappointment. 'Don't appear too grateful,' she had said when I had bounced through the doors of her pub and we told her. James's father then announced his intention to marry; he spoke of a double wedding. This idea not surprisingly died its own death without us having to address it. Most importantly, Craig was delighted. Indicating a ring on my finger to him by sign, we got the message across.

Then reality bit and panic threatened. There was more nail biting, body itching, vomiting, weight loss and nightmares. Pre-wedding nerves, I told myself. I wanted to be with James, wanted this wonderful day. Genuine feelings of joy, hope and happiness for the future wrestled and would not be reconciled with fear, mistrust and anxiety. Degrading and demeaning terms such as 'damaged goods' played on my mind – phrases to re-victimise a victim. It kept me in my place.

In keeping with my imperfect self-perception, I decided to get married in black! I could pull it off easily with my Punk background. This also allowed me to avoid the cliché of a virginal bride martyring herself at the altar of marriage, which was anathema to my slightly skewed feminist beliefs. It would and did seem like fun to get married in black. Another plus was it took the edge of the complete seriousness of the occasion. It matched the perceived persona of me as a rebel. Incredulously, James agreed to get married in white. So the Western use of colour as symbolism was complete. I was bad, he was good; I was tainted, and he was pure. My altar sure was unforgiving.

As I pressed forward with plans to cement my own little family unit, I once again felt the pull to get answers about my past and where I came from – it always happened when presenting my birth certificate. With my confidence building and feeling that I would be more respectable when wed, I had written to the Family Finders Department in the hope that they could put me in touch with my mother. Inexplicably, I had not wanted to embarrass a family that I had not yet even found – my father's comment about the shame I had brought on his family obviously cut more deeply than I admitted. Now I felt that I was in a position to meet her.

Life for now had me lifted off my feet and as high as a kite. I was going on a holiday, and that holiday was my honeymoon. This meant flying. I was going to fly! James and I had got a great deal, and Calella on the Costa Brava was our honeymoon destination. We had gone to the travel agents to find out what was available and when she offered us a deal, we got carried away and booked there and then.

We planned to marry at Larkhall registry office. It was a meeting halfway for both – from Hamilton where I lived and from the semi-rural village on the outskirts of Larkhall where James lived. We had shopped for outfits and booked our honeymoon before deciding to deal with the legal requirements and paperwork. Getting down to the nitty gritty, we found the devil was indeed in the details. The cart had been put before the horse. Legally, the wedding banns had to be posted to declare our proposed marriage 21 days before the event. In our excitement, we had miscalculated by about one day. It appeared as though we would have to have the honeymoon first. Dismayed, but driven by logic and practicality, I asked the registrar, 'This must have happened before, what do you do in this situation?'

She had been anticipating this question and knew the solution. 'You have to apply for a special dispensation to marry.' Fortunately, the law in this instance allowed for human error and was flexible. We supplied proof of our honeymoon booking and got our special dispensation.

James had paid for all our outfits, right down to my underwear, and Craig had a beautiful blue suit and bow tie. Although we had got a last-minute cheap deal, he had also paid for the honeymoon. It went unsaid that I had no mother or responsible father (he was now on the drink again) to advise, shop or help out financially. Apart from dictating that I wanted to wear black, I asked for nothing else. As my aunt had feared, I did end up feeling grateful as well as embarrassed but said nothing. It was merely circumstances, I told myself: shoulders back and chin up. It certainly was not James's or my own fault.

In a moment full of unfettered joy, I bought a record. No Punk, no politics of Billy Bragg, no prissy pretentions of the New Romantics. It was Jefferson Starship's 'Nothing's Gonna Stop Us Now'. Cheesy, but the words captured exactly how I felt. I also picked a silver lizard for James to wear on the lapel of his jacket.

My aunt Helen came to see me on the eve of our wedding. 'Are you sure you want to do this?' she asked. It was the only time she openly questioned our actions.

'Yes,' I replied.

Nothing more was said on the matter. Craig was tucked up in bed, settled, sleeping and maybe dreaming. Pearl popped up from downstairs. 'That lassie's goat ma hert roasted,' she told my aunt Helen. Quite how I had caused her any bother, I failed to see. She never expanded on this, only continued with, 'So's ma bhoy's.'

We all lit up our cigarettes and drank our tea, though Pearl's teacup contained vodka. When Pearl left, her parting words were to my aunt, 'Ach, another wan caught, eh, Helen?' Tutting, she shook her head and closed the front door. Aunt Helen and I laughed, not understanding fully what she meant. Older woman knew stuff, I thought; perhaps I would know in time. We shared more tea and a more trivial conversation finished the night off. When she left, she gave me a card. Inside the card was a hundred pounds. Welling up, I slid it under my pillow.

It was a Sunday night. Craig's taxi had been cancelled as James and I had decided to take him back to school ourselves. His blue suit lay over his toy box in his room, bow tie placed over his white shirt. We had kissed and cuddled enthusiastically, my boy and I, our radiant faces conveying our excitement for the following day and the hope it contained. In the run-up to the wedding, James, Craig and I had spent every weekend together as family. (Looking back, that was what Craig and I were searching for, a family to belong to.) James had begun to learn sign language – the only one apart from me in our lives who tried.

Our big day came and went. Aunt Helen signed the register for me as my witness. As the registrar read out the declaration, she had to physically hold my knees down. My teeth ached and rattled together. I stumbled over my words and could not hear myself speak. My ring got stuck, and then it was all over with a whisper in my ear by my new husband. He whispered he loved me and called me by my new legal name. Yet another one to add to the collection!

Aunt Elspeth from Fernlea turned up to see me. Hugging me and looking me up and down, she said, 'Congratulations! Look how slim you are.' She stayed for a photo and left. Our meal was a booking for ten people at the lunchtime buffet at the local Chinese. Even my sister Cathleen was there.

After the meal, we drove through to Edinburgh to drop Craig off at school. This was my only regret, as I wished he was coming with us. My aunt Helen's neighbour had warned me against this. She was the same neighbour who had turned up at the hospital when I was pregnant with Craig saying if I was hers she would 'skelp me one', the same neighbour who had been angry when, as a child in care, I was allowed to go on a school trip to Switzerland.

'You need time with your man,' she said, following up with, 'and you will have to give him a child. It's only fair, what with him bringing up another man's child.' James and I had never discussed having children! Perhaps she had a point. James never mentioned taking Craig with us on holiday, and I never broached the subject. It was his money, and I was feeling grateful enough. The guilt of leaving Craig now presented itself with a rising anxiety I had not foreseen, but Craig ran towards his school friends in the school corridor without looking back. I opened the champagne on the way to the airport, feeling both guilty and uptight.

I couldn't believe I was going on a plane for the first time! By the time our flight was called I had drunk so much champagne it did not matter. My black patent corkscrew heels teetered down the runway and onto the plane. Fear passed and the rush of adrenalin allowed me to enjoy the flight and finally the occasion. All my experiences now were new, shared and future plans ran riot in my head. Eventually, as usual, I burnt myself out, allowing contentment to seep in.

Sand that was so hot you could not walk on it with your bare feet, a bottle of wine for 50 pence, the smell of coconut oil wafting up the beach and from passing tourists in the shops all added to my sensory experience. Outside eating, al fresco! Though I had read of many of these things, it certainly was not the same as experiencing them. Bursting with joy and vitality, if it had been humanly possible to do everything my eyes could see in one day, I would have. Parasailing! I had to parasail. James was not so keen. He had spotted bikes. In spite of my past escapade with bikes and the Irish Sea, I wanted to do that too.

In the end we did both. James was persuaded to go parasailing by me going first. Strapped in on a rubberised platform, I was yanked from ground level at quite a speed. As I drifted high over the Mediterranean, alone under a yellow parachute, peace surrounded me. The air warm, the sea never ending to the eye, I did not want to come down. Looking down at the clear blue sea, I could see a man tucked away in a small rowing boat lying sunning himself; he was naked and waving up at me. I laughed, waved back and hit the landing platform with a thud. James went up next and was incredibly rattled. However, once up, his nerves disappeared and he too enjoyed the experience as I took photos.

I photographed everything. Toes in sand, lizards running up walls and even food on plates I decided deserved to be recorded. Swimming in the sea topless, the density of the warm salty water holding me up was as close to heaven as I had ever felt. It was intoxicating. Never have I been afraid of water, it was a symbol of freedom to me. During the day, in the evening and at night, in the pool I would drift into another world. I joked about seeing a puddle and wanting to take my clothes off.

Swimming and the salty sea made for a thirst. Fruit cocktails! That's what I said when I tasted sangria. So I drank some more, then some more. It was delicious and had real pieces of fruit chunks that I munched my way through. We ordered three jugs. I woke up the next day in our studio room. Neither of us remembered much, other than that I had strutted off in a comic huff, not wanting to go home. James had kept close behind me and watched me skid on discarded food before falling into the bins. The evidence was the kebab-style stains all down the back of my long white jacket. I was mortified! He laughed and laughed at me as he recounted the tale. The next night only one jug was ordered.

Bikes were next on the agenda. After initial instructions on how to ride them, to which I really listened this time, we were off for the day. A trip up the mountain had been decided upon. Having run up and down the beach area of the bike-hire stall, I realised these bikes were lighter and easier to ride in comparison with James's. No licences were required. Sand ripped up behind my bike as I turned successfully numerous times. Revving up, James told me to follow him. Onto the main road we went, me following his every move. I was wearing a bikini and sunglasses! No helmets. As we headed towards the mountain road, we followed some smaller roads. Tourists and locals cut in between us several times. Swerving to prevent crashing, I began to regret this venture. I was frightened to stop in case I fell off, fearing I was going to go over the handlebars.

Finally we reached the beginning of the inclined road that climbed the side of the mountain. The noise of the bikes and the wind in my hair egged me on to overtake James. It was wonderful; the road was empty and ours. Mostly I drove up the middle. All afternoon we drove, up and round, stopping to drink in the view before driving on some more. The scenery was breathtaking to me, a virgin tourist. Our bodies absorbed the cool mountain sunshine. To the left, a wide blue sea was separated from the golden strip of sand by a trim of white froth. Craggy dusty rock with little vegetation ascended on my right.

In the late afternoon, with a few rests and my excited rambles of how good a rider I was behind us, we decided to return. Our descent was more eventful. Traffic began to appear. Perhaps it was local people returning home from their day's work. In front and unable to make it understood that I wanted to get behind James and follow, I veered from the middle of the road to the side I was supposed to be driving on. Confused and exhausted, I managed to work out how to stop and what side I should be on. I followed James the rest of the way. Relieved but tired, we went back to our room and I fell asleep.

When I woke up, I was freezing but my skin burned, radiating heat like a bar on an electric fire. Needing to go to the toilet, I tried to stand up. I couldn't. It felt like the skin on my legs would burst open. James had to carry me to the toilet. Shivering and burning up at the same time, I became confused. The pain on my skin was a secondary concern at this point. All we had by way of covers were two light blankets and the starched white sheets. It was five quilts and a dozen blankets I desperately desired. Frightened, I pretended I was OK, but painkillers I had in my cosmetic bag helped. I spent the night in bed. Feeling guilty, I suggested that James go out. 'No point in the two of us being stuck in,' I said through chattering teeth. I preferred to suffer in private.

He brought me back a 'Lomo', our usual lunchtime snack. The Spanish sandwich of tomato and cheese with ham shook up and down as I tried to eat it. Sexy and desirable I certainly was not. Foolish and stupid were amongst the several things I felt. Shattered from shaking, I eventually fell asleep. The next morning it was a slow and painful walk to the toilet. My skin was as red as the tomato in the 'Lomo'. I managed a slow and considered walk down to dinner that night. Drawing my chair in under me, the contact between the wicker on the chair and my legs continually hurt. After dinner, it was back to bed and more painkillers.

Worryingly, my sexual experiences were not matching up with the literature I had read. Nothing I had read, be it the romantic poets, feminist writings or films, could explain what I was or was not feeling. Nor had I ever found a place for what had happened with Urquhart. As soon as these thoughts troubled me, I pushed them aside as being irrelevant, ever confident it would all be good in the end. Good intent was enough.

We ended our holiday with a tourist attraction. 'Authentic Fresh Pearl rings set in Silver and Gold,' the sign read. A well in the resort was filled daily with fresh oysters. A diver was paid to bring up an oyster from the contrived pool. Purporting to have all been X-rayed and containing pearls, we bought into it; a diver plunged in then burst back to the surface with my oyster. We left with my pearl set in silver on my finger. In the taxi ride home from the airport, as I playfully twisted the pearl ring I noticed a slight green band underneath around my finger, but being in no position to complain I just laughed.

36

Long and winding road

The one hundred pounds my aunt Helen had given me as a wedding gift was missing from under my pillow. Pearl's son Terry had been looking after Pebbles. I was sure his new girlfriend had stolen the money. The police interviewed her, but we never recovered the money. I never told my aunt Helen.

Plans were afoot on the home front concerning Craig's schooling. Dreaded meetings between the educational authorities and social work department were being arranged, as I had followed up my request that Craig travel to school on a daily basis rather than boarding. The problem, as always, was one of economics.

It tore me up that my son had to be boarded out for a better education. In my head, it was a similar set-up to being in care. Every Monday morning, I stood waving as the taxi vanished with my son, his face framed in curls as he waved till we disappeared from each other's sight. My son's well-being and safety were in other people's hands, as had been the case with me. We couldn't even communicate how we felt about this. On one hand, I knew that he was in his own community and peer group. However, I felt like a caretaker to my own son, his main influences being strangers who taught him and could communicate fully with him. Thoughts, feelings and views were all being imposed on him from outside. I was excluded as I didn't share a language with my son and he was excluded from me. I had finally managed to find sign-language classes but they had lasted only a few weeks; it was a short course covering the basics such as the alphabet. As his mother, I was therefore a failure by default. It seemed being 'handicapped' – deaf – meant sacrifices must be made. It felt almost like a punishment for both of us.

My guilt and the natural desire to have my child close and for us to have as normal a family life as possible ate away at me, worming itself deep into my own experiences of being sent away. My thoughts would turn dark and to worry. My own experiences in the homes had left their mark; I did not even need to revisit them in my head. All those little memories stored in neurons would light up and race around the circuit of my brain faster than a Formula One racing car. I just had to make sure it did not crash and blow up. My reactions of fear and thoughts were never shared, as I tried to keep up a mask of steel. Who would I tell and what words would I use?

I never had a language to communicate with my growing son, and I never had one to describe how I was feeling. I simply could not attach words to feelings or behaviours. The word paedophile still did not exist in my environment. Whilst I accepted my experiences like a true martyr, dreaming all might have been different if my mother had been alive, I was not prepared to tolerate any risk to my son. My son was different; his mother was alive. It had been intimated to me at the time of Craig enrolling in school that the situation could be reassessed. For me, the time had come to do so.

Other plans were also being put into motion. We had discussed moving to Stonehouse. New neighbours had moved in downstairs, but in my mind I could still see the dead body lying in the flat below me. Privacy was also an issue. My neighbour had heard James and me running around the flat laughing and squealing like the newlyweds we were. He commented to me one day in the street, 'I heard you two last night; we laughed at youse.' He meant it in good spirit, but it embarrassed me.

My flat in Hamilton was important to me. It was my security, given my previous homelessness and the circumstances that had brought it about. It was important to me not be dependent on others for a roof over my head. However, I felt that there would be more freedom available to us in the village where James had grown up. I loved the country walks and strolling along the river Avon. Also, the local park, once famous for having the largest chute in Britain, was filled with space. A fantastic view over the river and towards the viaduct added to its attraction. James's roots were strong in the village and his family were well known within the community. Craig would benefit from living in the countryside and I couldn't stop romancing the notion in my head.

James's dad was getting married in the September and would be moving in with Jessica, his wife to be. James wanted to stay in the family home, his mother's house, so we moved up to see how it felt for a few weeks, while going back and forwards to the flat. As it seemed to work well, we decided we would move, but we didn't tell anyone and we hadn't decided on the exact day to hand the keys in for the flat in Hamilton. Someone at the council found out, however, and two letters arrived almost in unison. One was from the Family Finders Centre in Glasgow who were contacting me to assist in my search for my mother. The other was a letter from the council and arrived at the Hamilton flat, promptly terminating my tenancy and asking for the flat keys.

Distraught that the final decision had been taken out of our hands and panicking at the loss of my flat and my independence, I walked out of the house and wandered. What were we going to do? We had nowhere else to go.

James's dad's marriage was pending. We had now received several letters from the council demanding that we move out of the family home. As they had done when I had lived with my cousin Bernadette, they insisted that James had no claim on the house. The only good news at that point was that my request that Craig be allowed to travel to school on a daily basis was granted. However, the dream of the normal family unit that I had craved and married into was disintegrating – we were to be made homeless.

37

Retracing and tracking

As we waited to hear our fate from the housing department, we went dully about daily life. I just did not know how to convey the news to Craig and my family. Staring out of windows and sighing became part of my day. In the small back garden, I was looking at the fence without seeing it when I heard the phone ringing. Discarding the tea towel I was holding, I rubbed my damp hands down my trousers before reaching for the receiver.

'Hello, is this Eileen?' I heard the voice ask.

'Yes, speaking,' I hesitantly replied.

It was Elsie, the social worker from the Family Finders department in Glasgow. Her next statement saw my jaw dropping and eyes widening. 'We have found your mother.'

Twenty-four years had passed for mother and daughter and my response to such momentous news was silence. My silence was not borne of being rendered speechless or dumbfounded. Calmness was washing over me, the anxiety of searching, of not knowing if she was alive or dead was over; so many unanswered questions would now be answered. It was only the beginning, my beginning!

I held that moment and savoured it. A deep, secret wish was coming true for me. My heart did not race, it slowed down as Elsie gave me more information on the situation. Perhaps, on reflection, there was an element of shock. I quietly listened while staring out through the slats in the venetian blinds and entwined the cord round the fingers of my right hand.

My birth aunt, my mother's sister, still lived at the same address as was on a file. Elsie had exchanged several calls with my aunt, whose name turned out to be Irene. Irene had said emphatically that my mother wanted to meet me. Elsie continued: 'Your mother has said she has waited years for this day to come.'

These were words I had dreamed of hearing. Confirmation that I had been missed and loved. I had mattered to someone.

'We will arrange a time where you can meet up in private, Eileen,' Elsie said as she ended the call. Replacing the receiver, I sat silently on the couch staring through the fire in front of me. Elsie had been delighted; these moments for her in her job must have been the most rewarding. Time neither passed quickly nor slowed down as I sat there. I felt a sense of disbelief or almost anticlimax at achieving a lifetime's goal, and my mind wandered over a hundred scenarios, all coming back to the moment I would hug my mother. Only when I finally phoned James and shared my news did I begin to feel an excitement. However, having broken my silence also brought with it a reality. My old friend 'fear' dusted its powder on my dream.

38

You

The time, place and day had been prearranged. James and I were to travel into Glasgow and meet up with Elsie in the tall glass-windowed building that housed the Family Finders department in Wellington Street, near Anderson Bus Station. After this, I was to be introduced to my mother. I had discovered from Elsie since our last call that my mother was taking the time before we met to tell her family about me. Her husband had no idea, nor did her children. Like me, she had kept secrets – all her life.

By now I had shared my news with my aunt Helen, who was not as enthusiastic or pleased for me as I had hoped. When I had left my adopted aunt, I felt a damping in my heart, and it confused me. Typically, I chastised myself as though I had done something wrong. It never occurred to me that my aunt, older and wiser, was protectively putting the brakes on the one-way train I was travelling in. '*Proceed with caution,*' her hand-held road sign would have read.

Although I was not a believer in anything preordained, this journey I had embarked on certainly had all the trademarks of destiny. It had begun before me, decisions and choices had been made without my knowledge or ability to change them. Wheels and events had certainly been long set in motion. However, I had chosen to unravel, explore and follow the leads left by events. With my experience and history, how could I not?

That night before our meeting, I lay awake fantasising about my mother, my brothers and sisters. Having very little knowledge left me with nothing but imagined scenarios and fantasies. Elsie had suggested that my mother was as keen to meet with me as I was to meet her. I had no names of my brothers and sisters. How had her husband reacted to the news of a child kept secret from him? What about the rest of her family? An even more daunting prospect, though desired, was that she would tell me about my father. I asked Elsie so many questions but most of these she didn't answer. She felt it would be better for me to keep my questions for my mother.

Worried I had brought trouble to my mother's door, I was determined to make this as easy as possible for her. I had to show her I held no grudges or underlying anger for her giving me away. My reasons for tracing her were pure, honest and hopefully guilt free. After all there were *'worse things than a baby'*.

Epilogue

WINTER 1987

The door before me was about to be opened. I would open it. In real time it represented the future, but by going through the door I was going to meet my past. I would be able to get answers to the continuous whirlpool of questions in my mind. Maybe she could bring them to rest, calm the undercurrent of ferocity and answer the questions that underpinned my teenage poetry. Who was I?

There she was in front of me, rising to hug me. I cannot remember anything about her clothes, shoes, or even if she carried a bag. Her short hair was the colour of wet bark, a shiny dark brown. The curls were unruly, like my son's but unlike mine. Her hands were mine but with long strong nails. There was no doubt. This was a momentous day but felt like a natural occurrence, almost like I had been born for it. It was always going to happen.

A relatively handsome grey-haired man sat beside her. He was introduced to me as Mick. After shaking his hand, I turned back to my mother. I was met with eyes that I recognised though I had never seen them before. We locked nervously into each other's gaze; her eyes wide, pale and blue, almost like my son's. The colour, though, was not as deep as Craig's; my mother's were an opaque blue, like the water lapping at the shoreline. The colour of Craig's was deeper, further out to sea. That nose, though, that nose belonged to both Craig and me.

'Oh God, you are the image of Gillian,' were her first words.

Was this a good thing? It seemed so. But who was Gillian?

Although we hugged like people who knew each other, her next statement threw me. 'I'm no going to cry. I've cried enough tears,' she said.

Momentarily I was confused, nodding as if I understood. My teetering tears of a genuine joy that could have fallen, receded. They stayed out of sight and remained unspilled. The tone had been set: we got down to practicalities. My mother and me!